Hearts and Minds

Deakin Studies in Education Series

General Editors: Professor Rob Walker and Professor Stephen Kemmis,
Deakin University, Victoria, Australia

Hearts and Minds: Self-esteem and the Schooling of Girls

Edited by
Jane Kenway and Sue Willis

 The Falmer Press

(A member of the Taylor & Francis Group)
London • New York • Philadelphia

UK   The Falmer Press, Falmer House, Barcombe, Lewes, East Sussex, BN8 5DL

USA   The Falmer Press, Taylor & Francis Inc., 1900 Frost Road, Suite 101, Bristol, PA 19007

First published 1990

British Library Cataloguing in Publication Data
Hearts and minds: self-esteem and the schooling of girls.
1. Australia. Schools, students, girls. Self-esteem
I. Kenway, James   II. Willis, Sue
370.15

ISBN 1–85000–739–X
ISBN 1–85000–740–3 pbk

Jacket design by Caroline Archer
Typeset in 10.5/13 point Bembo by
Graphicraft Typesetters Ltd, Hong Kong.

Contents

Contents

General Editors' Introduction

The Deakin Studies in Education Series aims to present a broad critical perspective across a range of interrelated fields in education. The intention is to develop what might be called a 'critical educational science': critical work in the philosophy of education, curriculum, educational and public administration, language education, and educational action research and clinical supervision. The series strives to present the writings of a rising generation of scholars and researchers in education.

A number of researchers based at Deakin University have been closely associated with the development of the critical perspective across these fields. For such reasons, people in the field have sometimes spoken of a 'Deakin perspective'. We do share some common views from which we hope to contribute to contemporary debates about the future development of educational enquiry; at the same time, our disagreements seem as fruitful for us as our agreements.

The Deakin Studies in Education Series provides an opportunity for extending this debate about the nature and future development of education and educational enquiry. It will include the writings of a variety of educational researchers around the world who, like ourselves, are interested in exploring the power and limitations of the critical perspective in the analysis of educational theory, policy and practice.

The central themes of the series will not be dictated by the alleged boundaries between 'foundational' disciplines in education, nor by an unexamined division of the tasks of education and educational research between 'practitioners' and 'theorists', or between 'practitioners' and 'policy-makers'. On the contrary, one of the tasks of the series is to demonstrate, through careful research and scholarship across a range of fields of practical, political and theoretical endeavour, just how outmoded, unproductive, and ultimately destructive these divisions are both for education and for educational research. Put positively, the central themes and questions to be addressed in the series include:

> the unity of educational theory and practice — expressed, for example, in the work of educational practitioners who research their practice as a basis for improving it, and in the notion of collaborative, participatory educational research, for example, in educational action research;

> the historical formation, social construction and continual recon-struction of education and educational institutions and reforms through processes of contestation and institutionalization — ex-pressed, for example, in the work of critical researchers into the curriculum and educational reform; and

> the possibilities of education for emancipation and active and productive participation in a democratic society — expressed, for example, in the development of critical pedagogy and the de-velopment of communitarian perspectives in the organization of education.

These are enduring themes, touching upon some of the central questions confronting our contemporary culture and, some would say, upon the central pathologies of contemporary society. They are all too easily neglected or obscured in the narrow and fragmented views of education and educational research characteristic of our times. Yet education is one of the key resources in what Raymond Williams once described as our societies' 'journey of hope' — the journey towards a better, more just, more rational and more rewarding society. Education has always aimed to nurture, represent, vivify and extend the values and modes of life which promise to make the best in our culture better. Finding out how this can be done, interpreting our progress, and appraising and reapprais-ing the quality of our efforts at educational improvement are the tasks of critical educational research. They are the tasks of this series.

Stephen Kemmis and Rob Walker

Acknowledgments

We wish to thank the Commonwealth Schools Commission which funded much of the preliminary work which led to this collection through its Projects of National Significance. We also thank all the writers for their generous and thoughtful participation in the project. Geraldine Connor helped us in the early stages, openly sharing her ideas, and we acknowledge and appreciate her assistance. We want, further, to express our appreciation to Kevin Keeff whose thoughts on certain aspects of the collection were valuable. Ann Stevens, Marilyn Walker and Leonie Taylor all helped with typing and formatting, and Joan Fox with proofreading; we are particularly grateful to each. Deakin and Murdoch universities provided institutional support for the project and we acknowledge a special indebtedness to both universities. Our gratitude also goes to Mary O'Connor who managed the project and assisted us most ably with many of its different components.

Preface

Buzzwords abound no less in education than in any other field of social relations. As they gain popularity and slip into everyday speech, they assume the status of common sense. The complexities surrounding their origins and their applications are lost, and they become a lazy lens through which to view social reality — forestalling thought and restricting the practices which flow from them. In popular explanations of girls' mode of participating in schooling, 'self-esteem' has assumed the status of a buzzword. Whatever explanatory power and educational value the concept of self-esteem and its history may have had, they are now in danger of being subverted in the deadening process of popularization over the last decade or so. This collection gathers together the thoughts of a range of specialists in education. Each was asked to consider critically the merits of current thinking on 'self-esteem' in relation to their field of expertise. Each concluded that what is demanded in their particular area is a radical reassessment of the current ways in which we think about self-esteem and its relationship to girls' schooling.

Self-esteem and the Schooling of Girls: An Introduction

Jane Kenway and Sue Willis

The relationship between gender and education has been conceptualized in a range of ways and from a variety of differing disciplinary, theoretical and political orientations. The early documentation of differences between the sexes with regard to such matters as achievement, treatment, attitudes and expectations was an important first step, both conceptually and politically. The use of a range of global measures to contrast boys with girls and women with men showed clear disparities across a whole range of circumstances, particularly educational and occupational. The use of such documentation as a feminist political lever was, and continues to be, invaluable. It also provides a database for ongoing attempts both to explain such differences and to develop strategies to improve the position of girls and women within the education system and society. Over time the range of explanations and their concomitant strategies for change have expanded quite dramatically. Indeed, there is no doubt that our understanding of the complexities of the relationships between gender and education and our recognition of the intransigence of the problem of sexist education and society have been considerably enhanced in the last decade.

There is now a number of different feminist discourses within the field of girls' education which, although overlapping in some areas (particularly in their use of each other's research findings), offer positions which vary in their intentions, scope and capacity for change. To an extent, these various discourses offer incompatible explanations and programs for action and, to an extent, compete for recognition, acceptance and funds. Within the field a particular literature has developed around the notions of self-concept, self-image and self-esteem. It is inspired by a blend of certain American psychological theories with certain feminist theories and consists of the following: research suggesting that girls have lower self-esteem and achievement than boys, particularly in certain fields; discussions about how sex role stereotypes affect girls, lowering their self-esteem and expectations and narrowing their achievements; and strategies to be employed to enhance girls' self-esteem and widen and improve their school achievement and life chances. Of course the litera-ture relating school achievement to students' self-esteem is not limited to that on gender. Low self-esteem has been used to 'explain' much educa-tional and social 'failure'. For instance, drug users and 'street kids' are seen to suffer low self-esteem. In addition, humanist teachers have in-sisted that good teachers must demonstrate a concern for their students' self-esteem, and so some curricula have come to incorporate this concern. Educators from various countries have demonstrated considerable interest in the applicability of the self-esteem literature to education. It has been acclaimed by many as a means both of addressing educational problems and of enhancing educational processes. This set of papers seeks critically to engage this wide-ranging international literature by bringing to bear upon it various issues and concerns which have arisen in the Australian context.

This collection arose from a strong sense of unease felt by a number of Australian educators about the apparently uncritical way in which the ideas associated with the self-esteem literature had slipped into popular educational thinking. The claims being made on its behalf as an explana-tion of school failure and as an elixir for both school success and the 'liberation' of girls seemed simplistic to say the least. Even though the self-esteem discourse was being both legitimated through government policy and underwritten by government funding for research and curricu-la development, and even though many teachers seemed rather smitten by the idea of smoothing their students' path to learning by improving their self-esteem, some hesitation seemed long overdue. We say 'hesita-tion', because, while on the one hand there was some suspicion about the regime of truth which had been developing around the notion of self-esteem, on the other certain merits were recognized in those educational projects which were centrally concerned with developing among students a positive sense of self in an atmosphere of mutual regard. Further, to 'come out' in opposition to programs designed to enhance students' self-esteem appeared dangerously akin to opposing happiness. Certainly there was no wish to condemn the efforts of humanist teachers. Along a different but related track, it was also recognized that, as improving girls' self-esteem had become such a central plank in the feminist educational agenda, its value as a slogan could and should not be high-handedly dismissed. Clearly, it was striking responsive chords, while at the same time proffering what we suspected was a very partial educational and political agenda.

In confronting these dilemmas it was decided that to 'throw out the baby with the bath water' would not only be an act of political naivety, it would also be one of bad faith as it would appear to undermine rather than advance the efforts of many concerned teachers and policy-makers. Rather, what this collection does is to recover something of the history of the field, offer an account of its current momentum across various cultural and educational circumstances and suggest a range of alternative, more full-blooded, ways in which it may be deployed in enhancing the experiences of all girls at school and beyond. Before we offer more specific introductions it is necessary that we clarify the object of our attention, place it in the wider context of feminist educational projects and offer at least some account of its development in policy documents and its application in schools.

Some Background

For more than a decade in Australia the self-esteem discourse has been very influential in the development of policy on girls' education and we will now provide a brief overview of its history.

Self-esteem in Australian National Policy Documents

Education in Australia changed dramatically in 1972 when the Australian Labor Party (ALP) came to power at the Commonwealth level. As part of its electoral mandate to inquire into and satisfy the needs of all Australian schools, the ALP established a permanent statutory authority called the Commonwealth Schools Commission. Drawing its policy inspiration from the report of its Interim Committee (*Schools in Australia: Report of the Interim Committee of the Australian Schools Commission*, 1973), the Schools Commission took on board a concern for promoting equal educational opportunity. At the time the main policy concern was for the forms of educational inequality associated with 'socio-economic disadvantage'. However, gendered educational inequalities were also recognized, and in 1975 the Schools Commission published a landmark report, *Girls, Schools and Society*, which documented the causes and consequences of the inequitable distribution of educational benefits between girls and boys. A concern for girls' self-esteem constituted a strong thread running through this document.

Girls, School and Society drew attention to several Australian studies which provided evidence of gender differences in self-confidence and self-perception. The cross-sectional data from a study of 9000 Sydney adolescents (Connell *et al.*, 1975) showed that from puberty through to at least 20 years, girls' and boys' levels of self-esteem diverged slightly with girls' self-esteem remaining static and boys' increasing by a small amount. That the adolescent girls reported lower self-esteem than did the adolescent boys was given particular prominence by the Commission which, based on Connell's interpretation of the data, commented, 'the evaluation placed upon themselves by girls as revealed in this study could be expected to influence aspirations and even interests' (p. 106). It also pointed to other studies which suggested that girls were less confident of their academic abilities than were boys and typically underestimated their academic performance.

The Commission also discussed in some detail two studies which suggested that individual self-esteem may not be central in influencing girls' actions and choices. Patricia Edgar (1973, cited in Schools Commission, 1975) showed that those girls characterized as having high self-esteem were less like boys with high self-esteem and, in many ways, more like those boys and girls characterized as having low self-esteem. In particular, in her study 'high self-esteem' girls as compared to 'high self-esteem' boys were less certain about future careers, had lower job aspirations than their school achievement would suggest as appropriate, were less likely to be considering university, were more interested in passive activities and were less likely to regard themselves as powerful and as able to act upon the world and change it. Don Edgar (1974, cited in Schools Commission, 1975) offered evidence that girls often see themselves as academically less capable than boys but regard themselves as at their best with regard to interpersonal competencies. He argued, first, that they are 'under more pressure than boys to conform to parental demands and such demands are more frequently to behave maturely and "get along nicely" with other people than to achieve academically' (p. 109) and, second, that the lower aspirations of girls can be regarded as realistic responses to the reality of women's lives and the unequal distribution of social power.

In 1975 the Commission's conclusions about self-esteem were quite tentative and also sensitive to the complexities of the issues involved. Action was urgently needed, it argued, which 'assists girls towards a changed view of themselves and a new construction of reality in which their capacity to affect circumstances and take conscious decisions is seriously taken but the most effective ways of doing this are not self evident' (p. 111). While the reference to girls' view of themselves could be read as 'self-esteem', in the context of this report the Schools Commission seems more concerned to promote a positive identity for girls as a group. Indeed, it commented of the studies by Patricia and Don Edgar,

'Both studies strongly support the notion that there are forces acting upon all girls as females which, *irrespective of* social class or ability or *self regard*, cause them to see themselves as people incompetent to act upon the world' (1975, p. 111, our emphasis).

In 1984 the Schools Commission produced a second report on gender and education called *Girls and Tomorrow: The Challenge for Schools*. By this time its position had become considerably less tentative. A section of the report was devoted specifically to this topic, and the development of girls' self-esteem had become a major priority area, an end in itself. The Schools Commission should,

> ... cooperate with the Curriculum Development Centre to ensure priority is given to production of materials and approaches which will assist girls to achieve in mathematics, science and technology, especially computing, and which will raise girls' self-esteem (Recommendation 3: Curriculum, Part 2, p. 11)

> ... work with the Commonwealth Tertiary Education Commission, teacher training institutions, systems and schools to assist teachers in training and practising teachers to (amongst others)
> * promote girls' participation in the full range of activities and to develop ways of promoting girls' self-esteem (Recommendation 4: The Teachers' Role, Part 2, p. 12)

> ... through its own programs, in the influence it may bring to bear on other funding sources and in cooperation with states and territories, promote and support research into (amongst others)
> * girls' self-concept and self-esteem, in particular, the general decline in girls' self-esteem during adolescence
> * the nature, role and impact of role models on girls' self-esteem and aspirations. (Recommendation 5: Research, Part 2, p. 13)

While the precise relationship between policy and practice may be debatable (that is, whether policy merely reflects the state of play at any given time or whether it helps to form it), policy may be seen as a reflection of much current thinking on particular issues. Between 1975 and 1984 there was a rapid growth of interest in the question of girls' self-esteem and projects to improve girls' self-esteem became increasingly popular. Funds were forthcoming at both state and Commonwealth levels. Not only did this support initiatives in the area, it also helped to guide the direction of research, curriculum development and school practice. The most recent

Schools Commission publication on girls' education is *The National Policy for the Education of Girls in Australian Schools* (1987). Assisting girls to develop and maintain 'healthy' levels of self-esteem is, again, a thread which runs through this document, but there is considerably less explicit attention to self-esteem, as such. Indeed, there appears to be something of a return to the emphasis of 1975. While the arguments are at a more sophisticated level, reflecting the experience of the intervening decade, the focus of the policy is 'group esteem' for girls rather than 'self-esteem'. The following quotations illustrate this focus: 'Schooling is critical for girls' sense of identity, self-worth and purpose' (p. 22). 'Schooling for girls and boys should reflect the entitlement of all women, in their own right, to personal respect, economic security and participation in, and influence over, decisions which affect their lives' (p. 28). Furthermore, the report focuses much less on necessary changes in girls and much more on the need for fundamental curriculum reform. One of the central objectives of the *National Policy* encourages teachers 'to provide a supportive and challenging school environment for girls'. It is this objective which has given the self-esteem discourse a new lease of life as gender equity workers search for ways of responding to it. So, despite the *National Policy's* more sophisticated interpretation of the self-esteem literature, the field of educational practice still appears dominated by the more simplistic version.

Self-esteem Programs for Schools

'Self-esteem' is widely used to explain and justify school programs which vary considerably in scope and intentions. For some, the promotion of girls' self-esteem is regarded as central (although often as a means for improving behaviour or achievement) and is addressed explicitly, while for others it is regarded as a by-product of other changes in girls' educational experiences. The latter kind can encompass educational reforms which range from improving girls' access to the 'forbidden' but empowering male domains of mathematics, science and sport, through to the development of gender inclusive curriculum, or, even further, to a fundamental restructuring of the whole school curriculum. However, more visible, more common and more 'acceptable' are the projects which focus on the development of self-esteem as such. As those projects are the focus of much which follows, we intend shortly to indicate something of the range. But first let us reveal a little mischief by noting that the language of self-esteem has sometimes been very useful as a form of leverage — a legitimating discourse for getting certain projects up and running even though their relationship to self-esteem, as it is conventionally defined, is at best tangential.

Given its popularity, 'self-esteem' can be a powerful term for people to use in their quest for public acceptance (and financial support) for their educational endeavours, and it is now possible to identify a variety of programs which use self-esteem as an organizing concept even when self-esteem is not, strictly speaking, what the project is about. For example, as the following quotations indicate, interest has increased recently in the relationship between sport and self-esteem for girls.

> The lack of recognition of female sporting success and physical potential has implications not only for girls' general physical fitness but also for their self-esteem and perceptions of their own capacities. (Schools Commission, 1984, p. 30)

> Research has indicated that during adolescence girls' enthusiasm for and participation in all forms of sport and physical education declines dramatically, with an accompanying decline both in fitness levels and in self-esteem. (Schools Commission, 1987, pp. 44–5)

The Schools Commission has recently funded a large-scale South Australian project, Girls' Achievement and Self Esteem: The Contribution of Physical Education and Sport, the aim of which is to 'investigate the contribution which physical education and sport in schools can make to increasing girls' self-esteem and, through this, to improving their levels of achievement in all aspects of life' (Dyer, 1986, p. iii). Increasing girls' participation in physical activity seems, for reasons of health, companionship, pleasure and confidence, to be a commendable aim in its own right and, indeed, this appears to be what the project really was about. It is interesting, therefore, to speculate on the emphasis on self-esteem as a mediating variable for increasing girls' achievement generally and difficult to escape the conclusion that the language of self-esteem is often used precisely because of its value as rhetoric.

Returning now to versions more 'pure', one version involves the allocation of a certain period of the school week (perhaps for a term) to self-esteem raising activities for girls only. This may be in the form of a unit in the English or social studies curriculum or in the context of personal development courses, leisure-time programs or 'home room' activities. *Improving Chances for Girls* (Transition Education Unit, 1981), for example, is a curriculum package for Year 10 girls which is designed to open up their career options through confidence building. This program draws heavily on consciousness and confidence raising programs for young women. Activities range from having students draw up lists of all their skills (encouraging them to set goals in a wide range of circumstances) and developing job interview skills through to developing assertiveness and the skills needed for dealing with anger. All of these are developed in the context of encouraging girls to consider a wider range of options than they previously might have. Within the very real constraint of a total program of approximately sixteen hours' duration, they learn about women and work and the impact of subject choice on career options, and they discuss possible conflict between jobs and marriage. Thus, although the development of self-esteem underpins the project, the focus is on building girls' confidence in their ability to make choices and to take decisions. Such thinking resonates strongly with that of the 1975 Schools Commission Report.

'Crisis management' is the purpose both of this program and of a later version of it designed to be used in classes of boys and girls (Transition Education Unit, 1983, p. 2). The need for such crisis management, the project officer suggests, 'implicitly calls into question what has been happening to girls in the schooling prior to Year 10 and means that further evaluation of the negative experience girls have had at school is necessary so that long term change can be planned and undertaken' (p. 3). Although in the later version some attention is paid to the 'hidden curriculum' of schooling, in particular the inequitable distribution of teachers' time between the sexes, this program does not offer a critique of girls' educational experiences nor, indeed, is it able to offer alternatives to girls' current educational experiences.

A particularly influential project is *Wings* (Tasmanian Education Department, 1983), which was also funded by the Schools Commission (through a funding program called the Projects of National Significance). The authors of *Wings* recommend the establishment of structured programs for small groups of secondary school girls (about ten being preferred) explicitly to develop their self-esteem. Although the authors state that the program should 'be reinforced by attitudes and approaches throughout the school' (p. 13), the course is designed to be used adjacent to the rest of the curriculum. The authors focus particularly on the teacher's role in self-esteem programs and comment that 'the teacher's role is difficult and different from that adopted when teaching traditional subjects' (p. 47). A variety of activities is recommended (pp. 16–17) to assist girls increase their knowledge of themselves (e.g. autobiographical time line, listing skills and abilities, collage of self, personal silhouette and relaxation exercises), build their self-esteem (e.g. communication skills, decision-making and standing up for rights, giving and receiving compliments, dealing with anger and negativity, looking at different levels of relationships, fantasy, imagery and visualization) and extend their self-awareness of roles and possibilities (e.g. long- and short-term goal setting, looking at heroic roles, stereotyping, self-defence skills, grooming and physical exercise). The difference in focus between the projects offered by the Transition Education Unit and this is quite marked, and consistent with the change in focus previously identified in the 1975 and 1984 Schools Commission reports. Although some consideration is given to consciousness raising, the development of high self-esteem has become the major aim.

The program offered by *Wings* is strikingly similar to the self-esteem technologies represented by such American publications as *100 Ways to Enhance Self Concept in the Classroom* (Canfield and Wells, 1976) and *Self Esteem: A Classroom Affair — 101 Ways to Help Children Like Themselves* and *Self Esteem: A Classroom Affair — More Ways to Help Children Like Themselves* (Borba and Borba, 1978, 1982 respectively). In Australia many such programs have been developed by guidance officers and social workers (Beecher, n.d.; Thomson, 1984; Fahey, 1986; Connor, 1986a), their origins being counselling and their intentions therapeutic.

A recent project of the Equal Opportunities Branch of the Education Department of Western Australia (*Self Esteem: Teachers Hold Some Keys*, 1986) was written for teachers working in pre-primary and primary schools and seeks to pre-empt the presumed lowering of girls' self-esteem as they proceed through primary school. It cannot, therefore, be said to involve 'crisis management'. Drawing heavily on *Wings* for its inspiration, its scope is somewhat broader in at least three ways. First, according to the author Gerry Connor (1986b), while the project addresses sex role stereotyping, it attempts to do so by embedding 'the issues of sex-related self esteem levels within the context of personal development for both boys and girls' (p. 24). Furthermore, the purpose is, more broadly, to expand 'children's self awareness in an environment free of sex-role and cultural stereotypes' (p. 18). Second, it is much more explicit about the importance of good classroom relationships generally, arguing that changes in traditional teaching styles are necessary. Teachers are urged to be more positive and sensitive to the esteem needs of all their students. Finally, the project considers the role modelling effect of teachers' self-esteem on children's. In this regard, since 'a teacher's self esteem could be threatened by such factors as being faced with an over-load of work and handling tasks that were defined in ambiguous terms, the project sought to circumvent these sources of stress by offering clear, concise and manageable suggestions and having teachers participate in short in-service sessions to supplement the Handbook' (p. 23).

At the other end of the spectrum in this category of projects mentioned thus far, and with lots of permutations in between, are the approaches concerned with relationships within classes and in the school as a whole (see Pugh and Thomson, 1984; Thomson, 1984). The emphasis in such 'school development programs' is upon cooperation and positive mutual regard between students (not just girls) and between students and teachers; there is a concern with pastoral care, with classroom and school morale and climate. Activities often range from classroom lessons of the kind recommended in *Wings* through to the involvement of the whole school (students, parents and teachers) in a major undertaking which stretches their capacities in many ways (for example, a sponsored cycle and run relay from Adelaide to Perth [3500km] to raise funds for charity). Such projects typically are not part of equal opportunity strategies for girls and will not be a particular focus of this collection. Nonetheless, as Peter Renshaw points out in Chapter 1, like girls' self-esteem projects, they are directed at children who might be regarded as educationally disadvantaged. Some of the observations which will follow, therefore, may also apply to such activities. However, let us now return to our focus on self-esteem programs for girls and to our endeavours in this collection.

Purposes of the Collection

Earlier we pointed to the general levels of acceptance which the self-esteem literature on girls (and by implication students generally) has had in education systems in Australia and elsewhere. While recognizing the value of much that is offered in the guise of improving girls' self-esteem, it nonetheless seems appropriate that we take stock and look more closely and critically at certain features of the discourse. In doing so, certain themes have emerged. These relate to the nature of the evidence supporting self-esteem programs in schools, the intersection of these programs with girls' community cultures, and the curriculum implications of adopting self-esteem strategies for change. With these three themes in mind, the following chapters ask of the self-esteem discourse a number of questions which usually remain unasked and bring to it a number of fields of inquiry which usually remain separate from it.

First, it seems that the early and often somewhat scanty research evidence has, in a number of instances, provided an unquestioned basis for feminist programs in Australian schools. Consequently, in Part I the quality of the evidence and argument on girls' self-esteem and education is examined. What exactly is the evidence about girls' self-esteem and its relationship to schooling, and what interpretations of the evidence are most appropriate? Peter Renshaw reviews the international research in its own terms, considering, first, the literature which compares girls' and boys' self-esteem and, second, the relationship between self-esteem and aspirations and achievements. Jane Kenway, Sue Willis and Jennifer Nevard subject the discourse to an ideology critique, point to some of its unfortunate silences and analyze some of its more subtle messages, asking, as feminists, whether these programs represent the most fruitful way forward.

Second, there appears to be a tendency in the literature to treat the issue of girls' self-esteem in a universalistic manner and thus to ignore the specific cultural circumstance of girls and the manner in which their culture intersects with gendered educational achievement and ambition. Five chapters make up Part II, their collective intention being to interpret 'self-esteem' in socially and culturally relevant ways, taking into account Australia's cultural diversity and the unique circumstance of particular subgroups of girls and the way in which their cultures mesh with girls' education and anticipated futures. Georgina Tsolidis provides a broad analysis of some of the assumptions which underpin strategies for overcoming 'cultural disadvantage' and relates these to the use of self-esteem programs with ethnic minority girls. She points to the rather perplexing possibility that, by implicitly undervaluing and condoning a negative view of particular girls' cultures, seeking to raise self-esteem in one setting, or in certain ways, may well tend to diminish it in another setting or in other ways. In the second chapter in this section Pat Dudgeon, Simone Lazaroo and Harry Pickett raise similar concerns with respect to Aboriginal girls and, in particular, they explore what self-esteem programs such as those described earlier have to offer girls who only very partially and ambivalently accept the values of the dominant culture. Jackie Wenner, in the following chapter, highlights a possible conflict between what teachers from Anglo-Australian backgrounds and students and parents to Indo-Chinese backgrounds regard as appropriate and useful skills, values and behaviour and considers the implications of such conflicts for self-esteem programs. Johanna Wyn analyzes the perspectives and priorities of girls from working-class neighbourhoods and points to the ways in which these girls define value and to the implications which such definitions have for their view of school. Finally, in her paper on privileged girls Jane Kenway asks whether high self-esteem is an unproblematic good and demonstrates the connection between high self-esteem and certain dominant social and educational values. These papers suggest that seeking to raise self-esteem within the terms of the educational and social status quo may well have the effect of underscoring the dominant sex, class and ethnic groups in society. They point to the importance of a cultural perspective in addressing the intransigent problem of girls' education and provide various frameworks for thinking about the specificity and universality of the experience of certain groups of girls.

If the self-esteem discourse is to move forward, if it is to achieve more than it often currently appears to, and if various deliberations are to be of consequence, then it is appropriate to explore at least some associated curriculum concerns. Part III in this collection thus focuses on curriculum, identifying some significant matters which may help practitioners think through and move beyond current constraints to new possibilities.

In the first chapter of Part III Bill Cope and Mary Kalantzis suggest an alternative social science curriculum approach based on the concept of 'social literacy'. In mainstreaming issues of gender, class, race and ethnicity and focusing on both cultural pluralism and social equity theirs is a serious attempt to improve self-esteem in ways that are socially effective. Next Pam Gilbert draws parallels between the English curriculum and the self-esteem 'curriculum', informed as they both are by 'personal growth' models, and reflects on the apparent paradox that girls' much quoted success in school English has not brought them success and recognition even in fields where language skills might be regarded as central. The third chapter here deals with girls and school mathematics. Sue Willis analyzes some of the evidence which focuses particularly on girls' lower participation in mathematics than boys'. She asks whether self-esteem strategies for overcoming differences in participation in mathematics do not inadvertently define the problem to be with and of girls and, hence, overlook more productive strategies for change. In the final chapter in this section Pam Jonas offers a study of one school's efforts to take a 'whole school' approach to changing the educational experiences of girls. These included rethinking school decision-making structures, curriculum content, processes and assessment and reporting strategies. She also indicates some of the difficulties, dilemmas and rewards experienced by the school community.

We have limited most of our discussions to secondary schooling because the adolescent years appear to be the focus of much attention and because the self-esteem programs directed explicitly at girls are generally designed for secondary schools. Nonetheless, pre-primary and primary education for girls and other curriculum areas are important areas for study and deserve considerably more attention than they have hitherto received.

The purpose of this collection is to make problematic the dominant tendencies in the self-esteem discourse on girls' schooling. The collection proclaims neither definitive nor closed and agenda-setting status. It seeks to provoke, to stimulate and to open up a range of possibilities which will then further provoke and stimulate. To date the self-esteem discourse has suffered the weakest possible interpretation. Yet, given its popularity, it should not necessarily be abandoned; rather, educators should seek to shift its connotations so that it may be used as a more powerful educational lever. If this is to happen, it will need to be 'read' differently, encompass different versions of girlhood and imply different educational strategies. Provoking ideas about what these differences might be is what this collection is about.

References

BEECHER, S. (n.d.) *The Self Esteem Teaching Program*, 4 Paradise Avenue, Roseville NSW 2967.

BORBA, M. and BORBA, C. (1978) *Self Esteem: A Classroom Affair — 101 Ways to Help Children Like Themselves*, Minneapolis, Minn., Winston Press.

BORBA, M. and BORBA, C. (1982) *Self Esteem: A Classroom Affair — More Ways to Help Children Like Themselves*, Minneapolis, Minn., Winston Press.

CANFIELD, J. and WELLS, H. (1976) *100 Ways to Enhance Self-Concept in the Classroom: A Handbook for Teachers and Parents*, Englewood Cliffs, N.J., Prentice-Hall.

CONNELL, W.F., STROOBANT, R.E., SINCLAIR, K.E., CONNELL, R.W. and ROGERS, K.W. (1975) *12 to 20: Studies of City Youth*, Sydney, Hicks Smith and Sons.

CONNOR, G. (1986a) *Self-esteem: Teachers Hold Some Keys*, Perth, Education Department of Western Australia, Equal Opportunities Branch.

CONNOR, G. (1986b) *'Reflections on the Project "Self-esteem: Teachers Hold Some Keys"'*, Unpublished working paper for the project 'Girls, Self Esteem and Education: From the Universal to the Specific'.

DYER, K.F. (1986) *Girls, Physical Education and Self Esteem: A Review of Research, Resources and Strategies*, Report to the Commonwealth Schools Commission, Canberra Publishing Company, ACT.

FAHEY, J. (1986) *Teaching Is Inviting: Activities for Building Self Esteem*, Blackburn, Vic., Dove Communications.

MELGAARD, G. and BRUCE, W. (1982) *A Confidence Building and Self Esteem Program for Year 7–10 Girls*, Adelaide, Education Department of South Australia, Woman's Advisory Unit.

PUGH, D. and THOMSON, L. (1984) *Kids Helping Kids*, Cyril Jackson Senior High School, 53 Reid Street, Bassendean WA 6054.

SCHOOLS COMMISSION (1975) *Girls, Schools and Society*, Report by a Study Group to the Schools Commission, Canberra, Australian Government Publishing Service.

SCHOOLS COMMISSION (1984) *Girls and Tomorrow: The Challenge for Schools*, Report of the Commonwealth Schools Commission Working Party on Education of Girls, Canberra, Australian Government Publishing Service.

SCHOOLS COMMISSION (1987) *The National Policy for the Education of Girls in Australian Schools*, Canberra, Australian Government Publishing Service.

THOMSON, L. (1984) *Social Development in the Classroom: A Plan of Action*, North West Metropolitan Region, Education Department of Western Australia, Priority Schools Program Project.

TRANSITION EDUCATION UNIT (1981) *Improving Chances for Girls: A Strategy for Confidence Building*, Adelaide, Education Department of South Australia.

TRANSITION EDUCATION UNIT (1983) *Transition Education for Girls: Confidence Building for Year Ten Students*, Adelaide, Education Department of South Australia.

Wings: A Pilot Project to Enhance Self Esteem in Girls (1983) Hobart, Education Department of Tasmania.

Part I
Critique

Chapter 1

Self-esteem Research and Equity Programs for Girls: A Reassessment

Peter Renshaw

Introduction

The psychological literature on self-concept and self-esteem has a long history, stretching back to the American work of James (1890), Cooley (1902) and Mead (1934). Self-psychology has been cast as an alternative, initially, to the dominant paradigm of behaviourism and, more recently, to the cognitive paradigm which has grown in strength from the influence of both information processing theory and Piagetian theory. Self-psychology found expression in various educational reform movements that emphasized the importance of human feelings and emotions (Jones, 1968), as well as the need for a holistic approach to schooling (Silberman, 1973). Given its oppositional stance, it is not surprising that self-psychology is part of the current attempts to reform educational opportunities for various disadvantaged groups, including girls.

In this chapter the terms 'self-concept' and 'self-esteem' will be used interchangeably, to refer to evaluations of oneself with regard to either a specific activity (for example, mathematics self-concept or self-esteem), or in some global or general manner (global self-concept or self-esteem). While researchers have tried to distinguish the content of one's self-perception (self-concept) from the evaluation of those contents (self-esteem), in practice the distinctions are often blurred.

The purpose of this chapter is to assess the research which has been employed in recent writing on girls' self-esteem. First, the descriptive or correlational research comparing the development of girls' and boys' self-esteem is examined. The assessment of this literature suggests that there is no convincing evidence that girls have a self-esteem deficit. Second, research is critically examined which places self-esteem in a mediating position between various social practices in schools and differential outcomes for individuals. The research literature examined is based on attribution theory, expectancy theory and intervention programs for the disadvantaged. Each of these three bodies of literature has the potential to highlight the powerful influence of social structures and social practices on individuals' learning and identity, but within the context of the 'self' discourse, they succeed only in highlighting the deficits within individuals and thereby reduce the perceived need for fundamental reforms.

Empirical Evidence for Girls' Self-esteem 'Problem'

In Australia the notion that girls have a self-concept or self-esteem problem has gained credence largely through inquiries funded by the Commonwealth Schools Commission (*Girls, Schools and Society*, 1975; *Girls and Tomorrow*, 1984), and through the resultant intervention programs designed to raise the self-esteem of girls within schools (e.g. *Wings*, 1983). The composite image emerging from such sources is of a girl with a declining level of self-esteem, which leads to underestimation of her potential, eventual underachievement and restricted career choices. The empirical evidence that girls' low self-esteem is the cause of the problem, however, is surprisingly thin.

Social theorists assumed that females would have lower self-esteem than males because of the myriad aspects of current society, including the devaluing of traditional female roles, beliefs in the inherent inferiority of females, derogation of the female body, promotion of male images as superior and so on, which undermine the female identity (Skaalvik, 1986). When data were collected comparing the self-esteem of females and males however, the theoretical expectations were not confirmed. The American review by Maccoby and Jacklin (1974), for example, examined thirty-nine comparisons of female and male self-esteem, and found no differences on twenty-four, females scored higher on nine, and males scored higher on six comparisons. Wylie (1979) in her exhaustive review also found no conclusive evidence of sex differences in self-esteem. However, the failure of the empirical research to confirm the theoretical expectations may be due to inadequacies in the self-esteem instruments. Wylie, publishing in the United States, was critical of the research, and others, including Skaalvik, publishing in Scandinavia, have noted serious problems with subject sampling and the reliability and validity of the self-esteem instruments.

Australian studies supporting the view that girls have a self-esteem problem are scarce. The report *Girls and Tomorrow* (Commonwealth Schools Commission, 1984) relied mainly on the research of Taylor

(1981) and the earlier study by Connell *et al.* (1975). Neither study provides unambiguous evidence for the claim that girls have low self-esteem. The Connell *et al.* data suggest that an impressive majority (of adolescents) are persons whose self-evaluation is confident and steady. Although the self-esteem of girls was found to be slightly lower than boys', the differences were modest — on average only half a scale point lower on a six-point scale. When the adolescents reporting very low levels of self-esteem were examined, more girls (10 per cent) than boys (6 per cent) were found. Although these students are cause for concern, they do represent only a small fraction of both the male and female school populations. Thus these data do not suggest that there is a major problem with the self-esteem of girls in Australia.

The Connell *et al.* data are used also to claim that the self-esteem of boys and girls diverges during high school, and they do suggest a very slight divergence. The self-esteem of girls was found to be remarkably stable for each cohort in the high school, whereas boys' self-esteem scores rose ever so slightly across the high school years — less than one-quarter of a scale point on a six-point scale. Because it is easy to assume that divergence means 'boys increase, and girls decrease', it is important to note that girls' self-esteem did not show a decline in the Connell *et al.* data. Furthermore, the research design was cross-sectional. That is, at a particular time (September 1969) the self-esteem of students at various high schools in Sydney was measured. Since only one assessment was made, there is no direct evidence that the self-esteem of any particular individual increased, declined or remained steady. Cross-sectional designs confound cohort and age effects, so differences in self-esteem may be due to events that are unique to particular cohorts. For example, the introduction of new curricula, or the reform of teaching practices, may affect the self-esteem of younger cohorts, but have a negligible effect on older cohorts. Developmental changes cannot be inferred from such cross-sectional data.

Taylor's research (1981) potentially overcomes the problems inherent in the cross-sectional study because it included a longitudinal design at three year levels — 8, 9 and 10 (with students on average 13, 14 and 15 years old respectively). The self-esteem of children was assessed in the three years at the beginning of the school year in 1976 and again in 1977. By comparing the self-esteem scores of the children across the one-year span, direct evidence of stability or change is provided. Using the data provided in the tables (Taylor, 1981, pp. 216–17), I calculated the change in average self-esteem scores for boys and girls at each grade level. In all but one group (Year 10 boys) the average self-esteem of boys and girls rose across the school year. There is no evidence here to sustain the claim that girls' self-esteem declines throughout adolescence. Taylor's study has been incorrectly interpreted because only the cross-sectional data which showed that younger cohorts of girls had slightly higher self-esteem scores than the cohort above them have been considered. An optimistic interpretation of the trend would be that schools may be having a progressively more positive effect on girls' self-esteem (if ever so slightly).

Research on the self-esteem of Australian primary and secondary students is substantially greater now than when the report *Girls and Tomorrow* was published in 1984. In particular, the research of Marsh (1985; Marsh *et al.*, 1985) is noteworthy for the large sample sizes, replication across different times of testing, and the span of age-levels included — from Years 2 to 12 (7 to 17 years of age). First, the data on primary school children will be examined. Marsh (1985) assessed the self-concept of 3562 males and females in Years 2–6 on academic (reading, maths, school) and non-academic self-concepts (physical ability, physical appearance, peer relations, parent relations). Overall, the differences between boys and girls in self-concept were small, with the largest differences favouring girls on reading, and boys on physical abilities. When the responses to all items were summed, boys scored slightly higher than girls (31.2 versus 30.5 on a scale with a range from 8 to 40), but this difference explains less than 1 per cent of the variance in children's self-concept scores.

Of more pertinence is the research on the self-concept of boys and girls in secondary schools, because it is during adolescence that girls are presumed to suffer a decline in self-esteem. Marsh *et al.* (1985) assessed the self-concept of 901 males and females in Years 7–12, on various academic and non-academic dimensions. The claim that girls suffer a decline in self-concept during adolescence, while boys' self-concepts rise steadily, should produce significant age by sex interaction effects, but none was found, so the assumption that schools have a decidedly negative effect on girls' self-esteem is not supported by these data. Looking in broad terms at sex differences in self-esteem, Marsh *et al.* (1985) found no differences in academic self-concept nor in total self-concept during the adolescent years. Sex differences were found on particular dimensions of self-concept that mirror domains which have been more clearly sex role stereotyped — girls had higher verbal/reading self-concepts than boys, whereas boys were higher in mathematical self-concepts. (The differences in mathematical self-concepts are discussed below by Willis; see Chapter 10.)

Examination of the changes in self-esteem across the high school years requires a longitudinal design, as noted earlier, and the Marsh *et al.*

(1985) study was cross-sectional, so it is impossible to reach definitive conclusions on the stability of self-esteem. It is worth noting, however, that there was no uniform decline in the self-esteem of girls from one cohort to the next. For both girls and boys, self-concept is highest at Years 7, 11 and 12. For boys, their lowest total self-concept score occurred at Year 9 (47.2 on a standardized scale), whereas for girls, their lowest total self-concept score occurred at Year 8 (47.1).

There is one consistency in both the international and Australian data that favours boys. If respondents are asked simply how proud, pleased or satisfied they are with themselves, then boys generally score higher than girls. Skaalvik (1986) argues that such a context-free measure is a more valid index of the individual's self-esteem because each respondent can answer from a variety of bases depending on aspects of their lives that are important and central. In reviewing studies published after Maccoby and Jacklin's (1974) and Wylie's (1979) articles, and considering only global measures of self-esteem, Skaalvik (1986) identified ten studies that met his criteria for adequately described samples and methodologically sound research. The ten studies included subjects predominantly in the adolescent age range of 12 to 18 years. In all ten studies boys scored higher than girls on general self-esteem, and the differences were significant in eight of the studies. Skaalvik's review of general self-esteem scores contrasts with the consistent finding in Marsh's research that, when boys' and girls' scores on various specific dimensions of self-concept are summed to provide an overall or total score, there are no differences between the sexes. How can these contrasting but consistent findings be explained?

Global, context-free self-esteem measures may be biased toward more stereotyped male characteristics. Males are expected to be proud, to think highly of themselves and to promote their own image. Females, in contrast, are expected to be more deferential and modest. When confronted with a questionnaire which requires self-aggrandizing responses, males may simply be more willing than females to 'blow their own trumpets'. For females to respond more positively to a general self-concept item is, in effect, to take on more of a stereotyped male identity. This argument is supported by research relating self-esteem to measures of masculinity, femininity and androgyne (Antill and Cunningham, 1979, 1980; Hall and Taylor, 1985; Marsh, 1987). These studies showed that self-esteem was correlated with measures of masculinity in both sexes, whereas the correlation with femininity was nil or negative. That is, the degree to which I am prepared to describe myself in stereotypical male terms (confident, independent, firm, boastful) will influence positively the likelihood that I will also report high levels of global self-esteem. The more I subscribe to stereotypical female descriptors (sensitivity, responsibility, patience), the less likely it is that I will report high levels of self-esteem.

It could be argued that the qualities of confidence, independence and boastfulness are the exact qualities that self-esteem programs for girls are designed to enhance. By focusing on specific characteristics, however, the debate shifts ground in a significant manner. Rather than focusing on self-esteem per se, which carries the assumption of being a universal good, the debate begins to focus on the particular qualities and values that might provide the basis of one's identity. If girls are being urged to become more like boys in terms of their self-confidence, are we implying that the feminine values of sensitivity, responsibility and patience are less worthwhile? Should not we urge boys to adopt the so-called feminine values?

The questions posed above raise the second major problem in interpreting differences in global self-esteem, that is, the assumption that *more* is necessarily *better*. General agreement could be reached, no doubt, regarding the undesirability of extremely low levels of self-esteem. One would be unlikely to accept as satisfactory a state where one was constantly unhappy with oneself. The obverse may be just as unsatisfactory. Exaggerated feelings of pride and self-satisfaction are not prima facie desirable goals to be pursued within schools. It may be better to describe an optimum range of self-esteem, rather than assume that higher scores indicate desirable states. From this perspective it may be that boys have a self-esteem problem, because more of them have unrealistic and exaggerated self-perceptions.

Several conclusions regarding girls' self-esteem need to be clarified. First, there is no empirical evidence to sustain the case that girls have a 'self-esteem problem'. The large majority of girls have a very healthy degree of self-satisfaction, and this maintains itself throughout the school years. At the beginning of secondary school in Australia there may be a drop in self-esteem, but this occurs for both girls (Year 8) and boys (Year 9). By Year 10 girls and boys have moved out of the slump, although conclusive evidence on this pattern awaits longitudinal research. These conclusions are quite different from those drawn in the earlier reviews, partly because more recent research has provided new evidence, and partly because the existing research was misinterpreted or its implications overstated. This review, however, should not be interpreted as an effort to endorse existing schooling practices, nor to suggest that girls do not confront real inequities within the educational system. Rather, the purpose is to show that reform movements based on self-esteem programs may be misdirected, and that other avenues for reform should be pursued. In the following section, I review the basis of a number of bodies of research literature which have incorporated self-concept or self-esteem as an important ingredient. In various ways these have been used to focus reformist energies on girls' presumed self-esteem problems rather than on the reform of social practices and structures.

Self-esteem as a Reform Tool

Self-esteem literature, particularly in its popularized versions, promotes the message that positive thinking and positive feelings are the keys to significant individual change and social reform. In various ways we are urged to be proud of ourselves, to believe in ourselves, to feel happy with ourselves, and it is assumed that from such a well-spring of self-esteem decisions and actions will flow which promote our real interests and welfare. Such a view is naive on at least two counts. First, there is no reason to believe that feelings of self-satisfaction are necessarily related to our real interests or welfare. People in an oppressed social situation may be urged to feel happy and self-satisfied in order to maintain their oppression, rather than to give them the personal resources to confront the source of their oppression. Second, the popularized self-esteem literature is naive because it assumes that individual change can occur in a social vacuum. By focusing attention and concerns inwards onto personal domains of feelings and self-evaluation, self-esteem programs imply that individuals can transform themselves without the need to confront larger questions of social conventions, social structures and the distribution of status and power in their social relationships.

Self-esteem does not have to be conceptualized on such narrow individualistic terms. The theoretical writing about the self by James (1890), Baldwin (1899), Cooley (1902) and Mead (1934) located the developing self firmly in an interactive social context. These early American theorists viewed the self as existing within the biological individual but, paradoxically, as being composed of concepts and categories that were provided by the society. Emerging self-concepts were seen as emerging social concepts. That is, descriptions of oneself such as 'I am a girl, a child, a black, an Australian' locate the individual's emerging self in established social groupings. The individual, therefore, learns simultaneously about the self and the society. If the social groupings to which one is attached are relatively low in status and power, then the concept of self that develops from growing up in such groups will include feelings of self-derogation and powerlessness. From this perspective, then, social change and individual change are inextricably linked.

Nonetheless, regardless of the way the theory has tried to connect self and society, when self-esteem programs are employed as the tools for educational reform, the focus of reform dwells on individuals rather than on social structures. To examine this proposition in more detail three areas of research will be considered: first, research on attribution theory and the intervention programs based on that research; second, the expectancy process derived from Rosenthal and Jacobsen's (1968) original research on the self-fulfilling prophecy; and third, the research on the relationship between self-esteem and achievement in the context of education programs for disadvantaged populations.

Attribution Retraining as a Reform Tool

The importance of attribution retraining for girls was highlighted initially by Carol Dweck's research on learned helplessness (Dweck and Bush, 1976; Dweck et al., 1978). For Dweck, as well as the original self theorists, self-esteem is closely related to feelings of control. Cooley (1902) wrote that self-esteem was linked mainly to ideas of the exercise of power, of being a cause. Subsequently, other writers have incorporated this notion of power and control in psychological constructs such as 'locus of control' (Rotter, 1966), 'self-efficacy' (Bandura, 1981), 'mastery orientation' or its negative image 'learned helplessness' (Dweck et al., 1978). The terminology itself has a masculine orientation with its emphasis on power, control and mastery. The person with internal locus of control, high self-efficacy or mastery orientation reacts favourably to challenges, has confidence that personal goals can be achieved and remains task-oriented in the face of initial failure. It is qualities such as these which girls have been presumed to lack and which many self-esteem programs for girls have been designed to promote.

Dweck conceptualized the individual's sense of personal power or control in terms of 'learned helplessness'. Learned helplessness exists when failure is perceived as inevitable. Dweck (Dweck and Reppucci, 1973) found that girls are more likely than boys to exhibit the helpless pattern of attributions. When confronted by failure, girls are more apt to blame a lack of ability for poor performance, and this occurs even on tasks for which girls are at least as proficient as boys. Given this particular attributional pattern, when evaluative pressures are high (closed examinations), or when there is an increased threat of failure (choice of a difficult subject), or immediately following an initial failure, girls are more likely to give up and show poorer overall performance (Dweck and Gilliard, 1975).

There is a puzzling paradox in this research. Girls' achievement in primary school surpasses that of boys in reading and mathematics; girls are regarded by teachers in a more favorable way than boys, and they receive less negative feedback than boys. Why, then, do they show a greater tendency than boys to develop the learned helpless pattern of attribution? In addressing this paradox Dweck (Dweck *et al.*, 1978) showed that teacher feedback may be the crucial factor. She compared the feedback received by boys and girls (Years 4 and 5, 9 and 10 years of age) from teachers in terms of its focus on form or content. Form feedback (non-intellectual aspects of the tasks) referred to such things as neatness and setting out. Boys were frequently criticized for such matters. Girls were criticized less than boys overall, but what criticism they did receive was directed more to the intellectual aspects of the task. Dweck argues that this is significant because girls may be getting the message, 'you are doing beautiful work even if you're not so bright.' Boys on the other hand may be getting the message, 'you are doing very untidy work but it doesn't matter, you're capable and bright.'

In evaluating Dweck's research I want to make two initial points. First, the research is compelling and creative. It locates a particular property of the self (how to make sense of success and failure on school tasks) in the dynamics of the social practices of teachers. The findings also very neatly solve a perplexing paradox regarding the development of learned helplessness in girls (more than boys) at the very time that they are achieving better results than boys. It is not surprising that this research is cited frequently in the literature on girls' achievement in school. The problem with the research, however, is the conclusion. In her discussion Dweck focuses on the self. The social dimension is important only to the extent that it forms the individual's attributional pattern. Dweck provides an intriguing explanation of the way boys and girls may transfer their attributional patterns from primary school to secondary school, with negative consequences for girls and positive consequences for boys. This is interesting, but the real message from the research was the powerful impact of social agents on self-concepts. The real implication is that both boys' and girls' attributions are susceptible to significant change, and that teaching practices need to be scrutinized to ensure that adaptive patterns of feedback are received by both groups. By focusing on the individuals Dweck inadvertently locates the problem within the girls as they become the unfortunate victims of their primary school success. The real conclusion is that the problem is located in the social practices.

Further analysis of attribution research reveals more problems in this regard. There are various intervention studies designed to help children acquire and use mastery-oriented attributional patterns (Dweck, 1975;

Andrews and Debus, 1978). In these studies children with learned-helpless patterns of interaction are selected. The selected children, whose attributional tendency is to explain success as due to unstable factors (effort, easy test), and failure as due to stable factors (lack of ability), are taught to attribute success to stable factors and failure to unstable factors, such as lack of effort. In both the Dweck and the Andrews and Debus studies children were able to adopt the new adaptive attributional pattern and showed increased task persistence subsequently. There is a major problem here, however, because the social context (namely the classroom) to which children will transfer such attributional patterns has not been described.

Consider a particular girl, who shows lack of persistence, gives up after failure and underestimates her ability. The classroom is also highly competitive — the teacher employs tests frequently and publicly displays the results. This girl participates in the attribution retraining program. She now attributes failure as due to lack of effort and begins to try harder. The spirit of academic competition in the class remains high, and the other children strive to maintain their own relative positions. Over time the girl's standing in the class does not improve significantly. She has been attributing failure to lack of effort and striving hard, but now confronts the fact that little progress relative to her peers has been achieved. The logical conclusion to reach is that 'I really am hopeless at this. I've persisted but I'm still a failure.' The outcome of the attribution retraining, therefore, could be to undermine the girl's self-confidence even further and increase her sense of helplessness.

This hypothetical case illustrates the problem of juxtaposing individuals and social contexts, rather than seeing how individual attributes are derived from social contexts, though not necessarily in a simplistic fashion (cf. Ames and Ames, 1984; Nicholls, 1979). The specific point illustrated above is that the competitive nature of schooling, which is a pervasive social phenomenon, provides the conditions which produce and sustain patterns of learned helplessness. More harm than good is likely to result from individually focused training programs which are directed at helping particular children without reforming basic social practices.

Expectancy Theory as a Reform Tool

Attribution theory has the potential to provide a research and intervention framework that maintains a dual focus on individual and social factors. So too has expectancy theory, which has been a major source of research on social processes and individual outcomes. In particular, the expectancy literature has illuminated the role of schools in reproducing established social divisions and status hierarchies. The expectancy model, in theory, locates the problem in the pervasive beliefs about the relative value of certain attributes, such as what to expect of particular races, ethnic groups, females and males, social class groups and so on. In theory at least the expectancy literature should lead to a critical analysis of the social attitudes and social structures that paint some groups in a negative light, rather than to a concern with individual self-concepts. In practice the expectancy literature is used to highlight individual deficits, which leads to compensatory programs for the victims, rather than to a more fundamental reconsideration of the underlying social attitudes and social structures.

The model of the expectancy process which grew out of Rosenthal and Jacobson's study of the self-fulfilling prophecy placed self-esteem in a central mediating position. It is argued that teachers' expectations can be assumed to act as powerful determinants of a child's learning only to the extent that the child internalizes and accepts the definition of self supplied explicitly and implicitly by the teacher's practices. If children resist the definition of themselves which is being offered, the expectancy process can be broken. Rogers (1982), in his book on the expectancy process, sees the individual's self-concept as the prime motivating force, initiating and directing the individual's behaviour. It is clear, then, why reformists from the United States and the United Kingdom respectively would seek to enhance the self-concept of children, particularly those from groups thought likely to be cast in a negative light by teachers. A resilient and strong self-concept may be thought of as an elixir, a dose of megavitamins to ward off the negative images offered by schools.

It is important to reflect again on the chain of logic in the expectancy process because it demonstrates the manner in which social and political problems are transformed from being the responsibility of those in power, to being the responsibility of the victims. The expectancy model identifies, quite clearly, that teachers' formation of negative expectations is based on widespread beliefs about certain groups — whether defined in terms of gender, class, race, family background, sibling reputation, physical appearance and so on. The widespread beliefs are tacit knowledge that remain essentially unassailable because the expectancy process works so well. The privileged groups have a vested interest in sustaining the discriminatory expectations because they justify and legitimate their position. The expectancy chain, by reproducing inequalities, provides apparently objective evidence that the original negative expectations were correct. It is unfortunate, therefore, that what could have been a powerful tool for challenging established social structures can quickly be turned back to suggesting deficits in the individual. The problem is transferred to the children. It is their self-concepts, expectations and aspirations that are preventing them from making the most of their opportunities. It is there, self-esteem enthusiasts argue, with apparent justification, that we need to direct our intervention.

Self-esteem, Achievement and 'Disadvantage'

The use of the self-esteem concept as a tool of reform is not unique to girls' education. Self-esteem occupies a central place in the discourse on educational programs for the 'disadvantaged' as it does, for example, in drug education. In this discourse high self-esteem is seen both as a necessary precondition for learning and as a desirable outcome from schooling.

On the surface it is difficult to argue against either proposition. The term 'low self-esteem' is associated with images of lethargy, defeatist attitudes, low motivation, self-derogation. Common sense would imply that children have to be lifted out of such a state before learning can occur. A key aspect of such thinking is the separation of self-esteem from the specific learning tasks. Self-esteem may be likened to the fuel that is required to raise the learning balloon, which then can travel across the school curriculum landscape. As self-esteem evaporates in the face of negative experiences, the learning balloon plummets. Books such as *100 Ways to Enhance Self Concept in the Classroom* (Canfield and Wells, 1976) support the artificial separation of learning and self-esteem. Likewise, the self-esteem curricula which have been prepared to complement traditional school subjects (*Wings*, 1983; Connor, 1986) are predicated on the view that a certain level of self-esteem is required before learning can occur, and that specific self-esteem lessons can provide that minimum level. There are two problems with this view. First, by separating self-esteem from the main elements of the curriculum, reform can by-pass the curriculum itself. If children are lethargic and low in motivation, it may be that the curriculum is not being presented in a manner that connects with their experience or interests. The focus of educational reform, then, should not be the individual's self-esteem deficit, but the content and presentation of the curriculum. A second problem with the view that self-esteem is a necessary precondition for learning is the assumed empirical relationship between self-esteem and achievement.

A positive correlation between self-esteem and achievement has been found consistently. Indeed, it would be worrying if self-esteem in a particular domain were not related to one's actual competencies or achievement in that domain. The correlation, however, is more modest than often assumed. Hansford and Hattie (1982) completed a meta-analysis of a large number of studies on this issue and found a positive but low relationship (r = +.24), the overall relationship being similar for girls and boys. This positive correlation, however, is often misinterpreted as suggesting that self-esteem causes achievement, that is, changes in self-esteem are assumed to precede and cause changes in achievement (the hot-air balloon model of learning). Reviews by Scheirer and Kraut (1979) and West *et al.* (1980), however, suggest that changes in self-esteem follow rather than precede changes in achievement. That is, as evidence grows of increasing competence and achievement, the self-esteem of the individual rises. There are good reasons to be cautious, therefore, in assuming that the achievement of disadvantaged groups or girls will be promoted if out-of-context, feelings-based self-esteem programs proliferate in schools.

I turn now to an examination of how in Australia self-esteem is considered as an outcome of schooling for disadvantaged groups. Kenway and Willis' (1986) critique of self-esteem programs for girls suggested that the underlying message was one of 'niceness' and 'political quietism'. It is informative to examine the recent history of the Australian Disadvantaged Schools Program for the politics of 'niceness and quietism'. The Priority School Program in Western Australia (Education Department of Western Australia, 1984) has emphasized self-esteem as an important outcome for the disadvantaged. It is intriguing to note also that self-esteem language is used widely in framing educational objectives for alternative upper secondary school curricula which are designed primarily for groups defined as 'disadvantaged' but forced to stay on at school. It would appear, however, that self-esteem is placed as a second best option — those who have the capability are expected to strive for success within the mainstream academic curriculum, whereas the failures can 'do self-esteem'. Such a view invites teachers to 'give-up' on teaching worthwhile competencies. A successful self-esteem program may do no more than prepare disadvantaged youth for a compliant acceptance of academic failure at school and eventual unemployment. This is the politics of 'quietism' in its most insidious form.

In support of the above contention I offer a brief analysis of a booklet prepared by one school district to promote self-esteem programs in schools (Thompson, 1984). The ideas in the booklet for improving self-esteem emphasize the importance of feelings, physical contact and social acceptance. In the final statement in the booklet the author provides an account of a meeting with a group of unemployed youth. The author's purpose is to draw together various themes in the booklet and convince the reader of the long-term benefits of self-esteem programs. In doing so, however, the connection between political quietism and self-esteem curriculum is vividly drawn.

> Until recently I lived a short distance from one of Perth's most beautiful beaches, I would watch in awe and wonderment at three young adolescents matching their wits with their surfboards against the wiles of the surf. The three laughed and joked with each other as they glided along the face of the waves. There was a certain 'air of confidence' about their presence, they appeared happy, content, and at one with their world. One morning as they walked past me, surfboards tucked under their arms I commented, 'Hi fellows — that's a good way to start a day's work.' They laughed and one replied, 'Not likely Mr. We're off to the Greenwood C.E.S. [Commonwealth Employment Service] to try our luck once again.' The boys had been unemployed since they left school and had been caught up in a fruitless search for work for the previous ten months. Yet they were coping. They were optimistic, not bitter, in their own way they remained positive, productive and motivated. On numerous subsequent mornings I would chat with them and never ceased to be amazed at their down to earth realism and sense of purpose. You see, through their surfing, through the support they had received from their teachers, parents, and 'significant others' in their lives, the boys had found value in their 'own totality of being' and could take pride in their own creative expression. (Thompson, 1984, pp. 81–82)

It is churlish, indeed, to be negative about young people who are confident and positive despite their unemployment. My churlishness is not directed toward that outcome, but to the assumption that self-esteem programs in schools could or should prepare young people to cope happily with an unacceptable status of poverty or dependency on welfare.

To summarize, a consistent distortion emerges in the three fields of study which incorporate self-esteem as a mediating variable between social structures and individual outcomes. By placing the self-esteem of the individual centre stage under the spotlight, the literatures have relegated to the shadows the social context and social structures that have formed and supported the development of that self-concept. This individualistic reading or interpretation of the literatures, of course, is not the only one that is available. As was pointed out earlier, each literature could be read as demonstrating the need for a more fundamental reassessment of teaching practices and curriculum. The individualistic perspective, however, has been influential in leading some educators to believe that the key to reform is the individual's self-esteem. Such a view has the unfortunate consequence of implying that the curriculum and schooling practices can remain unchanged, except for the addition of a self-esteem curriculum. Such a curriculum is unlikely to enhance the achievement of disadvantaged social groups, and may simply be a palliative which keeps students contentedly but unproductively occupied at school, and quietly passive afterwards.

Conclusion

Self-esteem programs for girls have been based on two widely accepted assumptions: first, that girls have a lower and gradually declining self-esteem compared to boys; and, second, that increased self-esteem is not only desirable in itself but can lead to increased achievement. Neither of these assumptions can be supported unequivocally. The evidence on the level of girls' self-esteem suggests that only a fraction of girls (perhaps 10 per cent) have very low self-esteem, and there is no evidence that schools have a progressively detrimental influence on girls' self-esteem. Throughout the whole school-aged group, boys' and girls' total self-esteem is remarkably similar. There are differences between girls and boys in specific aspects of self-esteem, and these differences parallel domains that have been more clearly sex role stereotyped.

The second assumption, that self-esteem can influence achievement, may be true, but current evidence suggests that changes in self-esteem follow rather than precede achievement. The implication of such a pattern highlights the importance of examining the quality of teaching and resource allocation for girls rather than focusing on presumed deficits within individual girls.

References

AMES, C. and AMES, R. (1984) 'Systems of student and teacher motivation: Toward a qualitative definition', *Journal of Educational Psychology*, 76, 4, pp. 535–56.

ANDREWS, G.R. and DEBUS, R.L. (1978) 'Persistence and the causal perception of failure: Modifying cognitive attributions', *Journal of Educational Psychology*, 70, 2, pp. 154–66.

ANTILL, J.K. and CUNNINGHAM, J.D. (1979) 'Self esteem as a function of masculinity in both sexes', *Journal of Consulting and Clinical Psychology*, 47, pp. 783–5.

ANTILL, J.K. and CUNNINGHAM, J.D. (1980) 'The relationship of masculinity, femininity and androgony to self esteem', *Australian Journal of Psychology*, 32, pp. 195–207.

BALDWIN, J.M. (1899) *Social and Ethical Interpretations in Mental Development: A Study in Social Psychology*, New York, Macmillan.

BANDURA, A. (1981) 'Self-referent thought: A developmental analysis of self-efficacy', in J.H. FLAVELL and L.R. ROSS (Eds), *Social Cognitive Development: Frontiers and Possible Futures*, Cambridge, Cambridge University Press.

CANFIELD, J. and WELLS, H. (1976) *100 Ways to Enhance Self Concept in the Classroom: A Handbook for Teachers and Parents*, Englewood Cliffs, N.J., Prentice-Hall.

COMMONWEALTH SCHOOLS COMMISSION (1975) *Girls, School and Society*, Report by a Study Group to the Schools Commission, Canberra, Australian Government Publishing Service.

COMMONWEALTH SCHOOLS COMMISSION (1984) *Girls and Tomorrow: The Challenge for Schools*, Report of the Commonwealth Schools Commission Working Party on Education of Girls, Canberra, Australian Government Publishing Service.

CONNELL, W.F., STROOBANT, R.E., SINCLAIR, K.E., CONNELL, R.W. and ROGERS, K.W. (1975) *12 to 20: Studies of City Youth*, Sydney, Hicks Smith and Sons.

CONNOR, G. (1986) *Self-Esteem: Teachers Hold Some Keys*, Perth, Education Department of Western Australia, Equal Opportunities Branch.

COOLEY, C.H. (1902) *Human Nature and the Social Order*, New York, Charles Scribner's Sons.

DWECK, C. (1975) 'The role of expectations and attributions in the alleviation of learned helplessness', *Journal of Personality and Social Psychology*, 31, pp. 674–85.

DWECK, C. and BUSH, E.S. (1976) 'Sex differences in learned helplessness: I. Differential debilitation with peer and adult evaluators', *Developmental Psychology*, 12, pp. 147–56.

DWECK, C. and GILLIARD, V. (1975) 'Expectancy statements as determinants of reactions to failure: Sex differences in persistence and expectancy charge', *Journal of Personality and Psychology*, 32, pp. 1077–84.

DWECK, C. and REPPUCCI, N. (1973) 'Learned helplessness and reinforcement responsibility in children', *Journal of Personality and Social Psychology*, 25, pp. 109–16.

DWECK, C., DAVIDSON, W., NELSON, S. and ENNA, B. (1978) 'Sex differences in learned helplessness: II. The contingencies of evaluative feedback in the classroom and III. An experimental analysis', *Developmental Psychology*, 14, pp. 268–76.

EDUCATION DEPARTMENT OF WESTERN AUSTRALIA (1984) *Priority Schools Programme: Guidelines 1984/5*, Perth, Education Department of Western Australia.

HALL, J.A. and TAYLOR, M.C. (1985) 'Psychological androgyne and the masculinity and femininity interaction', *Journal of Personality and Social Psychology*, 49, pp. 429–35.

HANSFORD, B.C. and HATTIE, J.A. (1982) 'The relationship between self and achievement/performance measures', *Review of Educational Research*, 52, 1, pp. 123–42.

JAMES, W. (1890) *Psychology*, New York, Fawcett.

JONES, R.W. (1968) *Fantasy and Feeling in Education*, New York, New York University Press.

KENWAY, J. and WILLIS, S. (1986) 'Girls, self esteem and education: From the personal to the political and from the universal to the specific', Paper presented at the Annual Conference of the Australian Association for Research in Education, Melbourne, November.

MACCOBY, E.E. and JACKLIN, C.N. (1974) *The Psychology of Sex Differences*, Stanford, Calif., Stanford University Press.

MARSH, H.W. (1985) 'Age and sex effects in multiple dimensions of pre-adolescent self concept: A replication and extension', *Australian Journal of Psychology*, 36, pp. 197–204.

MARSH, H.W. (1987) 'Masculinity, femininity and androgyne: Their relations with multiple dimensions of self concept', *Multi-variate Behavioural Research*, 22, pp. 91–118.

MARSH, H.W., PARKER, J. and BARNES, J. (1985) 'Multidimensional adolescent self-concepts: Their relationship to age, sex and academic measures', *American Educational Research Journal*, 22, pp. 422–44.

MEAD, G.H. (1934) *Mind, Self and Society*, Chicago, Ill., University of Chicago Press.

NICHOLLS, J. (1979) 'Quality and equality in intellectual development: The role of motivation in education', *American Psychologist*, 34, pp. 1071–84.

ROGERS, C. (1982) *A Social Psychology of Schooling*, London, Routledge and Kegan Paul.

ROSENTHAL, R. and JACOBSON, L. (1968) *Pygmalion in the Classroom*, New York, Holt Rinehart and Winston.

ROTTER, J.B. (1966) 'Generalized expectancies for internal versus external control of reinforcement', *Psychological Monographs*, 80, 1, whole No. 609.

SCHEIRER, M. and KRAUT, R. (1979) 'Increasing educational achievement via self concept change', *Review of Educational Research*, 49, pp. 131–50.

SILBERMAN, C. (1973) *The Open Classroom Reader*, New York, Random House.

SKAALVIK, E.M. (1986) 'Sex differences in global self esteem: A research review', *Scandinavian Journal of Educational Research*, 30, 4, pp. 167–79.

TAYLOR, SANDRA C. (1981) 'School organisation and sex differences and change in adolescent self esteem', in M.L. LAWSON and R. LINKE (Eds), *Inquiry and Action in Education, Volume 1*, Papers presented at the annual meeting of the Australian Association for Research in Education, Adelaide, pp. 214–20.

TAYLOR, SANDRA C. (1982) *Girls and Education: Issues and Priorities*, Symposium presented at the annual meeting of the Australian Association for Research in Education, Brisbane, pp. 308–43.

THOMPSON, L. (1984) *Social Development in the Classroom: A Plan of Action*, Perth, Western Australian Education Department Priority Schools Program, North West Metropolitan Region.

WEST, C., FISH, J.A. and STEVENS, R.J. (1980) 'General self concept, self concept of academic ability and school achievement: Implications for "causes" of self concept', *Australian Journal of Education*, 24, 2, pp. 194–213.

Wings: A Pilot Project to Enhance Self Esteem in Girls (1983) Hobart, Education Department of Tasmania.

WYLIE, R.C. (1979) *The Self Concept*, Lincoln, Neb., University of Nebraska Press.

Chapter 2

The Subtle Politics of Self-esteem Programs for Girls

Jane Kenway, Sue Willis and Jenny Nevard

Our purpose in this chapter is critique, not as an end in itself, but as a possible stimulus towards new directions in our thinking on the issue of girls and schooling. We offer this study in the belief that as feminist educators we must be constantly and restlessly critical, not only of the implications of the sex/gender system for members of our sex, but also of our own discourses. For if feminism cannot criticize itself, it cannot 'serve as the bearer of emancipatory possibilities that can never be fixed and defined once and for all' (Elshtain, 1982, p. 136). Our focus is upon the self-esteem discourse as it manifests itself in discussions of girls' education. We believe it is important that a form of 'ideology critique' is conducted on this literature for the following reasons. Discourses often direct and affect our behaviour in subtle ways which we are not particularly conscious of and have wider social implications which, on quick inspection, are not apparent. Dredging such 'subtexts' to the surface provides us with a better sense of what we are meaning to others and to ourselves. It also allows us to ask whether this is what we intended to mean and, if not, what of our language, imagery, style, logic, etc. we need to change so that the effects of our politics may more closely resemble our intentions.

Let us first establish what it is that we wish to subject to critical scrutiny. The self-esteem discourse is a complex of interwoven strands, each having its own ongoing history. It consists of the research on self-esteem and on self-esteem and education, and the application of both to the study of girls and their schooling. More remotely, it also comprises the various theories, methodologies and ideologies which inform and help to structure this research (cf. Renshaw, Chapter 1 above). Arising from the research, often filtered through the media and constituting many distortions and simplifications, is popular thinking on the matter. Further, including both the research and its popular interpretation, along with hosts of competing ideas and interests, is state or federal government policy on self-esteem and the education of girls. Finally, part of this discourse is constituted by that work which incorporates the concept of self-esteem conducted by curriculum developers and teachers. Often this work is driven by the funding priorities of governments, and is as much informed by popular versions of the theory and research as by the more academic. Although what these various strands have in common is the desire to improve the circumstances of girls by deploying the ideas associated with the self literature, as the introduction to this collection shows, the field is nonetheless characterized by a degree of diversity. Consequently, this discourse to date can be interpreted in a range of ways. Even so, within the range certain features dominate, and thus the discourse as a whole offers a strongly preferred interpretation, one which, we suggest, is quite limited in its scope. At the same time, however, we wish to emphasize the fact that the literature need not be, and has not always been, read in this way: that it offers the scope for different sets of connotations with much more emancipatory possibilities. Such an alternative reading is a major purpose of this collection.

An adequate ideology critique of this discourse is a grand undertaking and of necessity our intentions here are less ambitious. We seek to identify some of its major themes, and to indicate some of the underlying messages of the field, especially those for counter-sexist educational practice. We will point to the options which it privileges, those which it minimizes or closes off and the expectations and the possibilities it creates. Before proceeding to this task it is apt that we suggest, by way of examples, something of what the more complete critique might include.

Social science generally and specific disciplines within it have been subject to a feminist critique which has revealed a number of sexist tendencies. As Westkott observes, these include 'the distortion and misinterpretation of women's experience' (1979, p. 423). Women may be ignored, or considered and measured in masculine terms, defined only in relation to men, or defined as 'deviations' from, or 'negations of, a masculine norm' (p. 423). Women have been devalued in the social sciences no less than they have been devalued in society; the difference is that the former claim objectivity and produce knowledge which profoundly influences social organization. As Foucault's work on power/knowledge shows (Gordon, 1980), the social sciences provide knowledge which, when institutionalized through schools, hospitals, welfare agencies, prisons, industry, etc., distributes populations around 'norms', and confers on people an 'identity'. Given that the self-esteem discourse is immersed in phenomenological, social interactionist psychology and sociology, an adequate 'ideology critique' would place the self-esteem literature in their contexts and closely inspect the gendered assumptions which inform these fields of knowledge.

Equally, a critically self-reflexive feminism would subject to scrutiny the liberal feminism which inspires much of the girls and self-esteem literature; as such a critique informs much of this chapter, it is appropriate to identify key components. Liberal feminism draws much of its conceptual apparatus from social psychology and Parsonian sociology and includes notions such as sex role and role model, sex stereotyping, self-esteem and learned helplessness. The compensatory, access-oriented programs aiming to rectify girls' personal and educational 'deprivation' and 'disadvantage' which arise from these have had considerable public visibility, government sponsorship and teacher acceptance. Liberal feminism is feminism's most acceptable face; its language and its logic part of public discourse and powerful as rhetoric. Thus, as an important component of feminist political strategy, liberal feminism is valuable (see Eisenstein, 1980; Yates, 1986). But when one inquires why liberal feminism has slipped so readily into popular thinking, it is difficult to escape the conclusion that it is because of the harmony it has with dominant ideologies. Those feminists who are currently identifying some of the limitations of liberal feminism have pointed to the subtle connections between it and notions of free will, individualism, competitiveness, meritocracy, hierarchy and social mobility. These, it is argued, lead it to operate well within the tolerance threshold of the current structures of oppression associated with capitalism. Liberal feminism is much more concerned about girls' and women's access to current power structures than about offering a critique of them or constructing feminist alternatives. Ironically, in according such esteem to those spheres and to attributes most associated with males, liberal feminism is in danger of perpetuating some very sexist values (see Middleton, 1984; Kenway and Willis, 1986; Kessler *et al.*, 1985; Carrigan *et al.*, 1985).

Informed by the gist of these two examples, let us now focus more closely on the self-esteem discourse itself. First, however, we wish to make clear that not in any way do we wish to deny the importance of positive feelings, relationships and atmosphere or to decry, or discredit, the intentions of those generating and promoting this discourse. Our purpose is simply to try to capture some of its more subtle, broader-scale and longer-term directives. We will suggest that its preferred reading, and thus its most predictable outcome, is quite restricted in its understanding of power and in its view of education, society and social change and that ultimately, therefore, its capacity to fulfil its good intentions is limited. We are concerned that this is a discourse which individualizes, pathologizes and depoliticizes the issues of sexism in education and society and, further, that this has implications also for class, ethnic and racial educational politics which are of a similar nature.

Stereotypes, Pathologies and Ambiguous 'Compensations'

Within the literature girls' self-concepts and their self-esteem are seen to be inextricably caught up in processes associated with sex roles and stereotypes. Their underachievement and narrow range of choices are seen to be effects of the nature and transmission of sex stereotyped attitudes. Girls are held to be their compliant appropriators and victims, their attitudes leading them to 'fail' and to make 'wrong' choices, thereby restricting themselves and their opportunities. 'Girls' self esteem is constantly undermined by stereotypes which depict women as physically inadequate and often as total failures. This portrayal gives girls negative roles on which to model their behaviour' (*Wings*, 1983, p. 6). Within this particular type of discussion a pervasive and recurring theme is the individual girl's *lack* of certain attitudes, skills or characteristics. She lacks feelings of personal self-worth, confidence in her academic abilities, a belief in her potential for leadership, and indeed she lacks both an inclination and a belief in her power to act upon the world (Schools Commission, 1975, pp. 104–13).

In accordance with girls' deficient and 'victim' status and in recognition that they have been objects of discrimination, the self-esteem literature would have them compensated. Their compensation is often, but not always, a set of 'remedial' programs seeking to overcome the 'lack', to make them feel better about themselves in a range of situations and to encourage more rationality, autonomy and assertiveness so that no longer will they 'conspire in their own oppression' (see *Wings*, 1983; Melgaard and Bruce, 1982; Transition Education Unit, 1981, 1983). Not only does this discourse seem to blame the victim, it almost treats her as if the problem were hers in the first place. Compensation programs are conceived of at the level of the individual; in other words, it is a matter of tailoring the individual to fit the system rather than querying a system which confers on large numbers of students a deficient identity. Focusing intervention programs on the individual may have deleterious effects. For example, the problem may be seen less as a social problem and more as that of the individual and thus of small proportion and readily overcome. In addition, individuals may perceive of themselves as owning the problem and further, as a consequence of their being encouraged to regard themselves as autonomous and self-regulating, individualism is promoted at the expense of group solidarity.

In proffering its somewhat deficit view, the literature rather perversely constructs its own stereotypes of girls and these look strangely similar to those which it seeks to defy. Its girls uncritically absorb stereotyped messages all in similar ways. The following is one example of many. 'A girl internalizes that her role in life is to wait until asked rather than to initiate, to take what she is given rather than to ask for what she wants and to remain quiet rather than offer her own opinion especially if it differs from others' (Melgaard and Bruce, 1982, p. 4). Certainly, those females who negotiate a powerful personal position or operate against the constraints of engendered roles are often invisible, paradoxically though, emerging on occasions as role models. Generally, however, not only are the discourse's central characters submissive and dependent but also, in interpersonal self-esteem programs which are couched in the language of empathy and cooperation and which emphasize harmony and mutual positivity, they are encouraged to develop their 'discredited' nurturing capacities. Ironically, this stands in an uneasy relationship to the individualism noted earlier. While on the one hand girls are encouraged to operate in a masculinist mode as autonomous, rational and assertive, through such self-esteem programs they are also inducted further into a politics of 'niceness'. Such politics are certainly not new to women. *Wings* (1983, p. 35) exemplifies such a contradictory approach in the strategies which it offers for developing self-esteem. These include:

Communication skills, e.g. Active listening, identifying and expressing feelings.
Assertiveness training.
Decision making and standing up for rights.
Affirmations.
Giving and receiving compliments.
Resolving differences.
Dealing with anger and negativity.
Body language, non-verbal language.
Looking at different levels of relationships.
Movement, sound and role plays.
Fantasy, imagery and visualization.

Some feminists assert that although women's and girls' learned capacity for nurturance and collectivity may have been harnessed in the process of their oppression, such capacities may also be regarded as a particular strength. For instance, Chodorow (1978) argues that the social function of females in the domestic sphere is to provide the morality (the 'moral mother') that may be frequently missing from the public sector. Others (e.g. Ruddick, 1980; Rich, 1980) point to the potential benefits of 'maternal thinking' for the public sphere, suggesting, for example, that given the threat of nuclear war and environmental destruction, such thinking may well become humanity's saviour. In both cases, however, these 'female' capacities are celebrated, presented as a critique of public discourse, and heralded as a revolutionary way forward for society. In contrast, the self-esteem literature treats them simply as a means to gain access to the very power structures in which such capacities are derided. Contradiction seems to be at the centre of the self-esteem discourse, particularly as it manifests itself in projects for schools.

Self Politics, Individualism and Quietism

Let us reflect further on the matter of individualism. The self-esteem discourse is individualistic in ways beyond blaming the problems of the sexist outcomes of schooling mostly on the individual girl's attitudes. Although it urges girls to be concerned about the self-esteem of others, it is, as we implied earlier, not directed toward a sense of sisterhood or community. Like liberalism and liberal feminism, it implies a social benefit in collective self-interest, and so it primarily directs individuals inward to self-contemplation, 'purification' and enhancement. In suggesting that we can all maximize our achievement and our self-interest together, without conflict or cost, it appears innocent of current educational realities and constraints, expecting girls to take on board a Utopian view of the way education might be, without challenging the way it is.

There are limits to the sort of pluralism which is implied in the self-esteem discourse (see Giroux, 1985; Yates, 1985). Giroux (1985, pp. 30–2) argues that the discourse of pluralism 'signals an invitation for diverse cultural groups to join hands under the democratic banner ... and serves to legitimate the idea that in spite of differences manifested around race, ethnicity, language, values and life styles, there is an underlying equality among different cultural groups that disavows privileging any one of them.' This ignores the asymmetrical relations of power within which different cultures operate and, as he says, 'idealizes the future while stripping the present of its deeply rooted contradictions and tensions ... and refuses to posit the relations between culture and power as a moral question demanding emancipatory political action.' There are also limits to the social harmony promoted in the literature, particularly when the power and privilege of dominant social groupings are challenged. As we have suggested, the literature on self-esteem, in its more conservative manifestation, does not really mount an educational challenge. By and large it does not seek to promote critical consciousness or 'civic courage'. Even its language is that of political quietism. For example, in another, more politically contentious, body of thought, low self-esteem may be defined as alienation, and raising self-esteem might be defined as empowerment. Often in this discourse, for both teachers and students, the empowering 'why' questions, and thus the critical faculties, tend to be put to one side in favour of 'how to' questions. Technique supersedes political and ethical issues in the form of lesson plans or formulae. Witness the following,

THE FORMULA: When you are angry or miserable and don't know why and don't know what to do, use THE FORMULA.

THE FORMULA is: I feel ------------------
                  because ------------------
                  and I want ------------------
                  (Transition Education Unit, 1981, p. 31)

To argue that this discourse is individualistic is not to say that it ignores social interaction or society. Rather, it is to argue that its starting point is always the individual and that society is conceived of in a particular way. Unlike certain 'traditional' psychologies, which see society as the aggregate of all its individual members, this version arising from social interactionism sees the individual as the product of the interpersonal, intersubjective negotiation of meaning, and society as the aggregate of these interpersonal relations and meanings, i.e. its focus is always on the small scale. This has consequences for analysis and sexual educational politics. What it does not permit is sufficient recognition that certain social conditions also pre-exist individuals and their negotiations and, as such, individuals are, to a certain extent but by no means entirely or forever, the social relations into which they are born. Second, to focus on an individual's narrow range of interpersonal situations and to see her/him as a product of these, is to minimize the force of wider social processes, such as class. Interpersonal relations are clearly not a 'closed field'. This leads us to another implication of this perspective and allows us, moreover, to pick up an earlier suggestion that this discourse had apolitical connotations. The concentration on the individual and the interpersonal underplays the severity of the effects of the social *totality* in determining the relations between individuals and groups (see Henriques *et al.*, 1984). These points require elaboration.

In pathologizing girls' and women's position in the manner it does, this literature minimizes the historical, material and structural forces which have helped to generate such a position, at the same time as underplaying the possibility that women's position is, and has been, actively constructed by men. This perspective cannot adequately account for those relations of domination and subordination, those of power, gender and class which arise from material reality. It directs us to individual, intergroup change rather than social change or to an educational politics of general structural change.

What this means is that those features of the education system which sift, sort, grade, classify and, in the process, distribute and attribute value and valuelessness are not confronted. It neglects the power relationships which helped to produce the system, those that are embodied in its very operations and embedded in its curriculum with its hierarchies of value, not just for different peoples but for different knowledges and cultural, linguistic and personal styles. It places teachers in a double bind; while some of her/his efforts are directed towards the improved esteem of all, others are, of necessity, directed towards the esteem of a few. Clearly, schools don't (can't, won't) allow all students to be 'successes'. This discourse almost seeks to 'gentle the masses' into feeling good about failure and, ironically (maybe not), promotes individualism in an apparatus much of which is directed at conformity and social regulation.

Although this personal and interpersonal thinking resonates well with the feminist dictum that the personal is political, and although one would not wish to deny the importance of micro-politics, there is also no denying that the social condition and self-image of females generally are embedded in broader patriarchal and economic relationships in a range of complex ways (see Arnot; 1984). Let us substantiate this point, first, by considering the example of the patriarchal ideology which is embodied in the 'youth' industry which produces such profit for capital and, second, by mentioning matters more directly economic.

Patriarchal Politics and the 'Adolescent Girl'

There is no doubt that the image marketeers of the youth culture, leisure and fashion industries play a dominant role in defining valued *styles* of girlhood and that these, along with romantic (rather than domestic) ideology (see Taylor, 1987) and its associated temptations and trepidations, significantly impinge upon girls' hierarchies of value and conceptions of self. Although usually recognizing this with regard to adolescent girls, the self-esteem literature often fails to notice how the values of the youth industry have come to dominate the messages which the media now direct at much, much younger girls. As any viewers of programs for children on commercial television will quickly recognize, preparation for adolescent girlhood begins very early via, for example, the promotion of Barbie Dolls, 'pretend' make-up and jewellery, trendy designer fashions for children, 'junior hair gel' and the family-oriented rock-schmaltz young talent shows. As a consequence of such introductions to hegemonic definitions of feminine worth, many primary school girls are no less concerned about their body's adornment, display or concealment than their teenage counterparts.

Intervention programs might thus be far better directed at girls of 7 going 17 (and their parents) than at those girls already caught up in the logic of popular portrayals of valued adolescent femininity. One might also suggest that some self-esteem intervention programs are likely to reinforce a socially constructed self-consciousness in girls, to encourage them constantly to monitor their appearances with an eye to the sexist gaze. For example, take the self-esteem program at Riverside High School (cited in *Wings*, 1983, p. 70):

Week IV
1. Guest speaker on skin, haircare, make-up.
2. Discussion in small groups on health, appropriateness of make-up, pimples, embarrassment, money to buy make-up and why women use make-up.

Week V
1. Guest speaker on deportment, grooming, care of clothes, dressing appropriately, personal hygiene.
2. Planning a wardrobe, the money needed to buy clothes, dressing to suit figure and age.

It may well be appropriate for those feminist writers who are so firmly attaching the self-esteem discourse to secondary school girls to reject any ahistorical notion of adolescence and to consider the manner in which the 'adolescent girl' has been socially constructed across time by social scientists, policy-makers, the media and the 'youth' industry. The gendered assumptions embodied therein and the question of whose social interests are best served by the effects of such constructions are in urgent need of a feminist unveiling rather than reinforcement. Take the following as a case in point.

The notion of puberty is interpreted within the 1975 and 1984 Schools Commission reports on girls' education as a significant time when girls' sense of self undergoes change as part of a teenage crisis of self-identity and emotional change. Similar thinking appears in *Wings*: 'The beginning of adolescence is a disturbing time for self-image and females are most vulnerable at this key period' (1983, p. 6); and Melgaard and Bruce seek:

> 'to catch' girls at this stage and to give them skills to approach some of the difficulties which lie before them, . . . With the onset of puberty definitions of femininity and normalcy change and come precipitously closer to the stereotype. Girls find that behaviours that have previously been rewarded . . . are now viewed negatively by others. (1982, p. 6)

The implication in this literature is that suddenly as bodies change, so too do society's messages and girls' consciousness. That this is misleading is evident in the increasing body of literature on pre- and primary school girls' gendered socialization (see Davies, 1987). Even so, along with the notion of 'shock' goes that of 'crisis' which resonates disturbingly with some rather dated 'truths' about the connections between female biology and such emotional states as irrationality and irresponsibility. As Showalter (1985, p. 56) observes (citing Fielding Blandford, 1871), typical of such attitudes in Victorian times was the belief that 'the sympathetic connection existing between the brain and the uterus is plainly seen by the most casual observer.' Based on a psychiatric construction of the female life-cycle, Erikson (1968) extended the metaphor of a crisis at puberty to describe it as a stage of development when females break ties with the father in preparation for forming husband-seeking alliances. Here, the stages in girls' psycho-social growth are clearly marked by their relationships to males rather than by their own stages of development.

While the authors of the self-esteem documents noted above would want to dissociate themselves from either set of connotations of the notion of puberty crisis, they nonetheless have almost attributed to biology that which many feminists would consider primarily social. If, in our culture, growing through adolescence is a particular crisis for females, perhaps, as well as seeking to assist them through the difficulties, we should be asking why this is so. Why are menarche and a changing body shape often causes for shame and confusion rather than for celebration, as in some other cultures?

As the proliferation of posters and stickers on the general theme 'girls can do anything' indicates, the self-esteem discourse seeks to construct alternative and wider ranging definitions of valued girlhood. However, some of its attempts in this regard adopt a line of reasoning which asserts that 'I'm OK, you're OK', that 'Everyone is beautiful in their own way' (e.g. Brands, 1986, pp. 3–6). Commendable as such an approach to human aesthetics may be, this somewhat wishful thinking exhibits a naive faith in free will and rationality. It also fails to notice that although the youth image industry may ultimately have oppressive consequences, it is so effective precisely because of its capacity to produce notions of what is pleasurable and desirable. The patriarchal ideology embodied in popular literature, i.e. magazines, books, TV, films for girls (see Gilbert, 1987), does not simply regurgitate docile, unattractive, powerless female stereotypes. Rather, it 'identifies' the fields in which it is appropriate for females to be powerful and 'explains' the most acceptable ways in which such power may be displayed and exercised. Conversely, it attempts to keep the gate to 'male domains'. Either way the teenage girl is 'taught' that, for her, power and pleasure are best secured by acquiring and deploying the 'right' face, figure and fashion, and an interpersonal style which resembles the 'cool' and breezy sociability of the Coke ads. Therefore, to suggest that girls are duped by negative images of females is to fail to appreciate the capacity of patriarchal ideology to captivate and seduce through the use of 'empowering' images, while at the same time providing apparent avenues of escape from the drabness and dissatisfaction of the real into endless self-renewal through consumption, fantasy and romance. Also, as we will shortly elaborate, it fails to appreciate that the messages embodied in any social text cannot be equated with their reception.

Increasingly, feminists are exploring the subtle connections between the notions of femininity and gendered pleasure promoted by the youth industry and the wider culture of consumption and the gendered division of labour in paid employment and the home. Equally, they show how the domestic is often mediated through the romantic. However, the implications of the attractions of this ideological apparatus for girls' attachment or otherwise to school or to certain aspects of schooling are seldom explored. In defining girls as the hapless victims of stereotyping, the self-esteem literature refuses to contemplate the possibility that girls may, perhaps justifiably, anticipate some pleasures or rewards through the career and subject choices that they make. It is possible that they may read attempts to redirect their choices to, say, maths and science classes as encouraging them in part to 'suffer and be still' in spheres of activity in which they anticipate little immediate gratification. Pleasure and desire are actually produced through sex stereotypes and provide the means by which esteem is gathered and certain gendered forms of power gained while others are lost. Too often in the self-esteem discourse only 'male domains' are perceived as empowering; ironically, those areas in which girls and women conventionally succeed are defined as either power neutral or disempowering and thus are derided in a very sexist fashion (see Kenway, 1987). Either way, for schools' 'less able' girls, the promises of immediate gratification and happiness implied in both the youth culture consumption industry and in the romantic ideology associated with boy friends may well appear a better and more pleasant investment than the absence of promise or pleasure offered by a school system which defines only a minority as successful. If, for the price on the ticket, happiness can be bought, or if, at the cost of independence, relationships can be secured, then what value school? In short, if girls believe that what happens outside school provides a better avenue for constructing a positive identity than what happens in and through school, then this may, in many senses, be a realistic comment on what schools do to them and what they lack for them. It may also, of course, be an unfortunate and ultimately debilitating evaluation of what the culture of femininity offers.

It seems to us that the self-esteem literature undertheorizes power in many senses. Its girls don't have the power to make reasoned choices within constrained circumstances; neither do they have the power to resist, reinterpret or rearticulate oppressive stereotyping. In fact, a major omission in this discourse is any attempt to show either how girls actually receive and use the gendered cultural artifacts which constitute their worlds or how these intersect, in complex and contradictory ways, with the other aspects of their lives. In addition, there is little attempt to examine the ways in which girls respond to feminist discourse. Also there is no real sense of where the stereotypes come from and why they stay in place. They mysteriously provide their own ongoing conditions of existence. Consequently, the power relationships which help to construct a sex/gender system based on unequal relations between the sexes go unrecognized and thus oppositional politics are deprived of a focus. Instead, for instance, of pointing to males' 'will' towards power over females and the concomitant benefits of that power as a possible source, the literature urges girls to correct their individual thinking, to clarify their values and be more assertive.

The Self and the Economic: Some Subtle Imperatives

Let us now focus more specifically on the economic and the ways in which it is crucially implicated in the specific manner that working-class women and girls experience gender somewhat differently from women members of society's ruling groups. While the self-esteem literature does gesture towards the cultural differences associated with ethnicity or race (e.g. Liverpool New Arrivals Programme Workshop, 1985), class cultural differences are virtually unacknowledged. Yet valued ways of being female are class-related. Economic power is an ingredient which must be recognized in any feminist analysis. Too often feminists concentrate on males' power over females and minimize its many other dimensions. One of particular pertinence here is the power to determine meaning which often accrues to those with the economic power to manage or control the means of representation which, as we have just observed, often provide the parameters within which value may be defined. Those with the power to determine meaning also have the capacity to construct dominant definitions of what is valuable in education and elsewhere *and* to live according to those definitions. Notions of value invariably include a negative referent, and often those with the least power to popularize their own definitions will not only become a negative reference group for the more powerful, but will internalize at least something of a dominant definition. For example, working-class girls may move uncomfortably between various situations, some building a sense of self-worth, others undermining it. The personal anguish that such competing conceptions of value may cause are vividly demonstrated in Sally Morgan's moving autobiography *My Place* (1987). An Aboriginal, Sally was brought up as white. Her grandmother's and mother's experiences of an insensitive, exploitative and tokenistic white society explain why this is so. Here is an extract from Sally's mother's story. Separated from her mother and placed in an institution, she has a Christmas visit to the home of one of Western Australia's 'better' families in which her mother is in unpaid service.

> I remember one holiday at Ivanhoe when I was very upset. I was in the kitchen with my mother. She had her usual white apron on and was bustling around, when April came in with June. I couldn't take my eyes off June. She had the most beautiful doll in her arms. It had golden fair and blue eyes and was dressed in satin and lace. I was so envious, I wished it was mine. It reminded me of a princess.

> June said to me, 'You've got a doll too, Mummy's got it.' Then, from behind her back, Alice pulled out a black topsy doll dressed like a servant. It had a red checked dress on and a white apron, just like Mum's. It had what they used to call a slave cap on its head. It was really just a handkerchief knotted at each corner. My

mother always wore one on washing days, because the laundry got very damp with all the steam and it stopped some of it trickling down her face.

I stared at this doll for a minute. I was completely stunned. That's me, I thought, I want to be a princess not a servant. I was so upset that when Alice placed the black doll in my arms, I couldn't help flinging it onto the floor and screaming, 'I don't want a black doll, I don't want a black doll'. (pp. 261–2)

Although little acknowledged, class has a presence in this discourse beyond that already alluded to. Self-concept/esteem programs are most often conceived of for school 'failures', and school failures are most often working-class students who also tend to be the greatest school 'resisters'. Thought about in this way, the material takes on another dimension and other questions arise. To what extent does it become doubly compensatory offering working-class students camps, for example, and other pleasantries, while their differently classed peers get on with the academic mainstream? To what extent does the use of various tokens rewarding low-status achievement take the sting out of failure in the mainstream? (The use of rewards for 'low-status' achievement doesn't fool students for very long.) To what extent is it a means of classroom control in a humanist guise? The attraction which many teachers feel for the self-esteem discourse may be explained, not just by the appeal of such sentiments as caring, valuing individual worth and tolerance towards difference, but also by the desire, in increasingly difficult times, to maintain classroom control in a non-authoritarian manner. Indeed, some of the literature implies that self-esteem is best gained by conforming to school norms (see School Reports in *Wings*, 1983, pp. 67–8).

There are certain ideological conditions which benefit contemporary capitalist economies, and it is not totally implausible to suggest that the sorts of values both promoted and neglected by this literature could help to produce the sort of individualistic quietism which supporters of the economic status quo favour. Capitalist economies prefer compliant un-waged women, just as they prefer compliant paid workers of both sexes; and this discourse can be read as seeking to produce the 'quiet achiever', who, under current circumstances, is unlikely to complain as the education mandarins clone schooling closer to the interests of capital. The privatized individual matches nicely the privatized economy. Perhaps this approach really only seeks, on behalf of women and girls, to 'even up access to existing forms of success and failure' (Yates, 1985, p. 14). High self-esteem and individual achievement are the ultimate good.

It seems to us that the self-esteem discourse is probably too small an explanation for the vast disparities of power and social rewards which exist between men and women and women and women. So, too, is the notion that changing wrong-headedness will change a sexist society.

References

ADLAM, D., HENRIQUES, J., ROSE, N., SALFIELD, A., VENN, C. and WALKERDINE, V. (1977) 'Psychology, ideology and the human subject', *Ideology and Consciousness*, 2, October, pp. 5–56.

ARNOT, M. (1984) 'Male hegemony, social class and women's education', *Journal of Education*, 116, 1, pp. 1–25.

BRANDS, C. (1986) *Educating Our Daughters*, Perth, Women's Advisory Council of Western Australia and Equal Opportunity Branch of Education Department of Western Australia.

CARRIGAN, T., CONNELL, R.W. and LEE, J. (1985) 'Hard and heavy phenomena: The sociology of masculinity 1900–1980', *Theory and Society*, 14, 5, pp. 531–604.

CHODOROW, N. (1978) *The Reproduction of Mothering, Psychoanalysis and the Sociology of Gender*, Berkeley, Calif., University of California.

DAVIES, B. (1987) 'The accomplishment of genderedness in pre-school age children', in POLLARD, A. (Ed.), *Children and Their Primary Schools*, Lewes, Falmer Press.

EISENSTEIN, Z. (1980) *The Radical Future of Liberal Feminism*, New York, Longman.

ELSHTAIN, J.B. (1982) 'Feminist discourse and its discontents: Language, powers and meaning', in KEOHARE, N.O., ROSAEDO, M.Z. and GELPI, B. (Eds), *Feminist Theory: A Critique of Ideology*, Brighton, Harvester Press, pp. 127–45.

ERIKSON, E. (1968) *Identity, Youth in Crisis*, New York, Norton.

GILBERT, P. (1987) 'Stoning the romance: Girls as resistant readers and writers,' Paper presented at the ANZAAS Congress, James Cook University, August.

GILLIGAN, C. (1982) *In a Different Voice: Psychological Theory and Women's Development*, Cambridge, Mass., Harvard University Press.

GIROUX, H. (1985) 'Critical pedagogy, culture, politics and the discourse of experience', *Journal of Education*, 167, 2, pp. 22–41.

GORDON, C. (Ed.) (1980) *Michael Foucault, Power/Knowledge: Selected Interviews and Other Writings 1972–1977*, Brighton, Harvester Press.

HENRIQUES, J., HOLLWAY, W., URWIN, C., VENN, C. and WALKERDINE, V. (1984) *Changing the Subject: Psychology, Social Regulation and Subjectivity*, London, Methuen.

KENWAY, J. (1987) 'Is gender an issue in English teaching?' *Interpretations Special Issue: Gender*, 20, 1, pp. 17–27.

KENWAY, J. and WILLIS, S. (1986) 'Feminist single sex educational strategies: Some theoretical flaws and practical fallacies', *Discourse*, 7, 1, pp. 1–30.

KESSLER, S., ASHENDEN, D., CONNELL, R.W. and DOWSETT, G.A. (1985) 'Gender relations in secondary schooling', *Sociology of Education*, 58, January, pp. 34–48.

LIVERPOOL NEW ARRIVALS PROGRAMME WORKSHOP (1985) *Me No Good, Miss — Self Esteem and Social Skills — Strategies for Students of Non-English Speaking Background*, Sydney, Education Department of New South Wales.

MELGAARD, G. and BRUCE, W. (1982) *A Confidence Building and Self Esteem Program for Year 7–10 Girls*, Adelaide, Education Department of South Australia, Woman's Advisory Unit.

MIDDLETON, S. (1984) 'The sociology of women's education as a field of academic study', *Discourse*, 15, 1, pp. 42–62.

MORGAN, S. (1987) *My Place*, Fremantle, Fremantle Arts Centre Press.

RICH, A. (1980) *On Lies, Secrets and Silence*, London, Virago.

RUDDICK, S. (1980) 'Maternal Thinking', *Feminist Studies*, 6, 2, pp. 342–67.

SCHOOLS COMMISSION (1975) *Girls, School and Society*, Report by a Study Group to the Schools Commission, Canberra, Australian Government Publishing Service.

SCHOOLS COMMISSION (1984) *Girls Tomorrow: The Challenge for Schools*, Report of the Commonwealth Schools Commission Working Party on Education of Girls, Canberra, Australian Government Publishing Service.

SHOWALTER, E. (1985) *The Female Malady: Women, Madness and English Culture 1830–1980*, London, Virago.

TAYLOR, S. (1987) 'Empowering girls and young women: The challenge of the gender inclusive curriculum', Paper presented at the Annual Conference of the Sociological Association of Australia and New Zealand, Sydney, July.

TRANSITION EDUCATION UNIT (1981) *Improving Chances for Girls: A Strategy for Confidence Building*, Adelaide, Education Department of South Australia.

TRANSITION EDUCATION UNIT (1983) *Transition Education for Girls: Confidence Building for Year Ten Students*, Adelaide, Education Department of South Australia.

WESTKOTT, M. (1979) 'Feminist criticism of the social sciences', *Harvard Educational Review*, 49, 4, pp. 442–30.

Wings: A Pilot Project to Enhance Self Esteem in Girls (1983) Hobart, Education Department of Tasmania.

YATES, L. (1985) 'Curriculum becomes our way of contradicting biology and culture: Some dilemmas for non-sexist education', *The Australian Journal of Education*, 29, 1, pp. 3–17.

YATES, L. (1986) 'Theorizing inequality today', *British Journal of Sociology of Education*, 7, 2, pp. 119–34.

Part II
Culture

Chapter 3

Ethnic Minority Girls and Self-esteem

Georgina Tsolidis

Self-esteem has been central to the Australian debate on girls' education. As far back as 1975 it held a key position within the analysis offered in *Girls, School and Society*. Within the review of girls' education programs offered in the subsequent 1984 Commonwealth Schools Commission report, *Girls and Tomorrow: The Challenge for Schools* its central position was consolidated.

In some circles self-esteem is the pivot on which all other issues related to girls' education revolve; for example, girls-only classes, camps or schools are important as they raise girls' self-esteem; physical education programs or related sporting activities are important as they raise girls' self-esteem; methods of learning are judged in terms of their potential to raise or dampen girls' self-esteem; it is often argued that girls' self-esteem is not threatened in situations where they can work in small groups and learn cooperatively; role models are seen as important because they raise girls' self-esteem as girls witness their potential in the form of a woman whom they can both identify with and learn from. The issue of self-esteem has come to be an icon within the girls' education debate. To take down icons, even temporarily, dust them off and re-examine them is to risk the charge of heresy. However, a process of re-examination is necessary, not only for reasons of intellectual integrity but also for reasons of equity and access. We have consistently to re-evaluate whether the icons are worth worshipping but also whose icons are being worshipped, by whom and for what reasons.

Several questions need to be explored in relation to self-esteem. Is its prominence in the debate warranted? Is the issue of self-esteem central in the debate because it is more important than other issues, or because it is relatively easy to handle? Loss or gain of self-esteem implies measurement. How is it measured? Which situations cause loss of it or contribute to its enhancement? Additionally, we are, as educationists, obliged to explore such questions as they specifically affect the many subgroups which make up the category 'girls'. Are the factors which give rise to self-esteem the same for all groups of girls?

Self-esteem has become central because in many ways it is symptomatic of the ideology which dominates the girls' education debate. The type of feminism which has operated within this sphere can, by and large, be categorized as liberal feminism. It is a social analysis which has concentrated on the individual rather than on social structures. It has concentrated on the individual in terms of how teachers feel about themselves as agents of change, and in analyzing the students' situation and the panaceas it offers them. It has failed to take account of those social forces which along with patriarchy are responsible for the distribution and redistribution of power and privilege. By dwelling on the individual it allows debate on girls' education to side-step issues which are fundamental, for example, social divisions based on class, race and ethnic minority status.

Teaching has become an occupation riddled with complexities which reflect the inequities built into our society. It is difficult for teachers, often faced with staffing shortages and inadequate facilities and support staff, to ponder the social structures within which their hectic teaching day exists. Solutions to problems need to have a practical application; something that can be taught first period Monday morning. An issue like the raising of girls' self-esteem allows teachers to participate in a crusade which makes them feel good about themselves while at the same time they can avoid issues to do with power, its distribution and the role of schooling and the role of curriculum in power redistribution. These last issues leave little room for a feeling of success and optimism that something can be done about all that needs changing. It is simpler to offer socially compensatory programs than to challenge those educational institutions which keep disadvantaged students disempowered; for example, the assessment procedures and the hold universities have on post-primary curriculum. They can be more personally satisfying because teachers can achieve short-term results in ways which are less personally threatening. To deal with the feminizing of science as an issue, for example, without questioning which girls are gaining access to science, is to ignore structural inequalities based on factors such as class. If we are merely slipping a few privileged girls into the high status subjects of physics and chemistry without examining the need to democratize these subjects, we may be simply feminizing a structure of privilege and elitism. It is, however, more satisfying for the teacher to be able to point to an increase in the number of girls who pass Year 12 physics.

If we work on the level of the individual, we can avoid having to deal with groupings and therefore which groups of students are unrepresented and disempowered. Concentrating on the individual avoids questions of cultural hegemonies. Thus, the feminism which has dominated the education debate is one which, by default, pretends girls are a homogeneous group and that the only division is that between males and females. Because of this, issues of race, class, ethnic minority status and the relationships between them, on the whole, have not been integral to the analysis of gender and the practice which springs from it. The result in Australia has been practice which reflects the analysis and experiences, not of the widest range of Australian women and girls, but only that of a particular group of Australian women and girls.

Feminism, like other forces of social change, is not a monolithic ideology. The feminism which predominates within the established education debate in Australia is one particular type. To criticize it is not to be anti-feminist. It is not the only feminist analysis which is offered. Women bring their own personal experiences to any struggle, and the extent to which such differences can be voiced is an indication of the strength and maturity of that struggle. To be a black, working-class or ethnic minority woman is to have a different experience and interpretation of gender. Such differences require exposure and exploration.

The exclusion to date of the perspectives of the widest possible range of women and girls from the girls' education debate has been relatively uncomplicating. Programs can be distilled to a single issue and teachers involved can have a single goal, be it feminizing science, familiarizing girls with a broader range of careers or making them feel better about themselves as girls. By homogenizing a number of subgroups into a single category called 'girls', a single set of goals can be aimed for and a single set of strategies can be advocated. Thus, all individual girls need their self-esteem raised for the same reasons and by the same methods.

On occasions when subgroups of girls have been acknowledged in policy the perspective used to analyze their situation has been similarly mono-dimensional. Even when the view-finder has been moved to include a new set of subjects, the focus has remained unaltered. Social reality is filtered through cultural lenses. The critical questions are not only who is being observed but also through whose cultural lens. Cultural lenses exist and perceptions are filtered by these lenses regardless of what is being observed. One group of Australian girls particularly affected by these cultural lenses is ethnic minority girls. They and their communities are often assessed on the basis of perceptions not necessarily founded in an understanding of either their specific ethnic cultures or the culture which is a product of the migration process and the power inequities integral to it.

Girls, School and Society (Schools Commission, 1975) in a short chapter entitled 'Groups with Special Needs' acknowledged differences between girls. In this chapter, the report dealt with girls from rural areas, Aboriginal girls and migrant girls. However, the perspective offered was one which is steeped in the dominant culture.

> Some 11% of school going children in 1971 had at least one parent whose native tongue was not English. This fact, along with the lower levels of education of parents in major migrant groups, compared with the average of the adult population, and differing cultural norms affecting the status of women might be expected to result in lesser educational participation and success among migrant girls.... The Committee's special interest was to establish whether aspirations and performance were the same for boys and girls among major migrant groups of non-English speaking origin and whether girls were particularly affected by cultural differences between home and schools, and if so, how. (Commonwealth Schools Commission, 1975, p. 135)

The committee responsible for this watershed report outlines its starting point and main aims regarding ethnic minority girls in this paragraph, within which a number of assumptions can be challenged. Are these girls participating and succeeding less in education and, if so, is this because their parents have a native tongue other than English or a lower than average level of education, or are factors to do with the type of education these girls receive more relevant? Do different expectations for girls and boys have a cultural basis and, if so, on what grounds are such cross-cultural assessments being made? Can differences, if they actually exist, be explained by factors to do with ethnic background or by other factors related to the process of migration and its ensuing economic and social circumstances? To take an example:

> It has been suggested to the Committee that in some migrant communities this [school age girls staying home to do domestic duties] is also the case, perhaps even to the extent of girls being withdrawn from school before the minimum leaving age so that they can 'take over' while their mothers are at work. This situation needs looking into. We have no systematic evidence about it, but the suggestion has been persistently made. (Schools Commission, 1975, p. 139)

If the assumption can be made, for argument's sake, that non-English-speaking background girls, over and above other groups of girls, are kept home to mind younger siblings, is this because of their ethnic cultures' specific views of women? Could it be argued that if Anglo-Australian communities were in a situation where both parents worked and suitable child care facilities were not available, they too would opt for keeping girls rather than boys home to mind younger siblings? What should affront us more: the situation which forces parents to keep children home to look after younger siblings or that they may choose girls rather than boys to do the child-minding?

The analysis which has dominated the girls' education debate has, by and large, been ethnocentric. It operates within a schema which defines Australian in dominant cultural terms only. To be Australian is to be Anglo-Celtic and to be female and non-Anglo-Celtic is to be pitied. *Girls, School and Society* established this framework and is significant because many of the programs for which it acted as a catalyst trace their ideological foundations to the deficit model operational within it. It is a model which clearly defines ethnic minority status as a source of disadvantage rather than the butt of discrimination.

The deficit model applied to ethnic minority girls implicit in *Girls, School and Society* is based broadly on two main assumptions about Australian ethnic minorities and the women and girls within them, relative to the Australian ethnic majority and the women and girls within it. First, no investigation is made of the causes of sexism, so one is left with the interpretation that it varies in response to factors intrinsic to particular ethnic cultures rather than factors related to class, migration or personal belief systems. Second, it is assumed that a hierarchy of sexism exists which is related to ethnic origins. Ethnic minority cultures are considered more sexist than is the 'Australian norm'. This schema is riddled with fundamental difficulties. Whose standards are used to judge levels of sexism? Whose definition of 'Australian' and 'normality' do we accept? This is not to adopt a culturally relativist position. Sexism within any culture should not be condoned. However, in grading sexism we have to be careful not to imply that one form of sexism is worse than another simply because it is less familiar. Such gradings can have serious consequences for ethnic minority communities and the women and girls within them, particularly in a country where they already suffer discrimination.

What has all this to do with self-esteem? A program which seeks to develop girls' self-esteem, if based on an erroneous set of assumptions about ethnic minority cultures, could have grossly deleterious effects on non-English-speaking background girls. Because self-esteem programs operate within a framework which targets the individual victim as the cause of the problem rather than the system as the producer of disadvantage, they are unlikely to be beneficial to groups of girls who are traditionally discriminated against by the education system. For these girls such programs are next to irrelevant because they do not succeed at empowering them. In the case of ethnic minority girls they can be worse than unempowering but actually damaging.

In an effort to combat sexism, ethnic minority communities are often targeted specifically, as they are assumed to be more sexist. Implicit in this schema is the assumption that ethnic minority women are willing to put up with more male chauvinism than their ethnic majority counterparts. Such stereotypes exacerbate a syndrome of self-hate among ethnic minority girls, thus creating the opposite effect to that aimed for by such programs. As well, they condone a negative view of their cultures among other students, again making a positive sense of self more difficult to achieve.

An image of oneself is not formed in a social or cultural vacuum. A self-image is built on messages one is fed, sometimes force-fed, and the extent to which these messages are digested and internalized. There exists an image of ethnic minority girls which is based on assumptions about them and their cultures which are unexamined and stereotypical. These stereotypes are demeaning of these cultures and the women and girls within them. They portray ethnic minority cultures as having extraordinarily male supremacist views. The men within them are depicted as authoritarian, aggressive and domineering. The women are portrayed as passive, down-trodden and colluding in their own oppression. These families are seen as bastions of patriarchy whose closeness is stifling of individual expression and freedom. This is held to be generally true of all ethnic minority cultures, but is more so within certain ethnic groups, particularly those which do not share a Christian religion. The extent to which these characteristics are diluted is measured in terms of the degree of successful assimilation into Australian society and lifestyle. Once the problem is defined, the solution is then sought on the basis of the individual. How can individual ethnic minority girls be helped by their education to become self-assertive and embark on a road which challenges this intolerable oppression? The debate rarely side-steps this framework but within it discusses questions of tactics and the rights and wrongs of schools interfering with family life. Rarely is the thought entertained that the source of ethnic minority girls' problems may be other than their cultures.

Many ethnic minority girls have a different perspective of their ethnic culture and their role within it. Many are quite proud of their ethnic identity and are actively engaged in maintaining their mother tongues and cultural traditions. This is not to imply that they are totally uncritical of their cultures. They do, however, derive strength and confidence from their communities and ethnicity and feel alienated by the discrimination they experience in Australia. It is surprising then that self-esteem programs do not aim to help these students come to terms with discrimination as a means towards a positive self-image.

> Growing up as a Turkish girl in Australia is confusing as well as difficult.... Young Australians expect or think of us to be the same as them, but there are high mountains between us.... For example, take our religions.... Australians are quite different to us as they have no strict religion to go by.... At very young ages they go out with boyfriends, smoke, drink alcohol and do silly things such as kiss on the streets, swear in public and hurt and abuse each other....

> I really enjoy the Greek way of life, and I can see the advantages of being bilingual and being able to identify with the Greek and with the Australian cultures. I would like to see the traditions brought down to future generations, and our future sons and daughters to know how to speak and write the Greek language. But I very much fear that the future generations may not want to learn anything about the Greek culture, because our society is constantly changing. (MACMME, 1987, p. 64)

> Being a Greek girl in Australia has not been easy. As a young girl it was not a problem. I didn't feel any different to the other kids at school, the 'Australians'. Greek school would have been the only thing I did that they didn't, but this hardly ever came into our conversations. Life went on without any thought of being different. At high school, though, I began to feel different. I still had Australian friends, but there was something lacking. Somehow I didn't feel they understood me. For this reason I think, I drifted into the company of other migrant girls.... Now, although a few of my friends are 'Australian', I do tend to drift into migrant company, socializing mainly with Greeks and the odd Italian or other European. Most of them would know my parents. (MACMME, 1987, p. 59)

Stereotypes of ethnic minority cultures are firmly embedded within the dominant culture and as a result are often internalized by ethnic minority girls themselves. Ethnic minority girls will often deny their own reality because it does not coincide with what they are being told it is. So if an adolescent Greek girl is allowed to go to discos, she feels her parents are exceptionally liberal rather than an example of how the stereotype does not apply.

These stereotypes create divisions within families. Ethnic minority adolescents, who are already questioning so much about themselves and their environment, are also being told that their parents are socially unacceptable and inadequate. Their parents' status is diminished and insulted because of cultural dissonance, linguistic factors and economic dislocation. Messages about parents are also messages about their children. Clearly disassociating oneself from the family, under these circumstances, is to raise one's own status.

These stereotypes can also create divisions within communities. They not only have negative repercussions for women and girls within ethnic minorities but also on men and boys within these communities and women and girls within the ethnic majority. Of particular relevance for adolescents is the sexual aspect of cultural stereotypes. Ethnic minority girls are seen as overprotected by their parents and unable to participate in what is considered normal social interaction. They have an aura of sexual purity which is in marked contrast to the sexual image of young women portrayed through the media. Although the sexual double-standard which operates affects women and girls across all cultural groups, its consequences can be harsher on ethnic minority women and girls, particularly during adolescence, when life can be one long list of confusions and contradictions. The following excerpt from a study by the author on ethnic minority girls and education illustrates this point.

In discussions with these ESB [English-speaking background] girls it became apparent that the prevailing attitude to NESB [non-English-speaking background] boys was markedly different from that towards NESB girls. At co-educational schools, these ESB girls were more friendly with and towards NESB boys than they were towards NESB girls. One group stated that 'ethnic' girls did not like them and thought they were 'slack' because they 'went out and had fun' and did things like dye their hair and wear numerous earrings. Generally, these ESB girls thought that NESB girls were 'overprotected' by their parents because these parents did not trust 'Aussies'. What these ESB girls had developed was a view of their own reputation as girls not in relation to their brothers or fathers but in relation to the NESB girls at their schools. . . . Amongst these students there existed an image of NESB girls as 'pure' and ESB girls as 'promiscuous'. The NESB boys participated in this by 'looking after' their sisters' reputations. They also identified ESB girls as 'promiscuous' and commented that this, and their brothers' inability to contain it, was one of the dividing lines in the 'them and us' cultural dichotomy between NESB and ESB students.

ESB girls perpetuated this image by identifying NESB girls as 'pure' and 'overprotected'. They reserved their resentment for these NESB girls who were the least active participants and the most vulnerable in this situation. It seems that in some ways NESB girls earnt the wrath of the ESB girls because an image of 'purity' was being thrust upon them. This, then, provided a sexual standard that ESB girls could be measured against. This concretised the ESB girls' dilemma of needing to conform to the fashionable sexual image of youth culture and yet at the same time cope with the implicit social condemnation of this role. At co-educational schools this situation resulted in the ESB and NESB girls having little to do with each other socially. This stood in contrast to the boys who socialised with each other across ethnic groups. The most noteworthy consequences of these social patterns were that the NESB girls were the group of students who participated in the least cross group social interaction and the NESB boys were the only group who socialised across all groups of students. Thus, within the co-educational schools the NESB girls were the most socially isolated group and the NESB boys were the least isolated group. (MACMME, 1986, pp. 61–2)

This excerpt from a study conducted in Victorian state post-primary schools indicates that issues of gender cannot be separated from issues related to ethnic background. It was clear that, for the students involved, the two were interrelated. They did not simply divide the world into girls and boys, nor for that matter simply into 'wogs' and 'skips'. Educationists must come to terms with students' perceptions of themselves and each other and the role curriculum does and can play in reinforcing and altering these images.

How is the image of overprotected ethnic minority girls perceived by the girls themselves? Although it can be argued that to some extent the stereotype of overprotected ethnic minority girls has been internalized by the girls themselves, this would be to oversimplify the situation. Many of these girls were unhappy about the number of restrictions placed on them by parents relative to brothers or relative to their ethnic majority counterparts. What needs to be explored in this context is their perceptions of the reasons behind these restrictions. Most of them thought these restrictions unjust and considered them to be part and parcel of being part of an ethnic minority. However, they did not draw the conclusion that they were a product of the ethnic culture itself, but rather a product of living in Australia. These girls were keenly aware of the increased protectionism they experienced in Australia relative to their mother countries. They expressed the view that this was a product of their parents' lack of familiarity with, and confidence in, an environment that was alien to them.

> In Turkey my cousins are more free than me because there are hardly any other nationalities living in Turkey like in Australia. So there, their parents don't have to worry much but over here I'm not free because my parents are scared something might happen to me. My father is thinking of going back to Turkey forever in another one or two years time so I am looking forward to going back to my home country....

> My parents like Australia, but when it comes to me they'd feel safer in Yugoslavia because they are scared of the people living here because there's all different communities and because they think something will happen to me since I'm young and especially a girl. If they were in Yugoslavia, they'd have nothing to worry about, because the people are all Yugoslavian and they have the feeling nothing would happen to me. It's their country and there wouldn't be anything to worry about....

> My parents started not to let me out as much as they used to in Greece. I could not understand why at first, but then I realised myself that we were in a new country and we were surrounded by new people whom they did not know. I find that I belong in Greece. I like Melbourne but I find that the night life here is very boring. In Greece even sitting in a coffee shop entertains you because you know everyone, everyone speaks the same language and people talk to you even if they have never seen you before. Here in Melbourne, I find that people are snobs. (MACMME, 1986, p. 58)

An interactive and evolutionary view of culture must be adopted. Australian society, the ethnic minority culture as it operates within it as well as its country of origin, and the process of migration need to be considered. Similarly, a discussion of such issues must take in cross-cultural comparisons of class, education, political or religious beliefs. For example, fundamentalist Moslem schools should be compared to funda-mentalist Christian schools, not ordinary state high schools. How much is it the case of the more familiar appearing more palatable and less threatening than the unfamiliar and 'exotic'? How much is it a case of the values of middle-class, tertiary-educated Anglo-Celtic professionals being compared to those of people who have migrated from poverty and war to an alien country whose language and cultural milieu they do not neces-sarily understand, let alone share? Wealth and privilege can be mistaken for enlightenment. It is individuals who experience the luxuries of econ-omic comfort and political stability who can afford to contemplate the navel of alternative lifestyles.

Self-esteem is related to power and the ability to influence one's own destiny. For Australia's ethnic minorities, stereotyped images of them are simply one, perhaps relatively trivial, component of their powerlessness. Ethnic minority people, particularly women, are overrepresented in the worst, lowly paid jobs, they are still underrepresented in the decision-making structures of Australian society and in some ethnic groups, like the Lebanese and Turkish, their rates of unemployment are dispro-portionately high. Knowledge of the English language, access to jobs, adequate housing, health and education for the children tend to be issues of greater importance.

It is conceivable that in this context definitions of self-esteem, the emphasis it is given and the assessment of what causes it to inflate or deflate will vary enormously in response to economic, political and cultu-ral factors as well as specific circumstances. Teachers and ethnic minority parents are likely to have markedly differing opinions on these issues, particularly if teachers do not share the cultural and class origins of these parents and have not considered the impact of migration on families. If ethnic minority parents prohibit their daughters' participation in camps, for example, it may be not so much for reasons of moral and social etiquette, but because they may prioritize academic programs over and above ones perceived of as social in their emphasis. These parents are likely to prioritize programs which teach their children English over and above those whose aims appear ephemeral. These parents are likely to judge their children's progress in terms of academic results and the opportunities these create rather than success in programs centring on self-expression, for example.

In this context it is important to discuss the relatively high aspirations of non-English-speaking background communities and the resultant ex-pectations of schooling. Non-English-speaking background parents, girls and boys who participated in the aforementioned study were all in agreement that tertiary education was a top priority. Parents stated that this was the case both for daughters and sons and students, both girls and boys, stated that they perceived no difference between their parents' attitudes on this issue as it related to girls and boys. If anything, mothers were more concerned that daughters receive a tertiary education because they did not want them to share their experiences of degradation on the factory floor. Some non-English-speaking background girls commented that their parents' academic expectations of them were too high and that this created a pressure for them.

> My parents want me to be a doctor but they aren't forcing me to be that. They are the occupations which are needed more and easier to get a job if we go to Turkey. My parents' choice and mine is different because I think being a doctor is much harder and much more work. (MACMME, 1986, p. 32)

> I honestly believe that my parents want to give me what they were deprived of when they were young. They often say that they wish that they were educated so they wouldn't be treated like 'dirt' by the boss. I can always see tears forming in their eyes when we discuss the matter. This makes me feel a bit depressed because you can see that being uneducated really has its hardships. (MACMME, 1986, p. 40)

This stood in contrast to the view, as expressed in *Girls, School and Society*, that ethnic minority parents have lower aspirations for their daughters than those they have for their sons. For these students and parents, education was the medium through which their aspirations would be achieved. The sacrifices inherent in the migration process would be worthwhile if children could succeed academically and as a result experience upward social mobility. Because of this attitude schooling was a focus of attention. Many parents expressed disappointment at the schooling their children received as they saw it not offering them the opportunities they deserved. Many discussed its role in the preservation of a status quo which they saw as relegating migrants to the bottom of the pecking order. 'Australian teachers say that migrant parents are too ambitious because Australians want to keep migrants as slaves — discourage them from going to university so they can get somewhere ...' (MACCME, 1986, p.67); 'Migrant parents are not too ambitious — if the kids aren't good enough that's fine, but education here is negligent' (MACMME, 1986, p. 68). Teachers, on the other hand, often viewed these parents' expectations of schooling as unrealistic and a potentially conservatizing force. The parents' emphasis on discipline and structured assessment procedures was perceived as threatening hard-won reforms in curriculum development.

Ethnic minority girls indicated that their views coincided with those of their parents rather than with those of their teachers. As a group, they stood alone in their assessment of their schooling's inability to satisfy their expectations of it. They expected school to fulfil a myriad of functions, both academic and social. For example, they expected more academic rigour than they were experiencing. For many, school did not provide an environment in which they could learn adequately and comfortably. They lacked any confidence in their school's ability to facilitate the attainment of their aspirations. These aspirations were higher than those of their English-speaking background counterparts: 'I have to struggle against teachers and pupils to gain a serious working environment. I think there is too much mucking around. That means I can't get my work done at school....'; 'I want the teachers to teach us more' (MACMME, 1986, p. 39).

Teachers either thought that these girls had few career and/or academic aspirations, or if they were aware of their high aspirations, thought these were unrealistic. If high aspirations existed, teachers often thought they resulted from parental influence more than from any heartfelt desire by the girls themselves. Perhaps of most relevance here is the fact that so many teachers either saw these girls as aspiring to hairdressing, marriage and motherhood or as aspiring to university but capable of only hairdressing, marriage and motherhood. It is conceivable that a girl's self-esteem, particularly if she has high aspirations, would be dampened if she were being taught by people whose image of her was that of someone with little, if any, potential.

One of the ironies of this situation was that the parents were often considered as not valuing education for their daughters when more teachers than parents saw education as irrelevant for ethnic minority girls. Many teachers stated that ethnic minority communities expected these girls to marry young and become young mothers, and this was the expectation they taught to. How responsible are teachers for the creation of self-fulfilling prophecies?

A contradiction existed where schools were running programs which were conceived of as increasing girls' self-esteem while at the same time they were undervaluing and denigrating these girls' cultural backgrounds and aspirations. These ethnic minority girls identified closely with their mother tongues and mother cultures yet, more often than not, they were getting little if any reinforcement for these within the school environment. The curriculum ignored their experiences and those of their communities and often ignored their language. In other ways the school was teaching to images of these cultures which were negative. All in all, the message the schools were reinforcing was that which told ethnic minority girls that their cultural backgrounds were ones which they, particularly as girls, should be embarrassed about.

A school which was serious about empowering students would be seeking out ways in which their class and cultural backgrounds as well as their gender were being reinforced and built upon. Multicultural and counter-sexist curricula are not mutually exclusive. Nor is valuing the skills which students bring with them to the classroom condemning them to a 'mickey mouse' curriculum of crocheting and highlighting exotica for its own sake. Educational equality and access do not have to mean immersing working-class, ethnic minority, black or female students in the dominant cultural values. Ethnic minority girls come to school with skills inherent to their femaleness and their culture. To ignore these is not only pedagogically unsound, it is also taking the easy way out. The status quo needs to be made flexible enough to accommodate, acknowledge and value other than the dominant culture. This point can be illustrated with an example from a Melbourne school.

Exhibition High School draws a lot of its solely female population from the nearby Housing Commission flats (government housing for low income families). It is part of the Disadvantaged Schools Program and is generally considered to have a population which ranks among Melbourne's most socio-economically disadvantaged. In terms of the traditional deficit model its students are girls, working-class and the majority also come from ethnic minorities, often the most recently arrived. Some staff at the school have been innovative enough to incorporate what others would see as disadvantages into the curriculum, in ways which not only acknowledge the skills the students already have, but also create life options for them. For example, the community language course at the school was established in 1981 and is still continuing.

The school recognized early on that it would be unable to cater for the language needs of its students. Close to a dozen languages other than English were represented in the student population and that number of language teachers was out of the question. Instead the school built into the curriculum acknowledgment of, and assistance with, language courses the girls were doing out of school hours. This work was thus accredited and contributed to their Year 12 assessment. Thus, rather than treat them as a liability, the school was able to turn their mother tongues into something which enhanced their scores and facilitated the girls' entry into tertiary institutions. This stands in stark contrast to the many schools which offer bilingual students either token courses in community languages or courses in languages other than English which are totally foreign to them.

An issue that needs to be placed fairly and squarely on the feminist agenda is that of culture. Perspectives are culturally specific. To be feminist is not to avoid having a culturally specific vantage point. To examine this vantage point is not to dilute the importance of feminism. Australian feminism has come to mean the feminism of the dominant cultural groupings within our society. Ethnic minority women and the issues they are specifically affected by have not been part of the mainstream feminist debate.

It requires courage and confidence to walk out of the 'ethnic closet'. Because of physical characteristics, not all of us can hide our ethnic origins, but pride in these origins can certainly be denied. To stand up and say one is proud of being an ethnic minority woman in an environment which depicts such women as passive and down-trodden is tantamount to standing up and saying one is proud of being oppressed. Ethnic minority feminists can think they are exceptions to the rule because they are afforded few opportunities to meet each other and organize as such; so if one is a feminist, one cannot possibly also be proud of belonging to an ethnic minority culture. Hence a simple either/or choice is seen to exist; if you like your culture, you cannot possibly be a feminist, or if you like feminism, you cannot possibly like your culture. To the extent that these stereotypes are accepted they can become self-fulfilling prophecies.

The women's movement has to be broad enough to encompass issues as they relate to women other than those within the ethnic majority: for example, the recent campaign in Australia against cuts in the area of English as a second language, the multicultural education program and the proposal to amalgamate the two government funded television stations, the Australian Broadcasting Commission (ABC) and the Special Broadcasting Service (SBS), the latter being multicultural television. These decisions, if implemented, would have resulted in the drastic curtailment of life options for non-English-speaking background women and girls. Personal opportunities and rights are limited by different factors depending on personal circumstances. For some women, for example, not speaking English is far more limiting than a number of other issues which women within ethnic majorities have the 'luxury' of struggling for. Communication in English is still profoundly more important for self-esteem than a course in self-assertiveness training. When ethnic minority communities are still at a stage of having to fight to maintain the right to learn English, the issue of the number of women in principal positions within schools, for example, falls below first place on the personal agenda of struggle. It is not that ethnic minority feminists do not exist. At present the issues which affect us more dramatically and, as a result, are our top priority are being fought out on the agendas of organizations which are integral to our communities rather than the women's movement.

For teachers the issues which affect our communities are likely to be a higher priority. English as a second language teaching, community language teaching and issues which deal with ethnocentrism, prejudice and racism directly affect the life chances of non-English-speaking background women and girls in ways which they do not affect the ethnic majority. The question needs to be asked: which girls are being targeted and served by programs like the ones designed to increase girls' self-esteem? Are they really effective in increasing the life options of girls who are not part of the mainstream? Similar questions can be asked about issues prioritized by mainstream Australian feminism. Which women are getting into science courses? Which women are becoming school principals? To pose such questions is not designed to weaken the women's movement but to strengthen it. Definitions of feminism and feminists have to become broader and encompassing of women who do not share the dominant cultural assumptions so that the struggle does not become dissipated and divided.

References

AHMED, L. (1982) 'Western ethnocentrism and perceptions of the harem', *Feminist Studies*, 8, 3, pp. 521–34.

ANTHIAS, F. and YUVAL-DAVIS, N. (1983) 'Contextualising feminism-gender, ethnic and class divisions', *Feminist Review*, 15, winter.

APPLE, M.W. (1979) *Ideology and Curriculum*, London, Routledge and Kegan Paul.

ASHENDEN, D., BLACKBURN, J., HANNAN, B. and WHITE, D. (1984) 'A manifesto for a democratic curriculum', *The Australian Teacher*, 7, February, pp. 13–20.

BALLENDEN, C. (1984) *Facing the Future: Careers and Girls*, Occasional Paper No. 10, Melbourne, Victorian Institute of Secondary Education.

BARRETT, M. (1980) *Women's Oppression Today*, London, Verso.

BOTTOMLEY, G. and DE LEPERVANCHE, M. (Eds) (1984) *Ethnicity, Class and Gender in Australia*, Sydney, George Allen and Unwin.

CONNELL, R.W., ASHENDEN, D.J., KESSLER, S. and DOWSETT, G.W. (1982) *Making the Difference: Schools, Families and Social Division*, Sydney, George Allen and Unwin.

CUMMINS, J. (1984) *Bilingualism and Special Education: Issues in Assessment and Pedagogy*, England, Multilingual Matters.

EDUCATION DEPARTMENT OF VICTORIA (1983) *Women in the Education Department of Victoria*, Melbourne, Government Printer.

EISENSTEIN, H. (1984) *Contemporary Feminist Thought*, London, Unwin Paperbacks.

HANNAN, B. (1985) *Democratic Curriculum Essays on Schooling and Society*, Sydney, George Allen and Unwin.

JAKUBOWICZ, A. (1984) *Education and Ethnic Minorities: Issues of Participation and Equity*, NACCME Discussion Paper No. 1 ACT, Fyshwick, ACT, Canberra Publishing and Printing Co.

JEFFCOATE, R. (1979) *Positive Image: Towards a Multicultural Curriculum*, London, Chameleon Books.

JEFFCOATE, R. (1981) 'Evaluating the multicultural curriculum: Students' perspectives', *Curriculum Studies*, 13, 1, pp. 1–15.

MACMME (1986) *In Our Own Words: Multilingual Writing by Girls from Non-English Speaking Background at Exhibition High School*, Melbourne, MACMME.

SAMPSON, S.N. (1981) 'The role of the school in sex-role stereotyping', in GRIEVE, N. and GRIMSHAW, P. (Eds), *Australian Women*, London, Oxford University Press.

SARGENT, L. (Eds) (1981) *Women and Revolution*, Boston, Mass., South End Press.

SCHOOLS COMMISSION (1975) *Girls, School and Society*, Report by a Study Group to the Schools Commission, Canberra, Australian Government Publishing Service.

SCHOOLS COMMISSION (1984) *Girls and Tomorrow: The Challenge for Schools*, Report of the Commonwealth Schools Commission's Working Party on the Education of Girls, Canberra, Australian Government Publishing Service.

SPENDER, D. and SARAH, E. (Eds) (1980) *Learning to Lose: Sexism and Education*, London, The Womens' Press.

STRINTZOS, M. (1984) *To Be Greek Is to Be Good*, Cultural Politics, Melbourne Working Papers, Series 5, University of Melbourne.

THOMAS, C. (1980) '*Girls and counter-school culture*', in McCALLUM, D. and OZOLINS, U. (Eds) *Melbourne Working Papers 80*, University of Melbourne, Department of Education.

TSOLIDIS, G. (1986) *Educating Voula: A Report on Non-English Speaking Background Girls and Education*, Melbourne, Ministry of Education.

WEINER, G. (Ed.) (1985) *Just a Bunch of Girls: Feminist Approaches to Schooling*, Milton Keynes, Open University Press.

YATES, L. (n.d.) 'Curriculum becomes our way of contradicting biology and culture: An outline of some dilemmas for non-sexist education', Melbourne, La Trobe University, School of Education.

YATES, L. (1984) 'Is "girl-friendly" schooling really what girls need? Some reflections on the Australian experience', Melbourne, La Trobe University, School of Education.

YATES, L. (1985) 'Theorising inequality today,' Melbourne, La Trobe University, School of Education.

Chapter 4

Aboriginal Girls: Self-esteem or Self-determination?*

Pat Dudgeon, Simone Lazaroo and Harry Pickett

It is our contention that self-esteem theories and their associated education programs are inadequate as a way forward for Australian Aboriginal
students. Our intention is to demonstrate why this is so and to suggest
alternative directions. This chapter rests on the premise that without an
appreciation of Aboriginal history, culture and politics it is possible to
understand neither the ways in which Aboriginal girls relate to their
schooling nor the manner in which the education system can better serve
their interests. Of necessity our arguments are wide-ranging, dealing first
with Aboriginality generally before focusing specifically on women and
girls. We deal throughout with both the nature of Aboriginal identity and
self-esteem for girls — and their relation to education.

Some Historical Glimpses

> No child, whatever its creed or colour or circumstance, ought to
> be excluded from a public school. But cases may arise, especially
> amongst the Aboriginal tribes, where the admission of a child or
> children may be prejudicial to the whole school. (Harris, 1976)

Thus in 1883 the New South Wales Minister for Education defined
Aboriginal children as potentially a problem for mainstream education,
although he fell short of formally excluding them. Around 1912, however, 'an influx of Aboriginal pupils into European schools ... resulted
in those schools being closed to Aboriginal children for many years. No
provision was made for any effective alternative' (Hill, 1975, p. 71).

* This is an abridged and edited version of a critical review by the authors for the
Centre for Aboriginal Studies, Curtin University of Technology, Western Australia.

The Aborigine protection acts in the various states of Australia (Victoria, 1869; Queensland, 1897; Western Australia, 1905; New South Wales, 1909; Northern Territory, 1910; South Australia, 1912) gave complete control over the lives of Aboriginal people to white administrators and large numbers of Aborigines were forced onto reservations to live in appalling conditions. During this period Aboriginal children were excluded from mainstream education and every effort was also made to deny Aboriginal education to them. For example, in New South Wales one-third of Aboriginal children were removed from their families in the twenty years from 1909, 70 per cent of whom were girls who were usually sent to special training camps for domestic service (see further Huggins, 1987/88). 'One of the major functions of such a policy was the removal of Aboriginal women from Aboriginal customs and traditions so they could not learn the values and beliefs of their own culture' (Burney, 1987, p. 66). Thus Aboriginal girls, in particular, were used as a vehicle for cultural genocide.

The degrading separatist policies of the early part of this century were replaced by the so-called assimilation policies introduced in the 1940s. Aboriginal people were now expected to 'breed out' into the larger white society and welfare policies were designed to 'smooth the dying pillow' (Rowley, 1970, p. 103) of the extinguishing race. Just as Aboriginal people were to be absorbed into white Australian society, Aboriginal children were to be absorbed into mainstream education. This meant, of course, their subjection to an uncompromisingly Western education system.

During the 1960s there was increasing political activity by Aboriginal groups who were critical of the ethnocentrism and paternalism of assimilationist policies which 'failed to recognise the resilience and inherent worth of Aboriginal culture' (Daylight and Johnstone, 1986, p. 107). It was in this context that government policies of 'protection' and 'assimilation' gave way in the 1970s first to the notion of 'integration' and then to 'self-determination'. Under both assimilation and integration policies the participation and achievement of Aboriginal students in schooling remained at low levels. In the mid-1970s more than half of Aborigines and Torres Strait Islanders left school before they turned 15 years of age.

Reflecting the dominant mood of white education of the period, in 1975 Tannock and Punch reported that principals and teachers in Western Australia believed that 'under-encouragement by parents and lack of response to the teacher' (p. 38) were the main causes of low school achievement by Aboriginal students. They concluded that 'the Aboriginal child's "general attitude" towards school is regarded by teachers and principals as a significant impediment to scholastic progress, especially by comparison with white peers' (p. 38). This notion of cultural deprivation of Aboriginal children often led to 'compensatory' programs. According to McConnochie (1981), these typically provided intensive remedial education in an attempt to 'lift' cognitive and language skills and to facilitate the shift to mainstream Western attitudes and lifeways. This 'deficit' model, he argues, was essentially assimilationist, normative and prescriptive.

Only recently, and in the face of widespread failure of compensatory programs, 'have teachers begun to realize the heavy reliance on psychological evidence and explanation has misled them and have begun examining the failure of black education in terms of deficits in teachers, curricula and methods' (p. 131). But, even supposing that this is true, it is not enough. Aborigines demand the right to determine what, if anything, they want from the education system; that is, they demand the right to educational self-determination. Both educational achievement and educational strategies based on the concept of white culture (let alone 'superior' white culture) increasingly are regarded as being of questionable relevance to Aboriginal people, by themselves and even by the white majority. As Wilmott (1982, p. 13) suggests of Aboriginal education, 'there is no "simple solution". I believe we must look beyond curricula, educational technology or pedagogical skills. I believe that there is something fundamental and little understood which is plaguing . . . all of the schooling systems . . . it's almost as though some critical barrier has been reached.' This is, he suggests, both a resistance to assimilation due to the retention of primary identity as Aboriginal and an insistence on Aboriginal goals and process in education, determined and delivered by Aboriginal people and communities themselves.

In the 1980s the number of Aboriginal secondary school students has increased dramatically, but retention rates beyond junior high school are very low relative to the general Australian population. For example, in 1982 the retention rate into upper secondary school was 45 per cent for the general population and 10 per cent for Aboriginal people (*Aboriginal Education*, 1985, pp. 22–3). While participation rates are increasing, achievement levels remain low. In NSW, for example, 104 Aboriginal students (62 girls and 42 boys) sat for the Year 12 Higher School Certificate in 1985 but the aggregates of 74 of the 104 students were in the bottom 25 per cent of those for all students (Burney, 1987).

Furthermore, the majority of Aboriginal students are noticeably over-represented in the less academically oriented programs in most states. The situation is even worse in tertiary education courses (according to the *Survey on Aboriginal Access to Tertiary Education*, 0.3 per cent of Aboriginal students have tertiary qualifications compared to 2.2 per cent of all Australians: 1981, p. 14) Even though the numbers have steadily increased, particularly in teacher education, Aboriginals are 'the most starkly under-represented group in tertiary education' (*Policy Statement on Education for Aborigines...*, 1986, p. 1).

Despite the unfortunate history of Aboriginal contact with white education, common among explanations of Aboriginal students' under-achievement and underparticipation in mainstream education (and of what are often referred to as their 'social problems') is that they suffer from a lack of self-esteem. It is suggested that they have:

> lower individual self-concept/self-confidence/autonomy,
> lower individual achievement motivation,
> lower individual personal ambition,
> lower individual interpersonal competitiveness, and
> lower individual drive to power/dominance/status vis-à-vis non-Aboriginals.

Such explanations both 'blame the victim' and define the 'good students' with reference to white middle-class values. Nonetheless, typically it is considered that Aboriginal students' low self-esteem is a reflection of a general lack of self-esteem among the Aboriginal community. However, compared to matched socio-economic samples of whites there is often little difference, even reversals (Finch, 1973; Quine, 1973; Watts, 1970; Wright and Parker, 1978).

The relationship between self-concept and educational achievement is complex, requiring more than simple theoretical and methodological conceptualizations. There is little doubt that Aboriginal people are under-represented in mainstream educational and occupational attainments and have long been viewed as suffering from low self-esteem. However, it should be made very clear to educators that the nature of self-esteem for Aboriginal people and just how these educational and occupational under-representations relate to the self-esteem of Aboriginal girls and women, in particular, are anything but obvious. In the remainder of this chapter we will question, first, the applicability to Aboriginal people of the self-esteem concept itself and the strategies used in its measurement and, second, the appropriateness of applying self-esteem programs for girls to the educational and occupational experiences of Aboriginal females.

Self-esteem, Aboriginal Culture and Education

The purpose of this section is to describe the main arguments offered for Aboriginal people's lack of self-esteem and to identify some serious problems with this interpretation. We will then analyze some of the evidence regarding Aboriginal children's self-esteem and its relationship to their educational achievement, again highlighting the deficiencies of this line of thinking.

Aboriginal People and Self-esteem

In 1954 the psychologist Abraham Maslow argued that all people have a hierarchy of 'needs' and that attainment of needs higher in the hierarchy is impossible without a reasonable level of satisfaction of needs lower in the hierarchy. He suggested that self-esteem is a strong and central need essential to the effective functioning of the individual. Further, self-esteem develops out of a base of reasonable satisfaction of physiological and safety needs and, directly, from reasonable satisfaction of 'belongingness and love.' Erikson (1963) similarly describes self-esteem as growing out of early physical competence later reinforced through 'tangible recognition' in interpersonal, social and cultural relations developing a sense of general competence in life. In these terms it is not difficult to see how Aboriginal people may come to have low self-esteem. Their history has been one of physical deprivation ('physiological'), decimation ('safety'), dislocation ('belongingness') and degradation ('love') on a massive scale since initial contact with white culture 200 years ago.

Identity, self-concept and self-esteem — the ideas one has about oneself and how one feels about oneself — are determined in interaction with external referents or sources of feedback. That is, people's self-esteem is related to the congruency between their feelings about themselves and those provided by significant others, and it is important that there be some sense of unity in the various messages they receive. For Aboriginal people, these sources of feedback have generally provided incompatible messages: self-sustaining feedback from the Aboriginal community and denigrating feedback from the white majority culture. The very contact history of the Australian Aborigines has been devastating and the whole pattern of race relations one of denigration with an attack on Aboriginal self-referents and the provision of negative external referents. Finch (1973) draws a parallel between the Aboriginal situation and that of the American black.

Although there has been little research into Aboriginal self-concepts, one might reasonably conjecture that the effect, after many generations of cultural debasement, social ostracism, economic exploitation, and discrimination, would militate against the development of a healthy self-identity. In fact it has been suggested that these pressures have resulted in many Aboriginals identifying negatively with their race — 'black is bad'. (p. 46)

Thus, to the extent that there is an 'internalization of the oppressor', the Aboriginal self-referent system and confidence may also be undermined.

But it is also important to see that such 'low self-esteem' may be nothing to do with the fact of Aboriginality, but due directly to the kind of poverty that makes one dependent on others for sustenance. This may result from the difficulties experienced by many Aboriginal people in adequately meeting personal and family needs and so determining their ways and conditions of life. Low self-esteem is one of the effects of poverty dependency anywhere, and being Aboriginal adds an extra dimension and degree to this poverty and its associated powerlessness. Thus two of the main bases for any lack of self-esteem in Aboriginal people, it is argued, are denigration and poverty dependency.

There are, however, problems associated with this way of thinking about the relationship between Aboriginal people and education, and these should not go unnoticed. In the first place, it tends to treat Aboriginal people as a homogeneous and unchanging group. Also, as Aboriginal people are perceived as 'disadvantaged' and as Aboriginality is often held in contempt by the dominant culture, the assumption is made that their self-esteem naturally will be low. Finally, too few people ask whether the usual ideas from Western culture associated with self-esteem may be appropriately applied to Aboriginal people. Let us elaborate.

Diversity and Unity: Transition and Emergence.   Such analyses of Aboriginal people's supposed lack of self-esteem tend towards stereotyping and fail to recognize the many differences which exist among Aboriginal people. They also treat Aborigines as a category separate from mainstream Anglo-Celtic Australian society rather than interactive with it. Aborigines have roots and referents to some extent in both cultures. Further, their culture is not static but in dynamic interaction with the mainstream culture. As they have roots in both, an 'emergent' cultural reality is constantly developing (Berndt and Berndt, 1981, p. 530).

To reiterate, there is considerable diversity among Aboriginal people and this is greater now than before European contact. The traditional groupings across different geographical areas have been overlain by the widely different timing, extent and nature of contact, initially with Malaccans and Asians and, since colonization, with Europeans. This last contact has led to the dispossession of traditional land and to enforced disbanding and regrouping. Recently, further diversity has been wrought by new influences: from the 'outstation movement', various types of 'land rights', and the increasing numbers of Aboriginal people in local, state and federal government and in the professions. In one sense there is a 'transition' of Aboriginal lifeways, values and psychology from the traditional to the urban Western. At different times and places this involves reaction against traditional ways, and at others a resurgent interest in the old ways. Similarly involved is an attraction to and adoption of Western ways and also a rejection of them — a 'stopping short' of any sort of assimilation or identification. Elsie Roughsey (1984) puts this succinctly: 'we are not to go any further.' (p. 235), she says.

But there is also an increasing homogeneity overlaying this diversity. This is developing as Aborigines seek to rediscover their common heritage, to assert or reassert a common set of beliefs and values. Aborigines develop unity through a deep sense of belonging to the land which was originally clan land bequeathed by their ancestral beings. Further, Aboriginality involves a sense of being part of a broad group of people with its unique culture and with a long history of oppression and degradation. This emergent 'pan-Aboriginal' identity adds a new dimension to the sense of self which arises as a consequence of kinship bonds and communal life — the more traditional sources of psychological support and security. Associated with this development is the choice by 'part'-Aborigines to identify as 'Aboriginal'. This is a political stance caused by their persistent non-acceptance by the dominant culture. There is a rising sense of identity as a group which shares a common contact history and current minority status and conditions, giving rise to a level of commitment to the similarities between Aboriginal people and their situations, in a gradually unifying set of beliefs and ideals.

The Primary/Secondary Locus of Self-esteem.   In general, Aboriginal identity, self-concept and self-esteem are derived in the first instance from Aboriginality as the 'culture of origin' within which Aboriginal people seek to preserve and retap their primary roots. But also, as we have noted, Aboriginal life now exists within a dominant Western culture. Most Aboriginal people accept pragmatically the need for effective interrelation with that 'culture of access' so that their own culture may survive and so that they may acquire those aspects of the dominant culture which are considered valuable.

Naturally, the locus of the self-concept and self-esteem of Aboriginal people will correspond to their view of social reality. The primary source of self-esteem, however, is likely to be located within Aboriginal culture and the secondary source within the majority white culture. Gaining secondary self-esteem from participation in the dominant culture is, of course, only possible to the extent that there is access to that culture in a way that is meaningful, power sharing and leads to competence and the positive experience of success (by Aboriginal criteria). Increasingly, self-concept and self-esteem are derived from a newly emergent, exploratory and self-affirmative Aboriginality. There is no conclusive evidence that Aboriginal children or adolescents actually suffer low self-esteem. We will return to this matter shortly.

Aboriginal 'Communality' of Self-concept.   Another problem in applying the notion of self-esteem to Aboriginal people is related to the degree of communality, as against individuality, of self-conception. Self-concept is essentially a Western and somewhat masculine notion centred in the highly individuated male-dominated culture in which we exist both psychologically and socially. Western culture continues to lose the sense of community which, to some extent, existed historically for clans, villages and neighbourhoods. Although this 'cult of the individual' may be transitory, at present it provides a very significant dimension of difference between Aboriginal culture and dominant Australian culture. There are, then, likely to be very different dimensions to the self-esteem of Aboriginal and non-Aboriginal people.

For Aboriginal people, individual attributes such as personal name or even immediate family are less important than the 'local descent group' which gives them their place in the order of things such as country, ceremony and kin relationships, Their sense of self is also less distinct from their context. That is, Aboriginal people's idea of themselves is less separate and more intimately an overall appreciation of themselves as a small part of the continuity of things, persons and processes. In tradition-al Aboriginal society individual independence was played down and undervalued because group cooperation was an economic necessity. Kin-ship ties and associated obligations and mutually supporting responsibili-ties still are a dominant characteristic of Aboriginal life in rural, isolated and urban communities (Daylight and Johnstone, 1986). There is a par-ticular priority on retaining the identity and integrity of the group against assimilation and dissolution. Thus, not only is the consciousness of self and one's feeling not highly differentiated from the consciousness of the group, but there is, overall, little motivation to make it so. The press is not towards individuation but towards solidarity and oneness. The idea of focusing on one's own feelings and concerns can even be something of a taboo, against the prevailing cultural ethics and morality which empha-size the survival and well-being of the group.

So, in Aboriginal communities, whether they observe more traditional or more newly separate ways, the notion of self-esteem will be largely community-based. This will vary with the degree to which contact with the dominant culture has resulted in increased differentiation of self from community, but, generally Western notions of individual self-concept and self-esteem are likely to have less value and meaningfulness for Aboriginal people. For example, recently one of us studied the effectiveness of counselling for Aboriginal and non-Aboriginal students in a tertiary institution (Pickett and Stringer, 1985). The Aboriginal students studied were, like their non-Aboriginal peers, associated with and achieving within the Western educational system to a greater extent than Aboriginal people typically. Nonetheless, the two groups responded best to quite different types of counselling. One of the differences was that direct attention to the improvement of self-concepts and self-evaluations was productive for the non-Aboriginal students but quite unproductive for Aboriginal students who responded better to efforts to reinforce group structures. The results of the study suggested the appropriateness of community-oriented support for Aboriginal people rather than individualized approaches. In working with Aborigines a community referenced approach is more appropriate and meaningful because it relates to, and derives from, Aboriginal realities. The notion of self-esteem and self-esteem research should be seen as an ill-fitting imposition from Western culture, yielding 'results' and interpretations at odds with Aboriginal reality.

Aboriginal Students, Self-esteem and Schooling

Often educationists take for granted that Aboriginal students will lack self-esteem because of Aboriginal people's history of poverty and degradation during the last 200 years. Low self-esteem is frequently used to 'explain away' the limited benefits they gain from mainstream education. The research on Aboriginal students' self-esteem, however, is neither extensive nor conclusive. In 1971 Watts led a national workshop on Aboriginal education. She suggested that minorities tend to hold negative self-concepts and negative self-esteem, and linked low morale with educational failure for Aboriginal children. Although the workshop participants noted issues of powerlessness and lack of autonomy, the orientation of the early 1970s was largely one of 'cultural deprivation', and people saw a one-way causal link of low self-esteem leading to poor educational achievement. That is, it was assumed that Aboriginal children did not achieve in school because they lacked certain qualities, in particular, they lacked self-esteem.

Nonetheless, at the time of the national workshop Watts argued that 'adolescent Aboriginals may not be typically characterised by low self-concept' (p. 9) Two years later Finch (1973) reported that within their own environments Aboriginal people considered themselves equally socially adequate as their white peers. In particular, he found no significant difference in 'self as socially adequate' between rural Aboriginal and urban non-Aboriginal children. Wright and Parker (1978) also reported similar levels of self-esteem among Aboriginal and non-Aboriginal children. More recently, Callan and St John (1984) found little difference in reported self-concept between rural and urban Aboriginal and white youth. Often the dimensions of Aboriginality/non-Aboriginality, rural/urban, and employed/unemployed are confounded (e.g. Watts, 1970) so that we cannot say whether Aboriginality rather than, say, location or employment status is central. Finch (1973), for example, reported that urban Aboriginal children expressed more negative self-attributions than those on rural reserves, while Turney *et al.* (1978, 1980) and Sinclair (1983) have reported lower self-concepts with isolated children (including Aboriginal) compared to inner city or suburban children. Consequently, it is not at all clear that one can interpret Aboriginal students' educational underachievement and underparticipation in mainstream schooling in terms of generally depressed levels of self-esteem in Aboriginal communities.

In any case, the validity of most instruments used to measure self-esteem must be questioned. Even in their own terms, uni- and multi-dimensional measures often are not distinguished. Measures of 'general self-concept' or general self-perception are equated with 'self-concept of achievement' or self as measured against the standards and expectations of the school as a middle-class institution (Finch, 1973, p. 47). Even if such instruments were culturally relevant (and, as we have already suggested, they are not) and understood by the students, we cannot tell whether a particular instrument is measuring their attitudes toward themselves within the school system or their overall attitudes toward themselves, or whether these are one and the same thing for them.

Consider, for example, the following recent conversation with a girl in upper secondary school in Perth who was originally from an isolated community and is now one of only two Aborigines in a class of thirty white students.

How do you feel when you can't do something at school?
You know you're dumb.

Why?
'Cuz — 'cuz you're the only one in the class who can't do it!
Does that really mean you're dumb, do you think?
When we with each other [other Aboriginal girls] *we call each other dumb, but we don't really mean dumb. Just dumb at guddia* [white] *school.*

As suggested in this exchange, while low morale in the classroom may be typical of many Aboriginal students, general self-esteem and 'white' achievement self-esteem may well be quite separate. Aboriginal children may have negative views of themselves as students, but positive concepts of themselves as people using non-school life or the non-academic aspect of school life as referents. Also they may not accept feedback from schools as relevant to their personal and social values, nor as meaningful comment on their true abilities had they been given opportunities to develop these in the context of appropriate education. The main issue connecting self-esteem to educational achievement for Aboriginal students is likely to be the match between the locus of the student's identity (or self-esteem) and the education provided — its cultural focus and relevance, and who determines and controls it.

For many Aboriginal students, a major conflict exists between the desire to identify with Aboriginal groups and with the values, behavioural requirements and occupational outcomes of Western schooling. Those more oriented towards the dominant culture may well have to adopt behaviour patterns acceptable to that community and break off relations with other Aborigines, often their kin. The Aboriginal Women's Task Force (Daylight and Johnstone, 1986), after extensive consultation with Aboriginal women from all over Australia, commented that even confident and academically able students, who have coped with most pressures on them, find peer group pressure 'an insurmountable pressure. It means rejection of the group they identify with. To succeed where all others from the group are failing is perceived as accepting the school and staff and thus condoning the unfair treatment of other Aboriginal students' (p. 39). Not standing out in the group, but sharing and moving as one, is a strong emphasis in Aboriginal society and one particularly relevant to mainstream classroom expectations. Aboriginal people who achieve individual success as defined by white mainstream values can at times be seen as a threat, not only to their peers, but to 'community esteem'. While access and achievement in the wider society may be regarded as desirable, this must not be at the cost of cohesion of Aboriginal identity and community.

Many who identify with Aboriginal culture but attend mainstream schools find little satisfaction in schooling because it has no relevance to their lifeways. Typically, there is a lack of congruence between the locus of the student's identity and the education provided. The result is a negative view of Western schooling often leading to anti-school attitudes and absenteeism. But the result is not entirely what might be expected in terms of self-esteem. Often there seems to be a survival reaction on the part of Aboriginal students to preserve their identity and self-esteem by rejecting the education system as a referent for either. They simply focus their self-concept and hence derive their self-esteem in areas other than Westernized achievement and education, which become largely irrelevant. Consequently, while researchers continue to report that the success/ achievement dimensions of self-esteem are lower for Aboriginal Australians than for other Australians, and their educational attainment also is lower, they also report that general levels of self-esteem are no lower among Aboriginal people than among comparable white Australians, as mentioned earlier.

Where progress has been made towards a distinctive form of Aboriginal education, educational achievement rises and the educational process becomes more accepted into the set of referents determining self-esteem. Rather than being dissociated and in conflict, general and educational 'esteem' now interact more positively. But it is not quite as simple as this may sound. Cope and Kalantzis in this volume (see Chapter 8) describe the situation well with respect to minority students: 'it is a problem of (this) dichotomy between self-esteem through celebration of difference and self-esteem as access to dominant structures of education and social power.' Aboriginal people are attempting to develop a range of emergent alternatives which borrow from both traditional Aboriginal culture and Western culture but are limited to neither. For example, Yiyili in Western Australia is a traditional Aboriginal community where there is largely local Aboriginal determination, control and delivery of education. There is more educational relevance and a higher degree of congruence between what Aboriginal people identify with, what the education provides and how and by whom it is provided. 'An Aboriginal climate pervades Yiyili school which is in tune with the children and the social realities of their community' (Dickinson, 1985, p. 5). There is little doubt that there is a higher degree of enthusiasm among the children and their community for their schooling, and it serves to develop and reinforce their chosen identity and fosters educational achievement in and on their terms.

But there are still few Yiyilis. In most other situations difficulties remain. There invariably is a disjunction, sometimes huge, between what is chosen by Aboriginal people as important to them (and this will depend on their own context) and what the education system provides, the manner and style in which it is provided and who are the providers. Brandl (1983) notes that Aboriginal parents do not reject, for example, literacy. They want for their children many of the intellectual skills Western schools can provide, but 'above all, they want them to be Aboriginal.... Aboriginal parents are positive toward new skills and information, but not necessarily the cultural styles associated. Not wanting to deny their children access but wanting them imparted in ways compatible and not incongruent with or against the grain of their local cultures' (pp. 35, 38).

Self-esteem and the Education of Aboriginal Girls

While it is important that the educational situation of Aboriginal girls be appreciated in the context of Aboriginal history and culture, it is no less important that the gender dimensions to this cultural and cross-cultural history be acknowledged. What we will show in this section is that while the triple oppressions of sexism, racism and poverty constitute major themes running through this history, equally importantly a picture emerges of Aboriginal women's strength and resourcefulness in shifting circumstances of power and powerlessness. As we will now show, negotiating these contradictory complexities is the daunting task which both Aboriginal and white society set for Aboriginal girls.

Change and Diversity in Aboriginal Gender Relations

There is a debate in many Aboriginal communities about the extent to which Aboriginal men 'have embraced the sexism of the dominant culture' (Holland, 1987, p. 72). Janis Koolmatrie, for example, notes that due to both the maltreatment of women and the usurping of Aboriginal women's role by Aboriginal men supported by missionaries, anthropologists, sociologists and teachers, 'there has been a marked deterioration and destruction of the self-concept of many Aboriginal women' (1983, p. 124). Some believe that racism is the more central issue for Aboriginal communities and that discussions of sexism may be divisive. But for many Aboriginal women the two are inextricably linked. As Phyllis Daylight says, 'I am an Aboriginal woman. My sex is no less a part of my identity than my Aboriginality' (1987, p. 61). Either way, like the rest of Aboriginal culture, Aboriginal gender relations are diverse and dynamic.

In *Daughters of the Dreaming* Diane Bell (1983) describes gender relations in central Australia. Aboriginal male and female worlds are traditionally substantially independent of one another in economic and ritual terms. Men and women elaborate separate gender-specific power bases, 'a role of independence, responsibility, dignity and authority wherein they were enhanced as women, as members of their society, as daughters of the dreaming' (p. 23). Not dependent on men for survival, Aboriginal women were effectively autonomous. During the early years of contact with Europeans traditional gender equity was essentially maintained, but often this did not survive. 'Women worked beside their menfolk in the mines and on the stations, doing much of the same work, independently, until the arrival of white woman on stations and missionaries in towns. Women were then restricted to sex-specific tasks, less employment and reward, redefined as "dependents" and men classified as household heads' (p. 96).

But, as Bell points out, even in central Australia the situation varies between different communities. For example, the Katej and Alyawarra Aranda, from a social structure tightly mapped to the land, were able to remain in or near their traditional land and family groups. Women have retained more traditional status and functions, control and power base, and therefore their position with respect to men. On the other hand, the Warlpari, from the more diffuse social and land tenure systems of the more arid areas and also more subjected to missions and ration depots, were moved away from their lands to towns and settlements, living as large communities with other groups. Both groups suffered differently but terribly the 'violent and brutal pacification' (p. 151) drives in central Australia and the dislocation from their land which was the source of their physical and spiritual being, relationships and identity. There was 'damage to women's self-respect' and confidence 'was seriously shaken' (p. 151). Here men accommodated to their 'newly gender-dominated status as family heads and community leaders allocated by the male dominated colonial structure of Northern Australia' (p. 106). To this day women are still 'constrained by the male oriented and dominated European controls and policies which govern Aboriginal affairs' (pp. 161–2) so that 'they no longer enjoy the same status as full members of their society' (p. 179). This situation is aided and abetted by anthropologists ascribing to Aboriginal women a lesser status in accord with the current European society's attitudes, 'received male truths ... about women's lives' not necessarily related to the 'lived reality for women' (p. 237).

The situation in rural and urban communities often is different, although no less difficult, and opinions vary about how to interpret this. According to Vasey (1985), Aboriginal women have been able to adapt to white society more easily than Aboriginal men because 'women tend to be more resilient than men in general in this [identity] area. When their society is under disintegrating pressure, their identity is sustained by the nurturing role' (p. 45). Thus, she argues, females often take leadership positions in transitional Aboriginal society, even though this is usually not recognized as such by the majority culture. It is they who, in many instances, develop community strategies for coping with, or overcoming, problems of alcohol and drug abuse, deal with changed patterns of child care, fight for health clinics and participate most in their children's education in a system which, as we have noted, is often culturally foreign. Other Aboriginal women disagree with interpretations such as Vasey's, arguing that if Aboriginal women are better able to 'adapt' to white society, this is because they are regarded by whites as less threatening than Aboriginal men. Either way, they believe comparisons of this sort to be divisive.

Despite such debates there is no doubt that all over the country, in isolated, rural and urban settings, Aboriginal women are reconstructing a very positive definition of their womanhood. 'They are becoming active politically and taking charge of their lives, in spite of the difficulties which arise from this' (p. 46). But, says Vasey, many Aboriginal women reject existing white society as a model for relationships between women and men and also the visions offered by some of their white feminist sisters.

> They reject the unisex model which our society appears to be moving towards. Their own rich tapestry of life is woven around a two sex model in which women, although moving in largely separate spheres, are equal and complementary to men. They wish white society to recognise this and restore their economic independence by having split pension cheques, recognising the actual providers of children and restoring to them the ownership of their land. (p. 48)

Aboriginal women are demanding a return to the old ways where they were independently recognized as custodians of land. They believe that through land rights will come dignity and self-esteem, and they are demanding that they sit in their own right and as equals in land councils. Daylight and Johnstone report that women they talked to 'said that "in the old way no man spoke for them about their land like the way it is being done now"' (1986, p. 63).

But the lives of many Aboriginal women are grim. Helen Boyle (1983) describes their conflict, 'being forced to play the role of the submissive sex in the wider society but at the same time forced to play the role of the dominant sex within Aboriginal society because of the frustrations and alienation of Aboriginal men, which has been brought about by the racism and class structure in this country' (p. 47). The women now meet the responsibility for extended family and upbringing of children in a consciously Aboriginal environment, whereas before it was a more communal responsibility. A great many rear children without male support. While their role in the Aboriginal extended family is central and respected, 'they must carry out their difficult tasks within an overall environment which exacts heavy tolls on their health, strength, dignity and self esteem' (Daylight and Johnstone, 1986, p. 2). It is they who ensure that all family members residing with them are fed, clothed and bedded in situations often of dire poverty, ill-health, alcohol and drug abuse and the separation of families. Yet the structure of social services in Australia means that many have no independent access to funds. They are economically dependent on men who may experience many of the problems associated with alcohol abuse and frequent periods of imprisonment. Often they feel powerless to change their own circumstances or those of their children. Aboriginal women are also heavily relied upon to maintain Aboriginal values and practices, and they fear that many young people have lost contact with important aspects of their culture. The stress takes a heavy toll. As a result some, themselves, turn to alcohol or drugs, often leading to an early death.

Added to this is that a part of the colonization process involved the use of Aboriginal women as a means of sexual gratification for white men. In the interaction between Aboriginal women and white men, matters of race, sex and class are intertwined. Certainly white contact had a negative impact on the Aboriginal tradition that sex was uniquely tied to spirituality, ceremony and kinship relations. As indicated by Sally Morgan (1987) in *My Place*, wealthy white graziers often both employed Aboriginal women and had them sexually. It was not unusual for children to be the result of these exploitative sets of relations. In a similar vein but in different circumstances, early settler working–class European and Asian men often took Aboriginal women as longer-term sexual partners and as domestic labourers. While such treatment is less overt now, its effect is still vividly experienced. 'It is necessary to emphasise that historically Aboriginal women have been equated with permissiveness, thus our bodies and minds have been raped, battered and damaged in many ways' (Koolmatrie, 1983, p. 124). Racist and sexist name-calling still is a common part of the lives of many Aboriginal girls and women. As Wendy Holland suggests, the principles of colonization continue today and 'the impact on contemporary Aboriginal women is two-fold: they struggle against the racism of a colonialist society and the sexism inherent in its ideology' (1987, p. 72).

Aboriginal girls grow up with the evidence of this conflict and stress. Often they see their mothers, grandmothers and aunts as powerful and respected within the Aboriginal community and despised from without. Many experience racism and sexism from an early age. These, in conjunction with the emergence of the form of Aboriginal politics which protects and promotes Aboriginal identity, place women and girls in a paradoxical situation. To draw attention to the problems they experience associated with alcohol, drugs, unwanted pregnancies, rape and so forth is to denigrate further the public image of Aboriginal people. On the other hand, not to draw attention to such matters is to suffer them without using or extending the range of assistance available to help them both to cope and, more importantly, to change their circumstances. The question of what the education system offers these girls is one of resounding complexity.

Aboriginal Girls and Self-esteem Programs in Schools

While a large feminist literature has been generated on the education of girls in general, little has been written specifically on Aboriginal girls and their education. This may be because of the widely held view that the major 'problems' Aboriginal children experience are those associated with race and class and that gender, while important, is secondary. Nonetheless, the circumstances of Aboriginal girls are affected by race, class and gender in interaction and cannot be understood in terms of any one of these in isolation.

Studies of adolescent inner city working-class girls (e.g. Moran, 1985; Wyn, this volume, Chapter 6) show such a remarkable similarity to our experiences with Aboriginal girls both in the city and the Kimberlies that we are led to suggest that many of the processes are much the same despite cultural differences. Many Aboriginal girls seem driven by the need to establish for themselves a 'place' in the social and kinship network and this is so strong that often other options are not recognized or considered. The slightly older boys who have left school and who seem to the girls to be the main means of fulfilling this need are likely also to see their future wives as housekeepers and mothers only. This is not to suggest that Aboriginal girls, any more than the girls described by Moran and Wyn, are naive about their futures. They have few expectations and illusions about happiness as future wives and mothers. But what else is there?

Unemployment is high among Aboriginal people. Although work prospects are generally regarded as being better for teenage Aboriginal girls than boys, particularly in white collar jobs, this is not supported by the available data. In 1981, 37.1 per cent of Aboriginal boys and 37.6 per cent of Aboriginal girls between the ages of 15 and 19 years were registered as unemployed (the data for all Australians were 13.1 and 16.9 per cent respectively). Furthermore, the income of 60.6 per cent of employed Aboriginal males and 72.9 per cent of employed Aboriginal females was less than $10,000 per annum (for the total Australian population they were 29.1 and 62.6 per cent respectively). This means that there is greater disparity between the employment prospects of all Australian males and females than between those of Aboriginal males and females. Nonetheless, many Aboriginal girls face the grim reality that, regardless of education, their employment prospects are poor. The Aboriginal Women's Task Force (Daylight and Johnstone, 1986) were consistently told by women and girls of examples of racist and ethnocentric behaviour on the part of prospective employers:

> ... you never see ... a black shop assistant.

> ... it would always be the trainees with the lightest skin who got the jobs ... the situation occurred too frequently to be coincidental.

> ... she applied for a position in Commonwealth Education [and] was told to go to the DAA because they had more jobs for Aboriginals and she would really be happy there.

> ... the tone of voice of the interviewers is condescending ....

> The interviewee ... must process the question into his/her own language which takes time. The panel often assumes that the time lapse is indicative of the slowness or lack of intelligence of the interviewee. (p. 59)

Such poor prospects for the future are unlikely to encourage Aboriginal girls to commit their hopes and dreams to the mainstream education system which, itself, often provides them with evidence of the racism of the dominant culture.

> There are numerous accounts of young girls being called 'molls', 'sluts', 'whores', 'black bitches' and 'gins' by teachers as well [as students].

I wanted to continue my schooling but the teacher said to me 'You're fifteen, you're old enough to have babies. You should stay at home and do that. Isn't that what all your people do?'

A young girl [over the school leaving age] ... has a chronic medical condition [and has] over the years taken time off school to go to Sydney for medical treatment. Her mother ... was always meticulous about writing notes to the school after the absence ... on the last occasion her teacher said she was 'only making it up'. The teacher added that she was 'lying and being lazy and didn't really want to come to school'. Her mother was so incensed about the way her daughter had been treated that she readily agreed to her daughter's request to stay at home. (p. 35)

At times racism takes the form of ignorance and insensitivity.

I got into trouble with the domestic science teacher. She had asked us to do an assignment on the colour scheme of our home. I couldn't do it so she kept me in. I just sat there — I suppose I was rather stubborn. I tried to tell her we were only living in a one-roomed shack with a bough-shed and goat pen out the back. It was just built out of rusty kerosene tins built together.... We had no chairs, only kerosene tins.... The teacher kept me in till five o'clock but I wouldn't do it. Of course I couldn't do it and I wasn't telling a lie. (p. 34)

Most self-esteem programs in schools are directed either at girls (and sometimes boys) 'in general' (and, therefore, also at Aboriginal girls) or at girls who fit into some category regarded as 'at risk', for example, they may 'have behaviour problems' or 'not be choosing maths and science'. In a range of ways Aboriginal girls are educationally underprivileged and so such programs might be regarded as being in their best interests. In fact, a recurring theme through much that is written by Aboriginal people about Aboriginal education is the necessity for improved self-esteem. As we have already suggested, however, the individualistic notion of self-esteem which underlies most programs in school is not likely to be meaningful for Aboriginal people. When Aboriginal people speak of self-esteem (and self-determination), they are not suggesting a focus upon, or celebration of, the individual but rather of group identity and esteem (and determination). The National Aboriginal Education Council considers that Aboriginal and Torres Strait Islander girls need 'courses in self esteem based on cultural identity' (*National Policy for the Education of Girls* ..., 1987, p. 90). Pam Gilbert in this volume (see Chapter 9) also argues that girls do not need self-esteem but rather 'gender esteem'. Aboriginal girls need to feel respected and valued because of their Aboriginality and their femaleness.

Whether 'courses', as such, ever work well in achieving these ends is not clear. What is clear is that most of the self-esteem courses for girls which we have observed almost totally neglect matters of culture. They are likely to be inappropriate, unacceptable and unsuccessful for Aboriginal students generally and Aboriginal girls in particular. We have previously suggested ways in which such programs may be inappropriate and unsuccessful. The following two examples should clarify these points and indicate how the ethnocentric nature of such programs may also make them unacceptable to many Aboriginal girls.

Example One: Naming.

> Names *help to individualize people,* as a child's concept of self is built up from having a name that is reasonably different from others. Names also give a sense of belonging as they connect to a family with a past. They are passed down from generation to generation, and at one time had literal meanings, for example: Peter — rock, Phillip — a horse lover, Miller — a grinder of corn, Cooper — a barrel-maker and Margaret — a pearl.
>
> - The teacher might draw her family tree and discuss it as an example of 'belonging' to someone in the present as in the past.
> - Discuss the functions of a name, and ask children to find out names of their parents and grandparents.
> - Research the meaning of given names and surnames, and the reasons for the names chosen, for example 'Were you named after anyone?' 'Why?'
> - Allow pupils to draw up a family tree, or use photographs. (Be sensitive to children from broken homes as the exercise lies not so much in tracing the family as in determining relationships.) (Fahey, 1986, p. 9, our emphasis)

This extract is from a section entitled 'Belonging', and the author earlier states that we need to 'discover our basic unity as well as our uniqueness' (p. 9). Notwithstanding that the activity is, in a sense, about families, there is an explicit focus upon the individual; also only certain family structures are acknowledged. Many Aboriginal people's sense of the individual, family and clan are distinctly different from those of most Anglo-Australians. In particular, the personal name which, as the quotation above infers, is the main identification label of European Australians is much less important to Aboriginal Australians, A child's local descent group is much more important because this allots her a place in 'society's order of things, in ceremonies and relationships. Also important are the languages a child or person speaks and learns, the ceremonies he or she has participated in, their mother's country and language and those of their spouse and spouse's children. Each combination adds up to a unique identity' (Brandl, 1983, p. 37). Furthermore, most Aboriginal people have many personal names which are often difficult for outsiders to pronounce and so Anglo names are adopted only for convenience. Particularly, in classes where Aboriginal children are in the minority, close attention to Anglo names and family structures of quite different kinds to their own would be likely to make them feel overlooked and undervalued.

Example Two: Body Language. Most self-esteem courses include one or more sessions on body language (e.g. *Improving Chances for Girls*, 1981; *Wings*, 1983). Typically and quite unproblematically, it is suggested that a person's posture (tilt of the head, the length of the stride, the slant of the shoulders) reveals a great deal about their personality and mood. One associated activity is to have a group of students face away from a teacher and walk away as though they have just left a job interview in which they did well (or poorly) and got (or did not get) the job. Teachers have reported that certain Aboriginal students will find walking away quite threatening and want to face the teacher. Also for some Aboriginal students the arm actions and walk associated with happiness and confidence are likely to be different from those typical of Anglo-Australians. Aboriginal and Indo-Chinese girls may also find such activities an embarrassment. They are likely to react to such lessons angrily, going through the motions only or even refusing to participate in such an invasion of privacy. Of course, some Anglo-Australian girls may also respond in this way and not all Aboriginal and Indo-Chinese girls will. But certain ways of behaving are more valued and approved in some cultures than in others. Another activity frequently offered in self-esteem courses relates to maintaining eye contact. It is stated that eye contact is a measure of assurance. But in certain Aboriginal cultures avoiding eye contact is a sign of respect. Activities which require students to maintain lengthy eye contact may be quite an unpleasant experience for many Aboriginal students.

It is likely to be empowering to girls generally, and to Aboriginal girls in particular, to learn that some people interpret body language in quite ethnocentric ways. Such knowledge might help them to 'play the game' and avoid some of the worst consequences of the misreading of themselves by others. But the activities on body language typically present the Anglo-Australian version or interpretation as the 'normal' one. The cultural, and even gender, specificity of body language is either ignored or presented as a relatively minor matter. In the unlikely event that such activities do empower Aboriginal girls, it would be more from good luck than good judgment.

There are many examples of activities designed to improve the self-esteem of girls which may emphasize values and behaviour patterns which are inconsistent with those most strongly held by their communities. For example, an Aboriginal person is likely to be more embarrassed by making a mistake than admitting ignorance. 'I don't know' is not regarded as lazy or taking the easy way out but rather as 'I am not ready yet'. An Aboriginal child is not expected to perform a task in front of others until he or she feels quite confident in doing so. Certainly, 'having a go' and 'learning from one's mistakes', much approved in self-esteem programs, are not valued by Aboriginal Australians in the way they are by Anglo-Australians. As Brandl (1983) emphasizes, individual children may behave in ways which do not fit the prevailing cultural style. Some Anglo-Australian children hold back and some Aboriginal Australian children rush in. But Aboriginal and Anglo-Australian families are likely to vary in the value and emphasis they place on one behaviour or the other. Methods of conflict resolution, the appropriateness of personal comments, of focusing upon personal feelings and, as we have indicated, valued sex roles may also differ in quite significant ways.

We are not suggesting that activities focusing on such matters are necessarily inappropriate but they should, at the very least, be undertaken in full recognition of the large variations in cultural values and styles likely to be represented within a school. Ad hoc approaches (when a 'problem' occurs) are simply insufficient. Many self-esteem courses, while professing to value and support all girls, risk further alienating a great many of them. Not only are they almost insultingly inadequate to deal with the realities of many Aboriginal girls' lives, they may also be offensive. Returning to an earlier point, neither are we suggesting the improvement of self-esteem through a simplistic 'celebration of difference'. As Cope and Kalantzis state in this volume (see Chapter 8), and as Aboriginal communities know only too well, 'the project of social equity itself is often not a matter of cultural preservation, but of active cultural change.' It is also the responsibility of the dominant culture to undergo the kind of change that makes social justice possible. While education systems are not in a position to effect these changes in any broad sense, they can insist that schools, at least, provide a non-racist and non-sexist environment. To return to a point we made earlier, fundamental to the provision of such an environment for Aboriginal girls is respect for their Aboriginality and for their femaleness. By their actions schools must show Aboriginal girls that they respect their mothers, grandmothers and sisters, that Aboriginal womanhood is well regarded within the school. Aboriginal women traditionally and more recently have taken the responsibility for the education of their children; their advice will be invaluable in planning culturally relevant educational experiences.

Clearly, also, the curriculum must be inclusive of Aboriginal history and culture. Such a curriculum is necessary for *all* Australian children, who should know the history of their country and understand its cultural complexity. Self-esteem courses distract our attention from matters which include the following: history courses which marginalize Aboriginal history and women's history; home economics and social studies courses which present the nuclear family as the 'natural' form with a male as head of the suburban household; literature courses which implicitly devalue oral language and which ignore Aboriginal writers and poets and women writers and poets; and mathematics courses which exclude large numbers of children along race, class and gender lines. If schools are to assist Aboriginal girls to change their circumstances, then schools will have to change in some quite fundamental ways.

Conclusion

As Renshaw shows (this volume, Chapter 1), the concern for self-esteem was not developed entirely from a direct concern for the educational achievement of girls. Rather, self-esteem programs have become grafted onto education and have also been used in education as an avenue of influence for other socio-political agendas. The search for legitimizing correlation between self-esteem and educational achievement seems to be something of a rationalization in the making. If this is the case, it has come a full circle. Through its individualized focus, rather than serving to strengthen the cause of Aboriginal girls and women, it is in danger of subverting that cause.

Just a decade or so ago self-esteem became accepted as a valid outcome for the educational process, alongside educational achievement. So, too, for Aboriginal people, 'self determining education and education for self determination' have become regarded as a necessary educational process and educational outcome respectively. Further, self-determination has gradually become recognized as an underlying key to increasing both self-esteem and educational achievement, and social action. For Aboriginal people, this is essentially community rather than individual social action, community identity and morale and community competence. Thus for Aboriginal people (and also for women generally and therefore more particularly for Aboriginal women), self-determination does not place the individual as the focus but rather 'community'.

We need to be suspicious of the current tendency to locate the cause (and remedy) of poorer achievement within the individual. It should be recognized that this provides a convenient diversion from the real issues: educational dominance, arrogance and irrelevance, and the associated lack of access to the power of self-determination for Aborigines. It is a variation of 'divide and rule' further to disempower Aboriginal people from acting as a body on issues of broad social structure; a way of disenfranchizing, delegitimizing and discouraging group action against the structural causes of inequity and disadvantage.

Myths and strategies to make people feel happier and more passively accepting of their lot are common in the history of caste and class systems. They are invented usually by the privileged, internalized sometimes by the subjected, and serve, like much of establishment education, to preserve the status quo, that is, to entrench the power of the privileged to control and maintain inequity. For Aboriginal girls, as for Aboriginal people, self-esteem programs ask the wrong questions and offer the wrong answers. Community self-determination and individual self-determination are indivisible for Aboriginal people. Without them, self-esteem programs are irrelevant and contrived. If Aboriginal education is 'self-determined', self-esteem programs are unnecessary.

References

Aboriginal Education, Report of the House of Representatives Select Committee on Aboriginal Education, September 1985, Parliamentary Report No. 357/1985, Canberra, Australian Government Publishing Service.

BELL, D. (1983) *Daughters of the Dreaming*, Melbourne, McPhee Gribble/George Allen and Unwin.

BENDT, R. and BENDT, G. (1981) *The World of the First Australians*, Sydney, Lansdowne.

BOYLE, H. (1983) 'The conflicting role of Aboriginal women in today's society', in GALE, F. (Ed.), *We Are Bosses Ourselves: The Status and Role of Aboriginal*

Women Today, Canberra, Australian Institute of Aboriginal Studies, pp. 44–7.

BRANDL, M. (1983) 'A certain heritage: Women and their children in Northern Australia', in GALE, F. (Ed.), *We Are Bosses Ourselves: The Status and Role of Aboriginal Women Today*, Canberra, Australian Institute of Aboriginal Studies.

BURNEY, L. (1987) 'Meeting the educational needs of young Aboriginal women', in *Including Girls: Curriculum Perspectives on the Education of Girls*, Canberra, Curriculum Development Centre.

CALLAN, V.J. and ST JOHN, D. (1984) 'Self and other perceptions of urban and rural Australian Aboriginal and white youth', *Journal of Sociological Psychology*, 123, 2, pp. 179–87.

DAYLIGHT, P. (1987) 'Overview', *in Including Girls: Curriculum Perspectives on the Education of Girls*, Canberra, Curriculum Development Centre.

DAYLIGHT, P. and JOHNSTONE, H. (1986) *Women's Business: Report of the Aboriginal Women's Task Force*, Canberra, Australian Government Restructuring Task Force.

DICKINSON, R. (1985) 'Yiyili: An Aboriginal community school', Perth, Western Australian Institute of Technology.

ERIKSON, E. (1963) *Childhood and Society*, 2nd ed., New York, Orton.

FAHEY, J. (1986) 'Teaching is inviting: Activities for building self esteem', Blackburn, Vic., Dove Communications.

FINCH, K. (1973) 'A comparative study of the self-concepts of urban and rural reserve-dwelling Aboriginal children and non-Aboriginal urban children', *The Aboriginal Child at School*, 1, 3, pp. 46–52.

HARRIS, S. (1976) *Aboriginal Education in NSW, The Past, the Present and the Future.*

HILL, K. (1975) *A Study of Aboriginal Poverty in Two Country Towns*, Research Report to the Commission of Inquiry into Poverty, Canberra, Australian Government Publishing Service.

HOLLAND, W. (1987) 'Aboriginal women in education: A community initiative', in *Including Girls: Curriculum Perspectives on the Education of Girls*, Canberra, Curriculum Development Centre.

HUGGINS, J. (1987/88) '"Firing on in the mind": Aboriginal women domestic servants in the inter-war years', *HECATE, An Interdisciplinary Journal of Women's Liberation*, 13, 2, pp. 5–23.

Improving Chances for Girls: A Strategy for Confidence Building (1981) Adelaide, Transition Education Unit, Education Department of South Australia.

KOOLMATRIE, J. (1983) 'Aboriginal women in education', in GALE, F. (Ed.), *We Are Bosses Ourselves: The Status and Role of Aboriginal Women Today*, Canberra, Australian Institute for Aboriginal Studies.

McCONNOCHIE, K. (1981) 'White tests, black children: Aborigines, psychologists and education', in MENARY, B. and FINNANE, P. (Eds) *Aborigines and Schooling: Essays in Honour of Max Hart*, Texts in Humanities, Adelaide, Adelaide College of the Arts and Education, pp. 125–33.

MASLOW, A. (1954) *Motivation and Personality*, New York, Harper.

MORAN, P. (1985) 'Female youth culture in an inner-city school', in DWYER, P.J., WILSON, B. and WYN, J. (Eds), *Social Division, Economy and Schooling*, Geelong, Deakin University, pp. 85–97.

MORGAN, S. (1985) *My Place*, Fremantle, Fremantle Arts Centre Press.

National Policy for the Education of Girls in Australian Schools (1987) Canberra, Commonwealth Schools Commission.

PICKETT, H. and STRINGER, E. (1985) 'Developing counselling skills in Aboriginal education', Course Notes: A Short Training Course for Education Officers and Aboriginal Liaison Officers of the Aboriginal Education Branch of the Commonwealth Department of Education, Perth, Western Australian Institute of Technology (now Curtin University), Centre for Aboriginal Studies.

Policy Statement on Tertiary Education for Aborigines and Torres Strait Islanders (1986) Canberra, National Aboriginal Education Committee.

QUINE, S. (1973) *Achievement Orientation of Aboriginal and White Australian Adolescents*, PhD Thesis, Australian National University, Canberra.

ROUGHSEY, E. (1984) *An Aboriginal Woman Tells of the Old and the New*, Melbourne, McPhee Gribble/Penguin.

ROWLEY, C.D. (1970) *The Destruction of Aboriginal Society, Volume 1 of Aboriginal Policy and Practice*, Canberra, Australian National University Press.

SINCLAIR, K. (1983) 'Self-concept and the education of geographically isolated children', *The Aboriginal Child at School*, 11, 5, pp. 24–35.

Survey on Aboriginal Access to Tertiary Education (n.d., c. 1981), Canberra, Commonwealth Department of Education.

TANNOCK, P. and PUNCH, K. (1975) *The Educational Status of Aboriginal Children in Western Australia*, Nedlands, University of Western Australia, Department of Education.

TURNEY, C., INGLIS, C., SINCLAIR, K. and STRATTON, R. (1978) *Inner City Schools: Children, Teachers and Parents*, Sydney, University of Sydney Press.

TURNEY, C., SINCLAIR, K. and CAIRNS, L. (1980) 'Isolated schools: Teaching, learning and transition to work', Sydney, University of Sydney Press.

VASEY, M. (1985) 'Some aspects of the position of Aboriginal women in Australian society', *The Aboriginal Child at School: A National Journal for Teachers of Aborigines*, 13, 2, pp. 32–53.

WATTS, B. (1970) *Some Determinants of the Academic Progress of Australian Aboriginal Adolescent Girls*, PhD Thesis, University of Queensland, St Lucia.

WATTS, B. (1971) *Report of the National Workshop on Aboriginal Education: Priorities for Action and Research*, St Lucia, Department of Education, University of Queensland.

WATTS, B. (1976) *Access to Education: An Evaluation of the Aboriginal Secondary Grant Scheme*, Commonwealth Department of Education, Canberra, Australian Government Publishing Service.

WILMOTT, E. (1982) 'Schooling and identity levels', *The Aboriginal Child at School*, 10, 3, pp. 12–20.

Wings: A Pilot Project to Enhance Self Esteem in Girls (1983) Hobart, Education Department of Tasmania.

WRIGHT, M. and PARKER, J. (1978) 'The relationship of self-concept and locus of control to school achievement for Aboriginal and non-Aboriginal children', *The Exceptional Child*, 25, 3, pp. 167–79.

Chapter 5

Culture, Gender and Self-esteem: Teaching Indo-Chinese Students

Jackie Wenner

Teachers in Australian schools are daily confronted in their classrooms with students from widely divergent backgrounds, bringing with them a range of different experiences and interpretations of the world around them. All too frequently this divergence from the 'norm' becomes linked to lower educational achievement and to social disadvantage.

Given the complexity of the issues involved in accommodating such a diverse range of needs, and the limited resources available to teachers and to schools to do so, it is not surprising that Australian schools are still far from coming to grips with both the theory and the practice of accommodating diversity, while maintaining a cohesive and non-discriminatory education system. Meanwhile, classroom teachers must cope daily with the tensions and difficulties that diversity and difference can create. As a result, short-term solutions abound in our schooling system. A very real danger is that short-term solutions become long-term solutions, without any real analysis of their adequacy, their appropriateness or the problems inherent in them.

Those classroom teachers who are anxious to provide the best education for all the students in their classes will often solve the problem of diversity of student background by individualizing their teaching approach, attempting to build relationships with individual students and thus identifying and attempting to meet the students' individual needs. While recognizing that this is an appropriate, caring and demanding response from teachers, and that it may do much to assist individual students in the short term, this chapter seeks to draw attention to the limitations of such a response when it is adopted as the major solution to the difficulties encountered by students from 'disadvantaged' groups.

It will be argued that an adequate solution needs to focus not only on the micro-social level of individual and classroom interaction, but also on the macro-social level of class, gender and cultural interaction. Good education needs to consider students as individuals but also retain an awareness of the disadvantages individuals may be subject to as a consequence of their membership of certain class, gender and cultural categories within a stratified society. If this balance is not achieved, there is a danger that the disadvantages experienced by students from minority groups will be individualized to the extent that blame for failure will be located in the individual rather than in the educational and social system which discriminates in favour of certain groups and against others. There is a further danger that superficial descriptions and categorization of minority groups without an adequate analysis of the interactions between class, gender and culture will lead to oversimplified, stereotyped views of the individuals within those groups and their needs.

Since the 1970s, when the 'personal growth' discourse became fashionable, various programs for enhancing self-esteem and confidence have been developed and used in classrooms. Such programs have been used for all students, but often those perceived as needing them most are those students defined as belonging to minority groups and disadvantaged groups. Indo-Chinese students comprise one of the most recent minority groups to have entered our education system, and Indo-Chinese girls are readily perceived to 'suffer' the 'double disadvantage' of minority culture and gender. As such they may be seen as prime candidates for self-esteem and confidence building programs. This chapter examines if, when and to what extent such programs may be appropriate for this group of students.

Indo-Chinese Students: Socio-cultural Background

The category 'Indo-Chinese' is in cultural terms an artificial one, and its use has in many ways contributed to inaccurate and stereotyped views of the individuals who are included as members of this group. However, it has become a commonly used category in the discussion of education and minority cultural groups, and will no doubt continue to be used, so it is important to clarify what it really means.

Indo-China is a geographical region in South-East Asia which, in the nineteenth and early twentieth century, came under French colonial rule, and it is this colonization that gave it its conceptual unity. It includes three separate nations: Laos, Cambodia or Kampuchea, and Vietnam, each of which has within it several distinct ethnic and cultural groups. As a result of their imposed colonial unity, these three nations also share the common history of the struggle to regain independence from the French and to re-establish stable self-detemination, a complex struggle which came to involve the world super-powers and which manifested itself, in most Australians' consciousness, in the events of the Vietnam War and the horrors of Pol Pot's Khmer Rouge regime.

One consequence of these events was the eventual resettlement of significant numbers of Laotian, Kampuchean and Vietnamese refugees in Australia. It is these historical events which identify these individuals as a unified group in the Australian context: their arrival as refugees in the late 1970s and the 1980s, their high visibility as Asians and their shared experience of war and dislocation. These shared characteristics and experiences mean that individuals from these groups have much in common when it comes to assessing and accommodating their educational and social concerns and needs.

However, the cultural diversity which the category 'Indo-Chinese' embraces is often not recognized and, as a result, inappropriate educational strategies may be developed on the basis of overgeneralized stereotypes. A detailed discussion of the various cultures included in the category 'Indo-Chinese' can be found in several publications (Kelly and Bennoun, 1984; Department of Education and Youth Affairs, Cultural Background Papers, 1983; Storer, 1985). Here only some of the major characteristics of the group 'Indo-Chinese students' are outlined in order to demonstrate the degree of heterogeneity that exists within it.

The first major factor to consider is the variety of ethnic identities included in the term 'Indo-Chinese'. Not only are there three separate countries with separate histories, but within each of these there is a variety of ethnic subgroups. The most significant of these, all of whom are represented in the Indo-Chinese community in Australia, are the Viet, the Khmer (from Kampuchea), the Lao and the Mhong (from Laos), and the Chinese (from all three countries). Each of these ethnic groups (and there are further smaller groups which have not been listed) has distinct cultural traditions, different religions, languages and family structures and different economic and social status in each country. An indication of the extent of these differences emerges when one examines the long and varied histories these civilizations have had.

Whereas the Vietnamese culture has undergone extensive influence from Chinese traditions and social structures as a result of ten centuries of Chinese domination, Khmer cultural traditions have their roots and historic links with those of India and surrounding areas. The Lao people continue to have strong religious, linguistic and cultural links with Thai people, and the Mhong have a separate cultural tradition again, having migrated from China to the hills of Laos in the early nineteenth century. In all three countries there exists a substantial ethnic Chinese population, comprising both recent immigrants and descendants of earlier immigrants. These groups have tended to maintain a strong, separate cultural identity, their own languages, and often occupy particular economic and social positions within the country's social structure. The significant point is that, were it not for French colonial intervention and the subsequent wars in the region, these groups would probably not define themselves as a unified cultural group at all. It is the experience of colonization, war and resettlement as refugees that has caused them to be defined as a single group, but within this group there exist many differences and complex interrelationships.

A second factor which must be considered when defining the cultural background of these students is the significance of the rural/urban division in determining cultural attitudes and experiences. All three countries were predominantly agricultural nations before the recent political upheavals, and a large proportion of the population lived in small villages, isolated from the larger towns where local culture was more significantly influenced by colonial administrations. There thus arose significant differences in the values, attitudes and cultural practices of people coming from small villages and those coming from larger centres.

It is also important to distinguish between traditional forms of the cultures and developing contemporary forms. All too often descriptions of these cultures focus on traditional beliefs and behaviours and fail to take into account the effects the colonization, years of war, the extreme social upheaval of the Pol Pot regime in Kampuchea, post-war turmoil and the refugee experience have had on the cultures concerned.

No culture is static, and all minority cultures in Australia have been influenced by their interaction with the dominant Australian culture and the migration experience, but for the Indo-Chinese cultures the process of change and dislocation began long before their resettlement in Australia. For young people, in particular, traditional values may have very little meaning or relevance.

As educators, it is essential that we do not make assumptions about the attitudes, wishes, needs and aspirations of Indo-Chinese students and their families on the basis of simplistic cultural descriptions and over-generalizations. As with any cultural groups, it is important to recognize the degree of heterogeneity that exists within the group as well as the features which are held in common.

Self-esteem Programs as an Educational Strategy

Throughout the 1970s and the 1980s the notion of self-esteem and its relationship to educational success and achievement has increasingly been used to explain educational disadvantage, and a plethora of programs to improve self-esteem in disadvantaged students has emerged. In particular, programs based on the development of self-esteem have been popular as strategies to improve the educational achievement of girls, and of students from minority racial and cultural backgrounds (see introduction to this volume and Lippman, 1977; Liverpool New Arrivals Programme Workshop, 1985; Melgaard and Bruce, 1982; Slater and Cibrowski, 1982). As a consequence, teachers frequently turn to this notion of self-esteem, first, to explain the educational difficulties which students may be facing and, second, to provide strategies for overcoming these difficulties. In recent years there has been a recognition of the special needs of girls from minority cultural backgrounds, and the need to recognize the interaction between gender and culture and its implications for education (Tsolidis, 1986; Wenner, 1985; Kalantzis and Cope, 1986; Brittan and Maynard, 1984; Taylor, 1984). This debate has brought into question the appropriateness of many educational strategies when they are applied across cultural and gender divisions, and strategies based on the development of positive self-esteem must also be examined afresh in the light of these discussions.

Self-esteem strategies for the improvement of educational achievement have been criticized on a number of grounds. These are discussed in more detail in other chapters in this volume (Renshaw, Chapter 1; Kenway, Willis and Nevard, Chapter 2), but the following three points are particularly relevant to this consideration of Indo-Chinese students. First, there is a concern that self-esteem strategies provide a limited, individualistic explanation of educational disadvantage and thus 'blame the victim', rather than examining the social and educational system for discriminatory structures and practices (Brittan and Maynard, 1984; Stone, 1981). Second, there is some doubt as to the validity of assuming that there is a link at all between positive self-esteem and educational achievement (Kubiniec, 1970; West *et al.*, 1980; Bagley *et al.*, 1979). Third, methods of assessing self-esteem have been called into question, and some writers have suggested that groups who have been characterized as having low self-esteem (e.g. girls, black students) do in fact have quite positive self-esteem but based on criteria which are excluded by common forms of assessment (Fuller, in Deem, 1981; Brittan and Maynard, 1984; Sarup, 1986; Driver, 1982).

These issues all need to be examined more closely so that the value and appropriateness of educational programs to enhance students' self-esteem can be properly assessed. Needless to say, there are students in our classrooms who have low self-esteem and who may benefit from a teacher's efforts to help them see themselves more positively. The danger is that without an adequate theory of self-esteem and its relationship to learning, an understanding of the nature of the students, and of the world, we may, first, misdiagnose the problem and, second, expect too much of the solution.

Are Self-esteem Programs Necessary and Appropriate Educational Strategies for Indo-Chinese Girls?

One can find Indo-Chinese girls with low self-esteem and educational problems in Australian classrooms, but it would be a mistake to assume that these characteristics were causally linked, or that they necessarily indicate a general trend among Indo-Chinese students. Such conclusions have in the past been drawn with respect to other racial and cultural minority groups (for example, West Indian and Asian students in Britain, and black students in the United States), and recent work has pointed out that there may be negative consequences of educational programs which focus on improving self-esteem as a means of improving educational achievement (Stone, 1981; Fuller, 1981; various studies cited in OECD, 1986). A number of questions need to be answered, therefore, and a range of factors considered before we can be confident that the solutions we prescribe are appropriate and adequate. This is the task of this and the following section of this chapter.

Indo-Chinese Girls' Self-esteem

As a result of the commonly held beliefs that girls tend to have lower self-esteem than boys because of sex role socialization, and that students from minority cultural groups are likely to have lower self-esteem than those from the dominant cultural group because of the devaluation their culture is subjected to, there is a temptation to look for self-esteem problems among Indo-Chinese girls, who appear to be doubly at risk following this analysis. Before reaching any conclusions, however, such an assumption needs to be carefully checked.

Although no research was found that deals directly with self-esteem within the group of Indo-Chinese students in Australia, there are some research indications that when comparing levels of self-esteem between Indo-Chinese girls and boys, and between Indo-Chinese students and students from the dominant culture, there are no grounds for assuming the former group in each case suffers from generally relatively low self-esteem. Based on interview, survey and questionnaire material collected from Indo-Chinese students in the eastern states of Australia, Kelly and Bennoun recorded the following: 'As regards "coping" at school, 65% felt that they were. There was a significant gender difference with the girls being more confident that they were coping than the boys in Australia in contrast to the feelings of coping in their country of origin' (1984, p. 110). A five-year follow-up study of Vietnamese refugee children completed in the United States of America included an investigation of the children's perceptions of their own school achievement and capabilities: 'Among all the children, 64% ranked themselves as "equally smart", 29% ranked themselves as "smarter than" and 7% ranked themselves "less smart" than their American peers. This suggests these children have a good and realistic self-image thus far' (Sokoloff, Carlin and Pham, 1984, in Owan, 1985, p. 102).

Taking into account these results, and also considering the difficulties inherent in measuring self-esteem across cultural, gender and class groups, it is impossible to generalize and assume that Indo-Chinese girls as a group suffer from low self-esteem, although of course individuals within the group may.

The Relationship between Gender, Educational Achievement and Self-esteem for Indo-Chinese Girls

There is very little research evidence available on the relative educational achievement of Indo-Chinese males and females. A 1983 study of the Contingency Program for Refugee Children found no significant difference between boys and girls in the rate of improvement in English proficiency for South-East Asian refugee students (Department of Education and Youth Affairs, 1983). A South Australian study completed in 1986 followed up 159 Indo-Chinese students from Intensive Language Centres and found that among Vietnamese and Khmer students a higher proportion of boys than girls remained at school two years after leaving a language centre. However, among the ethnic Chinese retention rates were higher for girls (Wenner and Mckay, 1986). There is some evidence that Indo-Chinese girls value education highly and have relatively high aspirations (Wenner, 1985; Wenner and Mckay, 1986). Further research is required to clarify the patterns of educational choice and success among Indo-Chinese students, and a wide range of possible causal factors for any emerging patterns needs to be considered.

The Relationship between Self-esteem and Sex Role Socialization for Indo-Chinese Students

The assertion that girls tend to have lower self-esteem than boys is frequently linked to patterns of sex role socialization and stereotyping which narrow the acceptable options for girls and encourage them to underrate themselves (Melgaard and Bruce, 1982; *Wings*, 1983). There is a further tendency among many well-meaning educators to subscribe to the view that women in Asian cultures suffer greater repression on the basis of sex and are confined by even more rigid sex roles than we of the 'liberated West'. Finally, it is often concluded that to present alternative gender roles is inappropriate because it will cause a conflict for girls of those cultures.

The notion that girls have lower self-esteem as a result of sex role socialization has been challenged by recent work which has investigated the complexities of socialization and discarded the view of girls as passive recipients of a sex role ideology (Brittan and Maynard, 1984; Deem, 1978, 1981; Fuller, 1981). These studies focus on female subcultures and the definition of self-esteem in relation to these as well as in relation to the framework defined by the school, and suggest that girls do not passively internalize limitations prescribed by sex role stereotyping.

The assumption that sex roles are necessarily more rigidly defined or more restrictive for girls in Indo-Chinese cultures than they are in mainstream Australian culture is also problematic. The view that Asian women are somehow more oppressed than their Western counterparts in many cases reflects an ethnocentric view which takes superficial gender relations out of their cultural context, and which fails to be as critical of its own cultural characteristics as it is of the features of other cultures. This point has been clearly articulated by several British writers in relation to their Asian and West Indian communities (Sarup, 1986; Fuller, 1981; Riley, 1985). The following account by workers in a Neighbourhood Centre program for Indo-Chinese women illustrates the importance of recognizing the dynamics of gender roles within cultures other than our own, of recognizing that along with those aspects we might define as oppressive there may also be aspects which are very supportive and affirming of women.

> These women are able to maintain their cultural links and still find a place in Australian society where they have recognition, giving them the power to participate.... This is strongly linked with maintaining their own place in a 'women's culture' in their society. The strength of this women's culture seems to overcome

what Australian women may see as oppressive practices. The women appear to have an independence and confidence when this is present. It also seems to enable them to interact more in the broader Australian Society. (Nunawading North Neighbourhood Centre, 1986)

This example illustrates how important it is to view sex role expectations in a holistic cultural context and not to assume that because arranged marriages exist, or because women seem to be extremely polite and passive, or dress in a certain way that they are necessarily more oppressed than are women in Western society. Imposing Western notions of feminism and liberation may undermine the strength and support these women obtain from their own 'women's culture'.

However, this is not to argue that any conflict over sex role issues in minority cultures is inappropriate. The reluctance to challenge gender relations in cultures other than the dominant culture on the grounds of cultural sanctity reflects a narrow view that cultures are static and homogeneous, and that gender relations within minority cultures are fixed. This cannot be assumed, for, just as such issues are in a state of flux in our culture, so may they be in other cultural groups. Variations in attitudes to such issues as the domestic role of women, child care, roles within marriage, work, contraception, courtship and so on are evident among Indo-Chinese women and girls and can be related to differences in the various traditional cultures (Khmer, Vietnamese, Lao, Chinese), and to differences in social class, education, religion, and urban or rural backgrounds.

Further, the Indo-Chinese cultures in Australia continue to develop and change; they have not taken on a fossilized form. Life in Australia presents new and different challenges for the cultures to respond to. Work patterns are different — it is not as easy to find paid work that can be done in the home, for example. For many Indo-Chinese the traditional support of the extended family is no longer available, whereas welfare services provide a different form of support. Younger family members are more strongly influenced by Australian adolescent culture and thus create new problems for families to contend with. Knowles (1984) has documented some of the changes to role expectations that have occurred among women in the Vietnamese community of Perth (capital of Western Australia) and some of the factors affecting these changes. She identifies two major areas of change:

In Australia, older women experience a dramatic downgrading in their status and authority within the family [whereas] many of the

> younger women developed more assertive attitudes and began to
> demand and expect greater participation in the decision making
> related to their individual lives, their marriages and their house-
> hold arrangements. (Knowles, 1984, pp. 3–4)

It can thus be seen that the relationship between sex role socialization, minority cultures and the dominant culture is a complex one, and
any educational program which addresses self-esteem in relation to gender and culture needs to take these complexities into account. In particular, programs which are based on Anglo-Australian perceptions of sex
roles, and which fail adequately to understand the dynamics of relations
within the minority cultures may in fact undermine self-esteem which
girls derive from their role in the family and the local ethnic community.
As educators, we have a responsibility to ensure that students who are
disadvantaged in our society are provided with the means to greater
empowerment, but we must also ensure that the means we use to achieve
this recognize and respect both the individual and the cultural attributes
these students bring with them.

Criteria for Measuring and Assessing Indo-Chinese Girls' Self-esteem

The use of tests continues to be a controversial issue in education, an issue
which is of direct relevance to the application of self-esteem models to
groups such as Indo-Chinese students. There has long been a debate as to
the extent of cultural bias in intelligence tests, tests of achievement and
psychological and personality tests and whether or not such bias produces
poor results in 'non-standard' groups such as girls, working-class students or students from minority cultural groups. An even stronger argument suggests that not only may tests be biased and thus both unreliable
and invalid, but that their entire conceptualization may be a specific
cultural construct.

> It should not be thought that this cultural and ideological in-
> fluence is 'contamination' in the sense that the tests were generally
> acceptable but blemished by the cultural perspectives of their
> developers; in fact the tests are the products of their culture and
> ideology. The tests themselves are cultural artefacts, not merely
> bent at the edges by cultural biases. (Verma and Mallick, 1982,
> p. 183)

Self-esteem is a concept strongly rooted in a Western European context which stresses individualism. Thus this argument is likely to have considerable relevance to the application of tests and measures of self-esteem to students from an Indo-Chinese background whose cultures diverge from such individualism.

> To many, though not necessarily all, Indo-Chinese students and their families the suggestion that a student is doing badly at school because he or she has a negative self-image may be quite laughable, and attempts actively to cultivate positive self-esteem may be perceived as a waste of valuable educational time or an intrusion into the affairs of the family. To many Southeast Asian parents, psychological problems and conflicts do not make sense. Disturbed behaviour is perceived as being the result of either wilfulness or physical illness. "Talking" about it is not seen as helpful. Furthermore, talking to strangers outside the family is not acceptable. (Owan, 1985, p. 97)

This is not to suggest that we as educators should not offer such solutions, if we believe them to be appropriate. It does mean that we should understand if they are rejected and recognize that the family may have alternative solutions which are equally valid.

Apart from such potential cultural conflicts relating to the very concept being tested, there are also likely to be conceptual and linguistic problems in the interpretation or test questions. Even the use of translated tests or interpreters cannot prevent misunderstandings based on linguistic differences or cultural values. For example, many Indo-Chinese students and interpreters consider it of ultimate importance to give the teacher, researcher or tester the answer they want, the 'right' answer, rather than to express their personal feelings or opinions.

Specific terms or concepts may be difficult to translate and important nuances lost because of linguistic and cultural differences. Responses may also be misinterpreted by the teacher or researcher because of different cultural interpretation. For example, an item in the Coopersmith self-esteem inventory (Bagley *et al.*, 1979) such as: 'I have a low opinion of myself' may draw a strongly positive response from an Indo-Chinese student. This would contribute to a low self-esteem score, whereas the student may in fact have been responding in the context of a culture that highly valued modesty and humility and would have interpreted a negative response to such a statement as brash and impolite.

The same problems apply when teachers devise their own tests or rely on subjective observations. Even when exercising considerable sensitivity to the different cultural contexts involved, it is impossible for a teacher with limited time and resources to be fully cognisant of the many problems of cultural interpretation, and any assessment of students' self-esteem will be framed in the teacher's own cultural context. This is unavoidable, but is often forgotten when conclusions are drawn.

Factors to Be Considered in Self-esteem Programs for Indo-Chinese Students

The previous section drew attention to some of the limitations inherent in applying self-esteem theory to solving the educational difficulties of Indo-Chinese girls. However, this is not to deny that there are instances where it may be appropriate to use strategies designed to enhance self-esteem with an individual student or a group of students. This section seeks to examine some of the specific issues that may arise in relation to the self-esteem of Indo-Chinese students.

These issues arise frequently in work with Indo-Chinese students but, as has been indicated previously, not all such students will conform to these expectations, and educators must be wary of treating individuals on the basis of stereotypes, even stereotypes which may be sympathetic constructions. Not all of the factors discussed here are specific only to girls, but they have been included because they do contribute to an understanding of Indo-Chinese girls' experiences.

The Effect of Wartime and Refugee Experiences

Many Indo-Chinese students have had experiences, the horror of which it is difficult for us to comprehend, and clearly such memories and their feelings about the way they responded may influence the way these students now see themselves. Several studies have documented these experiences and discussed the implications for teachers and other professionals (Leak, 1982; Poussard, 1981; Kelly and Bennoun, 1984; Zulfacar, n.d.). In particular, some students may feel distressed and inadequate as a result of having left other family members behind in refugee camps or in their country of origin, of having failed to protect or rescue younger family members, of not being in a position to be able to sponsor other family members to Australia, of not earning enough money to help their family here, or family members still in refugee camps or in their country of origin, etc. This applies more to older students (and it should be remembered that many Indo-Chinese students in secondary schools may be young adults), but even some younger students may have borne responsibilities which they may feel they failed to fulfil. Now that they are in Australia these students feel an enormous pressure to take advantage of their new opportunities, to gain an education and a good job, and to earn money to assist their families. When this does not happen as quickly or as easily as they may have hoped, they may come to feel inadequate.

The Relationship between Racism, Prejudice, Cultural Conflict and Self-esteem

The concern that children from racial minority groups which are the subject of racist attacks from members of the dominant group will internalize the negative image ascribed to them is another factor contributing to the self-esteem debate. This analysis emerged in American work with black students (Fanon, 1970, quoted in Bagley and Verma, 1983) and has also been taken up by researchers working with West Indian and Asian students in Britain.

> Since an individual's self concept is based on his experience and since contemporary society has gone to great lengths to teach ethnic minorities that they are different hence they must be deficient, it has commonly been accepted that blacks in particular have somehow internalised this prevailing evaluation and made it their own. One consequence according to this formulation is that minority groups and blacks in particular experience a deficiency in self-esteem. (Bagley and Verma, 1983, p. 125)

The racist response that is unfortunately one element of Australia's welcome to Indo-Chinese communities may suggest that a similar pattern is likely to emerge for these students. However, there is a need to analyze carefully the processes of cultural or racial interaction and development of self-esteem, as overseas researchers have pointed out. The internalization of a negative image is only one possible response to racist attitudes and may not be the most common one.

Young and Bagley (1982) have argued that where individuals are presented with conflicting evaluations from different social and cultural contexts, they will exercise a variety of choices in which evaluations they regard as significant or insignificant. It is likely that members of groups which are defined negatively by the dominant social and cultural context will seek to create and identify with subcultures which provide them with a more positive evaluation. Evidence of this can be found, and has been documented in the case of working-class girls defining themselves in relation to an adolescent culture of sexuality (Kessler *et al.*, 1982) and West Indian students finding their pride in the Rastafarian revival (Stone, 1981).

> Working class and minority group children do have alternatives and do not need to accept the low status value which society places on their groups or to internalise it by developing low self-concepts or poor self-esteem. Their reference groups, unlike those of the middle class child, have different values from those which obtain in the school system. (Stone, 1981, p. 10)

Kelly and Bennoun (1984) found that the Indo-Chinese students they interviewed responded in a variety of ways to the negative attitudes they encountered. Some students expressed anger, some sadness, some seemed to have been sheltered from a perception of generalized racist attitudes by their strong identification with their ethnic community. It would seem that only a small minority of such students are likely to internalize a racist view of themselves.

One factor in determining whether or not a student is likely to maintain positive self-esteem in the face of racist attitudes is the availability of an alternative reference group in the context of which the student can construct his or her self-esteem. It may, therefore, be more important for educators to ensure that school structures, processes and content encourage the positive recognition and integration of minority group cultures into the mainstream, rather than introduce compensatory programs for minority group students that aim to enhance self-esteem as defined within the dominant culture's framework. By doing this, the personal cultural conflict experienced by a student can be minimized, and the positive support drawn from the student's own family and cultural background can contribute to the student's success at school without marginalizing these students into 'special' programs.

Apart from dealing with the racist elements in Australian culture, students from Indo-Chinese cultures are also engaged in the process of redefining their personal cultural identity in a new social environment where they have two, if not more, cultural frameworks to choose from. Inevitably there will be conflict and difficult personal choices to be made. Many of these students struggle to maintain self-esteem in two different social situations which measure respect and esteem according to different criteria. Again, it may be of more help to students facing these conflicts to provide them with a school environment which acknowledges their experience in the context of the general curriculum. Self-esteem programs, assertiveness training and social skills programs may provide students with the sort of skills Anglo-Australians would use to deal with such problems and conflicts, but they may not be appropriate skills for Indo-Chinese students. They may even intensify the conflict the students are trying to deal with unless they are contextualized within an understanding of the social processes that contribute to these conflicts.

The Importance of the Individual's Relationship to the Family

It is commonly acknowledged that Indo-Chinese students are likely to have a very different relationship to, and conception of, the role of their families. Cultural traditions are more likely to encourage them to perceive themselves primarily as part of a family unit, rather than as an individual, and this different cultural perception affects the relevance a concept like self-esteem will have for them. 'A person cannot act freely as an individual but must act in accordance with the wishes of parents and even distant relatives. All these people are so involved with an individual's life that they are in a very real sense a part of his or her triumphs, successes, defeats and losses' (Le, 1986, p. 41). It must be remembered also that for many Indo-Chinese students this traditional network of support and relationships has broken down, either because they are separated from all or part of their family, because they have lost all or part of their family or because in the process of resettlement traditional family relationships have broken down. As a result, students may have personal responsibilities beyond their capabilities, they may see traditional authority figures within their family lose their dignity and ability to provide appropriate leadership, or they may find it difficult to cope with the individual responsibility they now have for making decisions about their own lives.

Again, this cultural context must inform the kind of action teachers take in response to what they may perceive as low self-esteem leading to an inability to cope with the demands of school. The following example illustrates clearly how complex and difficult the application of solutions based on self-esteem enhancement are when used across cultures.

Kim, a Khmer girl, was 16 when she arrived, alone, in Australia as an unaccompanied minor. She had had less than three years of schooling in her life and was enrolled in a language centre for such students. At school she was quiet, polite and completed any work that was required, but she made very slow progress, both in learning English and in other subjects. She seemed somewhat apathetic, expressed few emotions and did not seem to make friends with other students, even though there were several other Khmer girls her age attending the language centre. She expressed dissatisfaction with her living arrangements and was moved from her first placement with an Anglo-Australian welfare worker and his family to a second placement with a single, Khmer, female welfare worker. This, however, did not seem to be a successful arrangement either. She continued to drift through her schooling, still making slow progress and apparently uninterested in pursuing her studies at high school but also unable to commit herself to a decision to take an alternative path. She continued as a student at the language centre for close to two years, and then announced that she was leaving to go and live in a country town where she was to be married to a young Khmer man. The marriage was condoned by the Khmer community, but nevertheless caused some consternation among staff at the language centre who were concerned about possible exploitation and felt that Kim was too immature to make such a decision. However, they did not seek to intervene beyond consulting with community welfare workers, and Kim left the language centre and was married.

Two years later I was interviewing former language centre students for a research project and had arranged to visit a young married Khmer woman, Sy, at her home. Much to my surprise the door was opened by Kim, holding a young child. Kim soon explained the situation. She was married to Sy's brother and the two couples lived together with their children and Sy's mother. Kim was a different person from the withdrawn girl I had known at the language centre. She was confident, poised and couldn't stop smiling. It was obvious that she felt she had made the right decision and was happy with her living arrangements.

This example illustrates the difficulties inherent in the superficial application of ethnocentric interpretations of sex roles in other cultures. When she was at the language centre, Kim presented as a classic example of a girl with low self-esteem, and many a well-meaning teacher would have tried to remedy this with some form of confidence building or assertiveness training program. It is likely that at best Kim would simply have not responded; at worst it may have intensified the distress she was experiencing as a result of her loss of collective identity. The solution which she found seemed inappropriate to many of the language centre teachers because it placed her in what they perceived to be an oppressive role in a culture which rigidly defined the role of wife as subordinate. However, it was that very role, and the social position in a family group and women's culture which it gave her, that seemed to have provided Kim with the self-esteem and confidence she needed.

The issues are complex and all of Kim's difficulties have not been overcome. She is still in a relatively powerless and disadvantaged position in Australian society, though within the sphere of her family and community she now has a power and sense of identity which she did not have before. What can be learned from this example is that middle-class Anglo-Australian conceptions of what contributes to self-esteem and confidence cannot be easily transposed cross-culturally.

The Significance of Age, Educational Progress and Self-esteem

Most Indo-Chinese students now in secondary schools are at least one or two years older than their classmates as a result of missed schooling and the need to learn English. Some may be trying to gain a secondary school education even though they are already in their early 20s. Some students may have had almost no schooling in their country of origin as a result of the wars, government policy and the social dislocation they experienced, and these students may begin their education in a new language at ages ranging up to young adulthood. This age factor can put added pressure on them to succeed quickly and can contribute to feelings of failure and inadequacy.

Although recognizing the long-term benefits of obtaining an education, older students may also feel responsible for earning an income to help support their family, and may come to feel that they are failing both in this respect and because their progress at school is slower and more difficult than they expected. To exacerbate the situation, it is often the case that younger siblings make faster progress in learning English and in adapting to the new routines and expectations of school life; this further undermines the respect for themselves older students can sustain.

Teachers also need to be aware of the age of such students and the many adult responsibilities they may have at home or within their community. Girls often bear demanding domestic responsibilities as well as part-time jobs while still at school (Wenner, 1985). The youthful appearance of many of these students, and the naivety and deference which they show, can be misleading, and it is easy for teachers to forget or not realize their age. However, it cannot do much for an older student's self-esteem and social standing to be treated like a child at school.

Self-esteem and the Social Environment

Research conducted by Kubiniec (1970) indicated that 'measures of self-perceptions employed should include perceptions of one's environment as well as perceptions of one's self' (Kubiniec, 1970, p. 333). The relationship between self-esteem and the perception of one's social environment may well be significant for Indo-Chinese students, particularly those who are recently arrived in Australia. Students are likely to find it difficult to define their own self-concept in the context of a social environment, the school, which they barely understand. Some of the responses to questions about self-concept, aspirations, etc. which may seem bizarre and contradictory can be explained by this lack of understanding of the social context. For example, several female Indo-Chinese students, when asked what sort of work they would like to do, listed such disparate occupations as 'doctor or sewing in a factory' (Wenner, 1985). Many students in the same research selected 'sewing' as a favoured occupation. This may not be an accurate indication of their perceptions of their own ability, but an indication of their inability accurately to assess their own potential in a new and unfamiliar social environment.

Conclusion

Educational practice based entirely on individualized, personal growth models, though seductive for the caring teacher, can never be more than a 'band-aid solution' and may often cause more harm than good. There is a danger that the ultimate result of educational programs that enhance self-esteem is to make students feel more positive about their lack of power and success in our society, rather than to equip them with the functional skills they need to succeed. Such programs may also encourage a false optimism that a positive outlook will overcome all obstacles, and students will fall even harder when they continue to fail in a sexist, competitive, stratified system where someone must fail, and that someone is most likely to be female, from a minority cultural group or from a lower socio-economic background.

An individualized approach to self-esteem enhancement will cause increased conflict for a student if the curriculum and other school systems continue to undermine and devalue that student's cultural background. Focus on such programs may also divert attention and resources from other pressing educational needs these students have, such as adequate teaching of English as a second language.

It is, of course, easy to be critical and far more difficult to come up with good, practical solutions. In conclusion, I do not wish to argue that programs which aim to improve the self-esteem, assertiveness and confidence of students have no worth and should be abandoned. My concern is that they be thoroughly contextualized in a framework that takes into consideration macro-social factors. Students need to come to understand the processes of social stratification and reproduction so that they are able to contextualize their personal experience in a way that is empowering. The contributions by Cope and Kalantzis (Chapter 8) and Jonas (Chapter 11) in this volume are examples of educational programs that attempt to do this by challenging some of the macro-social problems as well as addressing the individual needs of students.

Individualized educational programs must not be allowed to replace programs that challenge the structures and ideologies underpinning our education system. Curriculum, assessment procedures, the selective functions of schools, the interactions between the dominant culture and minority cultures and the distribution of resources are all issues which affect the self-esteem and educational achievement of students, and they must be addressed by educators who hope to bring about a genuine deconstruction of the patterns of discrimination and disadvantage in our society.

References

AUSTRALIA. DEPARTMENT OF EDUCATION AND YOUTH AFFAIRS (1983) *Cultural Background Paper — Kampuchea*, Canberra, Australian Government Publishing Service.

AUSTRALIA. DEPARTMENT OF EDUCATION AND YOUTH AFFAIRS (1983) *Cultural Background Paper — Laos*, Canberra, Australian Government Publishing Service.

AUSTRALIA. DEPARTMENT OF EDUCATION AND YOUTH AFFAIRS (1983) *Cultural Background Paper — Vietnam*, Canberra, Australian Government Publishing Service.

AUSTRALIA. DEPARTMENT OF EDUCATION AND YOUTH AFFAIRS (1983) *Schooling for Newly Arrived Indo-Chinese Refugees*, An Evaluation of the Contingency Program for Refugee Children, Canberra, Australian Government Publishing Service.

BAGLEY, C. and VERMA, G.K. (Eds) (1983) *Multicultural Childhood Education: Education, Ethnicity and Cognitive Styles*, London, Gower.

BAGLEY, C., VERMA, G.K., MALLICK, K. and YOUNG, L. (Eds) (1979) *Personality, Self-Esteem and Prejudice*, Westmead, Saxon House.

BRITTAN, A. and MAYNARD, M. (1984) *Sexism, Racism and Oppression*, Oxford, Basil Blackwell.

CRUICKSHANK, K. (Ed.) (1982) *In a Strange Land I Live: Stories, Poems and Interviews about Work and School*, Sydney, Materials Production Project.

DEEM, R. (1978) *Women and Schooling*, London, Routledge and Kegan Paul.

DEEM, R. (Ed.) (1981) *Schooling for Women's Work*, London, Routledge and Kegan Paul.

DRIVER, G. (1982) 'Ethnicity and cultural competence: Aspects of interaction in multiracial classrooms', in VERMA, G.K. and BAGLEY, C., *Self Concept, Achievement and Multicultural Education*, London, Macmillan, pp. 70–9.

FULLER, M. (1981) 'Black girls in a London comprehensive school', in DEEM, R., *Schooling for Women's Work*, London, Routledge and Kegan Paul.

KALANTZIS, M. and COPE, B. (1986) *Some Issues in the Education of Girls of Non English Speaking Background*, Sydney, NSW Department of Education.

KELLY, P. and BENNOUN, R. (1984) *Students from Indo-China: Educational Issues — A Resource Book*, Canberra, Australian Centre for Indo-Chinese Research.

KESSLER, S., ASHENDEN, D., CONNELL, B. and DOWSETT, G. (1982) *Ockers and Disco-Maniacs*, Sydney, Inner City Education Centre.

KNOWLES, J. (1984) 'Changing roles amongst Vietnamese women in Perth', Paper presented at the Fifth National Conference of the Asian Studies Association of Australia, Adelaide University.

KUBINIEC, C.M. (1970) 'The relative efficacy of various dimensions of the self-concept in predicting academic achievement', *American Educational Research Journal*, 7, pp. 321–35.

LE, V.D. (1986) 'Please understand me — Xin Hiu Toi'! *Pivot*, 13, 5, pp. 40–4.

LEAK, J. (1982) *Smiling on the Outside, Crying on the Inside: The Prevalence and Manifestation of Emotional Stress in Refugee Children from Vietnam, Aged 9–12 Years*, Adelaide, South Australian College of Advanced Education.

LIPPMAN, L. (1977) *The Aim Is Understanding: Educational Techniques for a Multicultural Society*, Sydney, ANZ Book Company.

LIVERPOOL NEW ARRIVALS PROGRAMME WORKSHOP (1985) *Me No Good Miss: Self Esteem and Social Skills — Strategies for Students of Non English Speaking Backgrounds*, Sydney, NSW Education Department.

MELGAARD, G. and BRUCE, W.A. (1982) *Confidence Building and Self Esteem for Year 7–10 Girls*, Adelaide, Education Department of South Australia, Women's Advisory Unit.

NUNAWADING NORTH NEIGHBOURHOOD CENTRE (1986) 'More than English is needed', *Ms Muffett*, 28, August, p. 17.

ORGANIZATION FOR ECONOMIC COOPERATION AND DEVELOPMENT (1986) *Girls and Inequalities in Education: A Cross National Study of Sex Inequalities in Upbringing and in Schools and Colleges*, Paris, OECD.

OWAN, T.C. (Ed.) (1985) *South East Asian Mental Health: Treatment, Prevention, Services, Training and Research*, Washington, D.C., US Department of Health and Human Services.

POUSSARD, W. (1981) *Today Is a Real Day: Indo Chinese Refugees in Australia*, Melbourne, Dove Communications.

PURVIS, J. and HALES, M. (Eds) (1983) *Achievement and Inequality in Education*, London, Routledge and Kegan Paul.

RILEY, K. (1985) 'Black girls speak for themselves', in WEINER, G., *Just a Bunch of Girls*, Milton Keynes, Open University Press, pp. 63–76.

SARUP, M. (1986) *The Politics of Multiracial Education*, London, Routledge and Kegan Paul.

SLATER, S. and CIBROWSKI, L. (1982) *What Do You Like about Yourself? — Developing a Positive Self-Concept!* Washington, D.C., Home Economics Education Association.

STONE, M. (1981) *The Education of the Black Child in Britain: The Myth of Multiracial Education*, London, Fontana.

STORER, D. (Ed.) (1985) *Ethnic Family Values in Australia*, Sydney, Prentice-Hall.

TAYLOR, H. (1984) 'Sexism and racism: Partners in oppression', *Multicultural Teaching*, 2, Spring, pp. 4–7.

TSOLIDIS, G. (1986) *Educating Voula*, Melbourne, Victorian Ministry of Education.

VERMA, G.K. and BAGLEY, C. (Eds) (1982) *Self Concept, Achievement and Multicultural Education*, London, Macmillan.

VERMA, G.K. and MALLICK, K. (1982) 'Tests and testing in a multi-ethnic society', in VERMA, G.K. and BAGLEY, C., *Self Concept, Achievement and Multicultural Education*, London, Macmillan, pp. 176–87.

WEINER, G. (1985) *Just a Bunch of Girls*, Milton Keynes, Open University Press.

WENNER, J. (1985) *Behind the Smiles: The Needs and Aspirations of Indo Chinese Girls in Australian Secondary Schools*, Adelaide, South Australian Education Department.

WENNER, J. and MCKAY, P. (1986) *Two Years Later: A Study of the Educational Experiences of Former New Arrival Program Students in South Australia*, Participation and Equity Program First Phase Language Learners Project, Adelaide.

WEST, C.K., FISH, J.A. and STEVENS, R.J. (1980) 'General self-concept, self-concept of academic ability and school achievement: Implications for causes of self-concept', *Australian Journal of Education*, 24, 2, pp. 194–213.

Wings: A Pilot Project to Enhance Self Esteem in Girls (1983) Hobart, Tasmanian Department of Education.

YOUNG, L. and BAGLEY, C. (1982) 'Self esteem, self concept and the development of black identity: A theoretical overview', in VERMA, G.K. and BAGLEY, C., *Self Concept, Achievement and Multicultural Education*, London, Macmillan, pp. 41–59.

ZULFACAR, D. (n.d.) *Surviving without Parents: Indo-Chinese Refugee Minors in NSW*, Sydney, University of New South Wales.

Chapter 6

Working-class Girls and Educational Outcomes: Is Self-esteem an Issue?

Johanna Wyn

For many years the educational outcomes from schooling for girls have concerned feminists, educationalists and some members of the community. Although in Australia girls have an equivalent participation rate in secondary education to boys, the quality of their schooling compared to boys' has come under question. In many schools girls' participation is different from boys. For example, 'technical drawing, computing, maths and physical sciences are male dominated at high school level' (*Meeting Young Women's Needs*, 1984, p. 23). This means that young women emerge from school with their options for employment already limited by the content of their school courses. Young women also have a lower participation rate in post-school training, further limiting their options for employment.

Occupational segregation in Australia reflects these differences in the form of gender divisions. In 1984, 64 per cent of female employees were concentrated in three major occupational groupings (clerical, sales and service), characterized by low pay, low status and few possibilities for career opportunities (Sawer, 1985, p. xiv). As this pattern of occupational segmentation continued into the late 1980s, many sought to alter the pattern by intervening in schooling practices. The processes that lead to differential outcomes from schooling have come under scrutiny, in particular, discrimination against girls.

Over the last decade the complexities of the situation have become more apparent. Early assumptions about objectives and strategies for change have been undermined by the persistence of occupational segregation (O'Donnell, 1984) and the apparent determination of many girls and women to place a continuing priority on relationships and domestic concerns (Connell *et al.*, 1982, Wilson and Wyn, 1987). What has emerged is a picture of the ways in which class, gender, race and ethnicity interrelate in shaping the educational and social outcomes of girls and young women in Australia (Kalantzis, 1986; Wilson and Wyn, 1987) and elsewhere (Deem, 1980; Gamarnikow *et al.*, 1983). In Australia an awareness of the significance of these differences among groups of women has been incorporated into policy formation. The recognition of the heterogeneity of girls is a step forward, but it is not enough if the ideas and strategies which have informed educational change over the last decade (such as self-esteem) continue to be used without question.

Young women and girls bring to school particular perspectives derived from their experiences of class, ethnicity and race. While there are some dimensions of life that many girls and young women experience in common, there is a danger in assuming on the basis of feminist theory that there are 'essential' experiences that all women share. As Yates points out, there are potential conflicts to be considered that may occur for women, between class, sex and ethnicity (Yates, 1987, p. 12). Strategies for change need to relate to the circumstances of specific groups of young women and girls. Wenner and Tsolidis in this volume (see Chapters 5 and 3 respectively) support this view, focusing on the way cultural background affects many aspects of girls' experiences of education and the decisions they make regarding their futures.

The interrelationship between ethnicity and class is complex. Young women and girls from any ethnic background whose parents are, for example, unskilled workers in factories bring quite different priorities and expectations to school than those whose parents are employed in professional occupations. It is no longer appropriate to treat girls as if they were a single category or as if the problems identified above are merely a matter to be solved through the treatment of individual girls. This recognition has implications for strategies aimed at changing educational outcomes. Acknowledgment of difference between groups of girls and young women implies taking seriously the perspectives that each group brings to the school and classroom.

During the previous decade or so the concept of self-esteem has been used frequently in discussion on girls and unequal outcomes, both in terms of an explanatory concept (often used in conjunction with 'sex roles') and in terms of a strategy to affect change. This chapter explores the relevance of the concept of self-esteem to the educational experience of girls from working-class neighbourhoods.

Working-class Girls

The research reported in this chapter draws particularly on two studies of young women (14 to 16 years) who attended schools in working-class neighbourhoods. The first is based on research I undertook between 1982 and 1984 (Wilson and Wyn, 1987; Wyn, 1987) on young people attending two inner city schools in Melbourne. Supporting evidence is drawn from the second study on working-class girls in Sydney by Moran (1983).

Both schools in the Melbourne study were located in areas which had traditionally depended heavily on the manufacturing industry for employment. With the decline in manufacturing industry, the areas suffered an increasing rate of unemployment. The schools also served communities with a high proportion of migrants, with 80 per cent of the students coming from homes where English was not spoken. One school aimed to provide an educational program that would mainly cater for students who wished to proceed to the Higher School Certificate examination at the end of Year 12. At the same time some teachers at the school were beginning to develop an alternative program that would suit a wider range of students. The second school offered programs to suit a range of students' needs.

Young women in these schools were asked about their experiences at school and their hopes for their futures. At both schools young women put a priority on 'traditional' choices and occupations. They aimed to work in jobs which involved relationships with other people (children were mentioned frequently), often in a 'caring' capacity. Some were not very specific, but simply wanted, like Amanda, to 'work with kids — anything really'. Another girl said that the kind of job that would best suit her would be 'I suppose with kids, because I can really talk to them, I can understand them.' Others were more aware of the types of work that would involve working with children. For example, Kathy said: 'I'd like to go on to teach physical education in a primary school. I prefer the younger kids up to grade 6, then I could really help them get interested.' Jeanette said she would like to work in 'some kind of nursing with kids or physically retarded people.'

Jeanette, and others like her, wanted to do some form of social work, but were discouraged from this option, because they felt they would not be able to get the credentials from school needed for tertiary study; nor was the prospect of tertiary or further study attractive to them. Hairdressing was also cited as a favoured occupation by a large group of girls, because of the opportunity it offered to meet people and because hairdressing was associated with feminine work. In some cases, however, young women were interested in less conventional options, but were not confident of their ability to make the necessary commitment to school work. Christine, for example, said: 'About last year I told my Dad — I told him I wanted to be a lawyer and he really wanted me to. But now I've changed my mind. I want to be a hairdresser.' When asked why she had changed her mind, she said: 'I just got sick of school. If I do law, I have to do that for about six years. I'm going crazy now at school.'

These young women were making choices about their futures based on their priorities. Even despite some support and in some cases pressure to consider more 'ambitious' careers, the majority opted for a traditional path. However, in some cases those who were interested in an occupation that had traditionally been the domain of males were pressured into changing their minds. For example, Mandy said: 'Actually, I wanted to be a mechanic. I've wanted to for years now, and my parents say it'd be no job.' Another young woman said: 'I wanted to be a plumber once, but my dad got angry. He doesn't like to see girls doing that job and guys in offices, when their body is more suited to doing those kinds of things. Women are built differently.' The result of these decisions was that these young women were aiming for a remarkably small range of occupations in the labour market. However, they were not unusual in doing this. Moran's (1983) study of girls attending school in a working–class neighbourhood in Sydney produced similar findings. She found that the young women whom she interviewed wanted to be beauticians, hairdressers, models, secretaries and nurses. The persistence of this narrow selection is an issue of major concern to those interested in improving the opportunities for young women.

The processes that produce these results are complex. On the one hand, there were pressures on some of the young women in my study to conform to traditional practices, and there was also some discrimination at school and in their homes. Pressure to conform came frequently from parents, in the form of concern that the young women should ultimately have employment that enhanced their chances of marrying. This concern was what lay behind the anger of the parents of the would-be plumber referred to above. Furthermore, a majority of the young women to whom I spoke were expected to carry a considerable responsibility for domestic work at home. Young women themselves identified this as a problem which interfered with their ability to complete homework, and which constantly reminded them of their restricted status, compared with their brothers. The school did little to challenge gender stereotypes. At the time that the research was conducted the careers teacher organized work experience for the boys and girls along gender lines; girls went to hairdressers and creches and the boys to mechanics' workshops and small businesses.

On the other hand, young women also took an active part in these processes. On occasions the girls contributed to the sex stereotyping of jobs through their belief that one's gender identity is maintained by one's work. For example, when asked whether it would be acceptable for a man to stay at home and his wife to be the breadwinner, Angela said: 'But if a man was staying at home and doing the cooking and dishes all day, he would be as a woman, and she would be as a man.' Practical considerations were also important. Perhaps because of their parents' experiences, they did not have a positive view of the combination of motherhood and paid employment. As Jenny summed up: 'For most of us, although we're up with the times, we want to go and work and all this — apprenticeships for girls coming in, also at the back of our minds is that . . . what about your family?' To reinforce the point, she added:

> I got a brother right, who is married, and they both work — they had to work to get a home, and they had to pay all the car and that — they need the car as well. They've got a daughter. She is only around a year, right. Every day they bring her around to my house for mum to mind her, and then they take her back when they come back, say around 8.00 pm. It's no good for the child and it's no good for the mother as well.

The narrow outcomes in terms of job prospects were in part the result of choices which reflect priorities based on their present experience of school and home, and their vision of their futures.

A closer look at the priorities of the young women in each of the studies revealed that they were systematic. That is, a number of fundamental priorities recurred, and two, which focused on relationships, were significant: establishing themselves as adults, and friendship. Young women in my study consistently placed a high priority on establishing a relationship with a male, usually aiming for marriage. Similarly, Moran comments in relation to her young women that 'all the girls regard marriage, children and domestic labour as their primary roles in the future' (1983, p. 88). This was despite the fact that many of the young women in her study expressed 'disillusionment' and 'cynicism' about their future as 'happy' wives and mothers. These young women, Moran reports, 'oscillated between believing romantic notions about relationships, and feeling anxious, disappointed and angry with the boys' (1983, p. 95).

The young women in the Melbourne study expressed the same orientation. They were not 'romantic' about marriage and relationships with men, but saw marriage, and particularly child-rearing, as an important feature of their future life. This is illustrated by Anna, who said, 'I'd like to get married actually, because I really wanted to have a baby when I turned 16.' She added, 'Actually, I'm not really for marriage. I'm more for de facto. You can stay when you want and go when you want. You understand each other.' In each of the studies womanhood was associated ideally with having a steady relationship with a male and ultimately having children. There was also a material element to the vision of womanhood, frequently expressed in the desire to have control over one's own domestic space.

Getting a job and gaining some independence were oriented towards the goal of establishing a flat (in contrast to the boys' priority on getting a car). One young woman imagined that when she left school she would: 'Go straight down to the CES, get a job, work for two weeks, get a bond, get a flat, and then I'd be set for the rest of my life.' In terms of their present life particular priorities also recurred. Although a majority of these young women were not performing well academically at school, they saw school as necessary because it appeared to provide a basis for getting a good job. However, most important to them at school were their friendships. 'Well, I can really appreciate being at school and not working. It's a lot different from the workforce, and also there's more social life, because being at school you're with your friends and so forth, so I really appreciate it.' For this young woman, a brief experience in the workforce was a lonely time and she looked forward to being reunited with her friends at school. For others, friends were a reason for leaving school: 'Most of my friends were leaving, so I wanted to be with them.'

Moran also found that friendship was significant.

> Going to school is important to each member of the group because of their friends/the group:
> D. That's the only good thing 'bout school, the friends.
> M. I guess we all come there because we all like each other so much, we've got a lot of friends and it's not like when you go home and you're with your brothers and sisters. Like, sometimes I go home an' . . . oh well, we can tell our secrets to each other. It's more better at school 'cause you get to say what you want to say . . . you can get to swear, you get to . . . do everything. (1983, p. 89)

The persistence of these priorities on friendship and on establishing themselves as adults in the context of feminine practices makes sense if we consider them as priorities resulting from cultural perspectives. That is, they are seen as deriving from traditions and collective experiences that result from their own and their families' lives, and the types of things that happen in their neighbourhood.

Despite the ethnic diversity of the young women in both the Melbourne studies and the Sydney study by Moran, there were important similarities in their views, goals and experiences of school and life outside school. This commonality does not imply support for the existence of a 'youth culture'. On the contrary, the difficulties with schooling, the ambivalence about further study and the lack of information about the range of options that education may open up place the experience of both groups of young people more in line with that of their parents than with other young people their own age, living in more prestigious areas of Sydney and Melbourne.

Cultural Perspectives

In the context of cultural perspectives the priorities of these young women are placed in a category of beliefs and actions that are more than whim or fashion. Instead, they are seen as the products of a process of cultural formation. In all societies people grow up in a cultural context that they take for granted and in which a majority are able to establish a sense of belonging and acceptance. At times people may challenge the beliefs and practices of their culture, and conflict is normally expressed through political and judicial systems that are accepted as legitimate by a majority of the population. 'In Australia, however, many working class people have routinely experienced subordination, alienation and exploitation resulting in a pattern of cultural formation marked by tension and conflict, as well as by ambivalence and co-option' (Wilson and Wyn, 1987). These processes contribute to a formation of cultural perspectives among Australians that broadly reflects the society's social division.

The high priority placed on friendship by these young women makes sense as an expression of a cultural emphasis on solidarity. This emphasis also helps explain the resistance that young women such as these frequently make to the competitive and individualized practices of some aspects of schooling.

The emphasis on establishing relationships with people in the workplace and on ensuring a particular type of domestic life is also consistent with their cultural perspectives. It is clear, in the environment in which they live and from the experiences of their friends and families, that maintaining domestic life is important to women. Paid work is a high priority in itself, but it is also a means of establishing a comfortable place to live, and supporting relationships with other people. Most of the young women in Moran's study did not envisage other options for themselves beyond marriage and motherhood. As Tsolidis and Wenner point out in this volume (see Chapters 3 and 5), within particular ethnic contexts, variations on this vision of womanhood are seen very positively by young women themselves. Furthermore, many of these young women have seen the debilitating effects of work in factories on their parents and perceive that the workforce does not hold much promise for them, unless they are able to succeed in gaining further training or qualifications and get a job with good working conditions.

Cultural perspectives provide a powerful basis for shared knowledge. If young women such as these are to improve their outcomes from schooling by choosing wider options for study, they need to do so in a context where they can explore their collective experiences, problems and strengths, in a framework which recognizes the social and political context in which they live. A focus on the shared understandings as well as the variations in knowledge and experience would address the 'gender esteem' of girls and young women in working-class neighbourhoods. In the Melbourne study the school's attempts to encourage a competitive academic style among its students at times led to conflict among students and teachers. Instead of the students being encouraged, failure to meet the academic standards required may have contributed to a lowering of individual self-esteem among the students.

Although school holds the potential to broaden the possibilities for these young women, it frequently serves to undermine them instead. If raising 'self-esteem' is seen as a means of advancing individual girls to develop their particular talents, and to encourage competition, then this strategy is in direct conflict with the priority these young women themselves place on friendship and solidarity.

A persistent theme in the discussions of these young women about school was its negative aspects. Apart from their friends, much of school was seen as boring, irrelevant and at times a source of conflict and negative relationships with teachers. Faced with these problems, the relationships that these young women develop with each other, and with male friends and boyfriends, provide a strategy for coping on their own terms. Their emphasis on solidarity provides a basis for maintaining a sense of dignity and some power over their circumstances. The strategies that they develop are based on a positive evaluation of themselves and of each other. Frequently, the strategy was to 'muck up' in class like Kirsty who said: 'I don't like sitting in classes 24 hours a bloody day, keep writing and all this and all the comprehension, and that crap, you know. But I like sitting in class and mucking about with me friends. They should have a smoking room for us, 'cos you know we always get into trouble, sprung over something.' At other times the strategy was to 'skip' classes, seeking refuge in the girls' toilets, or leaving the school entirely for most of the day.

The circumstances in which young women in working-class neighbourhoods live involve many complexities. In another study of working-class girls in a Sydney secondary school Carrington (1986) has illustrated some strategies and devices used by young women to respond to their circumstances. She argues that the girls' use of space in toilets as a 'graffiti room' reflected their experience that they were not free to use public space as boys were, and that through the graffiti they attempted to negotiate the implications of the sexual double standard in their relationships with males and with each other. Moran (1983) also notes the difficulties posed for girls by the sexual double standard. Even despite these difficulties, the evidence in these studies suggests that the young women approach their futures positively and hopefully as they face the difficult task of balancing the demands of school and home in anticipation of the conflicting demands of private and public life in their futures.

These young women are not compliant, or victims, making 'wrong' choices. The choices they do make are based on their knowledge and experience of life around them, in a context in which class and gender politics are experienced daily. Although some exploration of their individual self-esteem may be helpful, it would be far more empowering for them to have brought into focus and scrutinized in the classroom the contradictions, conflicts and struggles that particular groups of young women and girls face. What about the position most women are in, the work most women do, which is valuable and important but not recognized as such? Is the ambivalence that these young women feel about competing at school related to the fact that the workforce is structured in such a way that women have to make a choice between career or children? Questions such as these would be worth exploring with young women at school.

Conclusion

In practice there are barriers to fulfilling the good intentions with which the concept of self-esteem is used. Kenway, Willis and Nevard in this volume (Chapter 2) point out that the concept of self-esteem implies an approach which 'individualizes, pathologizes and depoliticizes' the issues of sexism in education and society, and avoids the issues of class, ethnic and racial educational politics. They make two criticisms of the way in which self-esteem is used: it makes girls appear to be compliant victims in the process whereby they become disadvantaged, and therefore in need of 'remedial' programs — the problem is seen as belonging to the individual girl; and it does not encourage girls towards a sense of sisterhood or collective action. Rather, it is oriented towards self-interest in the guise of achieving for all. The social benefits of 'collective self-interest' are individual ones, and in the current climate of many schools, imply the success of one person at the expense of her friends. These criticisms of the concept of self-esteem are particularly relevant to strategies for improving the educational experience of girls in working-class neighbourhoods.

The emphasis on the individual implicit in much of the literature on self-esteem ignores the perspectives that these young women bring to their schooling. Combined with particular schooling practices, the emphasis on the individual, and on competition, systematically undermines rather than enhances the attempts by young women to maintain a positive view of themselves. A more appropriate application of the sentiments behind self-esteem strategies would be to develop 'gender esteem', as Gilbert suggests (see Chapter 9). This approach would emphasize the collective experiences and circumstances of groups of girls and women.

The representation of girls in post-school course and training options and in employment is significantly different from that of boys. Overcoming these patterns is not just a matter of educational reform; it requires a challenge to the nature of social division which affects the society as a whole. Specifically, it requires challenging those processes which marginalize the experience and perspectives of girls and women, leaving some vulnerable, both materially and culturally. One means for doing this is to focus on the outcomes from schooling. However, the strategies associated with self-esteem are especially limited with regard to outcomes. The concept of 'gender esteem' moves the focus onto a collective level, but the attention is still on young women, leaving untouched the political issue of how their outcomes from schooling are to be assessed.

Currently, there exists much confusion about outcomes. 'Educational and social outcomes' has had a variety of meanings in Australian educational literature, especially in the documents produced by the Schools Commission (see Wilson and Wyn, 1987, p. 51). The Schools Commission employed the idea of 'equality of outcomes' as an approach which emphasized the valuing of all students and their backgrounds and encouraged learning strategies in which all students could participate equally and from which the outcomes would be equally worthwhile (1987, p. 30). The Commission tackled the criticisms that this approach implied a 'leveling down' and that individual differences were being ignored. It argued that all students were capable of excellent performance in their own terms, should be encouraged to have a vision of what is potentially achievable and to recognize that excellence can be displayed in many domains of life, not only through academic work.

As long as the curriculum implies a valuing of the concerns of men at the expense of women, and of particular cultural and class experiences over others, 'self-esteem' will be a problem. In practice, common outcomes that might be expected for all students should be developed to encompass the priorities not only of girls, but also of other groups whose social and educational accomplishments are marginalized at present.

References

CARRINGTON, K. (1986) 'Girls' toilet graffiti', Paper presented at the 1986 SAANZ Conference, University of New England.

CONNELL, R., ASHENDEN, D., KESSLER, S. and DOWSETT, G. (1982) *Making the Difference: Schools, Families and Social Division*, Sydney, Allen and Unwin.

DEEM, R. (Ed.) (1980) *Schooling for Women's Work*, London, Routledge and Kegan Paul.

GAMARNIKOW, E., MORGAN, D., PURVIS, J. and TAYLORSON, D. (Eds) (1983) *Gender, Class and Work*, London, Heinemann.

KALANTZIS, M. (1986) *Opening Address: Opening Doors, Educating Women and Girls in a Multicultural Society*, Adelaide, Australian Women and Education Coalition Conference.

Meeting Young Women's Needs (1984) Canberra, Australian Government Publishing Service.

MORAN, P. (1983) 'Female youth culture in an inner city school', *Educational Research and National Development: Policy, Planning and Politics*, Collected Papers of the Australian Association for Research in Education, National Conference, Canberra, pp. 281–90.

O'DONNELL, C. (1984) *The Basis of the Bargain*, Sydney, Allen and Unwin.

SAWER, M. (Ed.) (1985) *Program for Change: Affirmative Action in Australia*, Sydney, Allen and Unwin.

SCHOOLS COMMISSION (1987) *In the National Interest: Secondary Education and Youth Policy in Australia*, Canberra, Australian Government Publishing Service.

WILSON, B. and WYN, J. (1987) *Shaping Futures: Youth Action for Livelihood*, Sydney, Allen and Unwin.

WYN, J. (1987) *Schooling, Work and Social Division: A Study of Working Class Youth*, Unpublished PhD Thesis, Monash University, Melbourne.

YATES, L. (1987) 'Does "all students" include girls? Some reflections on recent educational policy, practice and theory', Paper given to Melbourne College of Advanced Education Centre for Urban Studies and Programs seminar.

Chapter 7

Privileged Girls, Private Schools and the Culture of 'Success'

Jane Kenway

The self-esteem and education literature tends to be dominated by these premises: that low self-esteem is a problem, that it is a problem for and of certain individuals, and that it prevents them making the best of their schooling and their lives. Further, the literature attributes low self-esteem to individuals who belong to those social groups which are least valued by and powerful in society. Hence a lack of self-esteem is often associated with groups other than the socially dominant. To overcome their lack is to overcome their problem and thus to open to them a pathway to success and happiness.

In my view the lack is in the self-esteem literature itself and the problem is the way the problem is conceived. The literature is far more concerned to define 'self-esteem' and to explain why it is a problem than to explore how it became a problem. Writers in the field seldom stop to reassess whose problem it really is, or whether high self-esteem may always be regarded as unproblematic. In this chapter I will do precisely what the literature does not and look at some of the processes through which individuals and social groups build a positive identity, suggesting that high self- and social esteem is not necessarily an unquestionable good.

My focus is upon privileged girls in one of Western Australia's most esteemed private schools for girls: the Ladies School of Perth (LSP).* As high social esteem is a deeply sedimented part of the history of expensive private schools in Australia, high self-esteem is deemed a natural consequence of a prestigious private school education. In the literature on girls' education such schools are not regarded as a problem; after all they have a reputation for producing confident, 'successful' young women (see Kenway and Willis, 1986). To raise self-esteem issues in connection with their girls is thus seen as akin to 'taking coal to Newcastle'. Given

* This chapter is drawn from a wider study of private schooling; see Kenway (1987a).

the connections between private schools, social power and dominant educational ideologies, it is hardly surprising that their success is deemed inevitable. However, I wish to argue that to the extent that LSP, as one such school, may be defined as successful, its 'success' is the product of hard ideological labour and is achieved through the intensive use of dominant educational and social categories of value. Second, I will demonstrate that this 'success' is built upon a number of premises and contrasts which have some very unfortunate consequences for some of the girls themselves, their state school counterparts, for feminism and society. One way of exposing these is to make audible the voice of the girls themselves.

Through what the girls say it is possible to identity some of the mechanisms by which a school seeks to construct a positive identity for itself and its students. By this means one learns how these girls read and use such mechanisms in constructing their own identities. Their narratives show the extent to which the culture of 'success' and the social esteem which are associated with such private schools are produced, in part, through a set of severe attitudinal restrictions and a series of damning comparisons with the values and practices of other institutions and social groups. It also shows how the logic of consumption is central to the school's and the girls' processes of social and self-definition.

It is useful to consider such processes under two broad headings drawn from Therborn (1980): the ego and the alter ideology. The ego ideology refers to the means by which social groups define themselves and 'the other' and in so doing develop a consciousness of themselves as a unified group whose interests differ from, are superior and in opposition to 'the other'. The purpose of the ego ideology is social bonding, positive mutual regard and defining insiders and outsiders. Outsiders are the negative referent upon whom a positive self-image is built: the negative other. The alter ideology is concerned more with the relationships between groups than with group formation as such; less with a sense of power than power *over*, and its purpose is ideological co-option or hegemony. It seeks to persuade 'the other' of the justice of a system of social relationships in which one's own group holds ascendency. Elsewhere (Kenway, 1987b) I have discussed the manner in which private schools have developed an alter ideology of great force; here I refer to it only in passing, concentrating, instead, on the ego ideology of the LSP.

The Self

How do the girls read their school's endeavours? What sorts of people do they believe that it asks them to be?

G: They expect us to be proper people in my view. They expect us to be upper-class people.

J: What does that mean?

G: Education and manners.

'Proper', 'right', 'perfect', 'correct', 'adult', 'successful': these adjectives dominate the girls' discussions of the school's messages about who to be and what to value. 'Education and manners' indicate the two primary categories running through their discussions. 'Manners' may be applied to the promotion of a certain style of girl-womanhood and 'education' to the academic curriculum, its associated values and career futures. Let us consider these two main message systems through the eyes of the girls. What does it mean to be 'proper people', to be 'upper-class people'?

Achievement and Success

High academic achievement, preparation for prestigious tertiary study and a meritorious career combine as one of the main messages from the school which the girls are conscious of receiving. Choice, meritocracy and investment, financial debt and waste are the central motifs in this discourse, which is diligently articulated by the school and the parents and absorbed and replayed, little altered, by the girls. Becoming its willing subjects secures for most girls not only a future as 'independent women' but also ensures that they achieve membership of an esteemed social class, in their own right rather than via their men. Further, the meritocratic logic which is at its core provides these girls with a rationale by which their membership of this class and others' exclusions from it may be justified. Hardly worried about getting a job, most are concerned about making the right career choice. The school and the parents are vigilant in directing this process of 'choice' and ensuring its appropriate resolution.

The fact of attendance at a private school is central to discussions of achievement and opportunity. It suggests that certain expectations are held, that particular efforts must be made and that some ambitions are more appropriate than others. Apparently 'being part of a wealthy school and wealthy families' *naturally* means that you will 'aim high' and 'do well'. Yet there is very little that is natural about the cultivation of academic confidence and career aspirations at the LSP. The girls are systematically taught that 'what you gain' through a private school education is 'a high standard of education'. They also constantly acknowledge that what they gain is an obligation to make good their parents' investment in their future, through hard work, 'high ambitions' and a meritocratic career. The greater the debt, the greater the dues.

G: If you come to private schools, you are not just going to leave and, and get married.

G: I feel I've got a duty to do something, like being a doctor or something because my parents have sent me to a private school all my life.

G: At *private* schools we sort of have it put upon us that maybe we shouldn't take jobs like — um —

G: A garage mechanic or something unskilled or just receptionist or secretary. They expect more of you. [Year 10]

Half-hearted application and an inappropriate future are to 'reneg on' the debt, a waste.

The term 'waste' is a popular one, applied to almost any future which does not involve tertiary study. To make alternative low status choices in the labour market or to opt for the domestic sphere is largely, although not entirely, regarded as 'waste of education', a 'waste of ability', and a failure 'to get my money's worth'. It is 'throwing education down the drain'. 'A friend of ours, when she leaves the LSP, she'll just go home to the farm, and we think "Oh god, what a waste of five years at a private school. She could have gone to a state school for that!"' [Year 10]. It is clear from what the girls say that this investment logic is constantly deployed by parents and the school as a means of committing them to the tertiary-bound path. With fees at its centre, a circuit of obligations and expectations is produced. Through the students' eyes one can see the school fulfilling its end of the bargain with great diligence, for obviously its interests as an educational institution in a competitive market are also involved.

Students are encouraged to and have a vested interest in 'getting the LSP's name up more and the name and grades and everything. You have to get the LSP a good name.' Making a 'wrong' career choice is one way of exhibiting a lack of concern for the school's good name and the great majority of girls 'automatically' expect to take up paid work in the form of a career, for 'that's the way it is'. The mechanisms for producing such 'natural' commitment, such docile beneficiaries, include the use of successful ex-scholars as models.

G: They always bring them back. They'll say, 'Oh there was a girl at the LSP and she became a such and such.'

G: She became something different. She did industrial design or

became a doctor or whatever — she was such a good student.

G: They try to show off our background to make other people
think, 'Oh that's a great school. My kids go there.'

G: It means we've got to keep up the image of the LSP.

Another mechanism is the use of guest speakers from the 'respected'
professions. However, the two main methods, according to the girls, are
the careers course in Year 10 and advice from the school's guidance
officer. The forms their efforts take are implicit in the following discussions.

The girls strongly emphasize that the school helps them to choose
what they 'want', what they will be 'happy in', 'what is best for me', and
yet they also make it quite clear that it limits their choice, that the 'aim of
the school is to turn out successful independent women', that they must
be 'ambitious' and set their sights on university. In effect they are told
what they want, and learn what will make them happy. They assert their
free will, while simultaneously pointing to the force of the constraints
upon them. Apparently many parents offer similar freedoms within constraint. One Year 10 wryly observed, 'Although I have previously said I
do not think they would mind what I did, I think there are quite a few
exceptions.'

Through what the girls say one sees a school intent on defining what
a valued future is, both in career and personal terms. Ambition and independence have very restricted connotations.

G: Do you remember careers at the start of the year, there were
all these lists on the wall?

G: Unskilled jobs and semi-skilled jobs and she said, 'Well you
don't need to look at the first list 'cos you won't be doing that
sort of job.' [Year 10]

Gender boundaries within the professions are less significant than the
very rigid distinction between careers and jobs, skilled and unskilled
work and mental and manual labour.

G: They don't say girls want to be teachers, nurses, secretaries,
they say look at another field — doctors.

G: And if you want to do something that women aren't usually
in, they encourage you to try hard to get into it.

G: It's very feminist. [Year 11]

University and the professions are the destinations, and considerable effort is spent 'pushing' girls in those direction and discouraging other possibilities. To leave 'early', to be a 'Year 10 leaver', carries considerable stigma. It signifies not only a lack of drive and ambition but, more devastatingly, a lack of ability.

The school promotes a belief that most of its girls have higher than average ability. Given that most have 'successful' parents and given that it is expected that they will be tertiary-bound, there is an accompanying assumption that, as a group, they will be skewed to the top of the ability range. Such assumptions are often 'confirmed' by batteries of tests conducted by the guidance officer. The girls learn very early what the school regards as their ability level, whom to 'push' and where. The concepts of ability, intelligence, capacity, achievement level and potential are central to the girls' definitions of themselves and their futures. Many make apparently unselfconscious reference to their own high capabilities.

Those who have learned that they have ability have also learned that it must not be wasted. Indeed, some girls imply that a 'challenging', 'exciting', 'stimulating' career is their due because of their proclaimed high levels of ability. They want and expect work which is 'satisfying and fulfilling' (a common expression) and 'worthwhile' (not quite as common). For them, work should offer 'prospects for advancement and responsibility', and should allow them to 'use' their 'ability to its fullest capacity'. Most work not associated with some tertiary study is regarded as 'dull' and 'dead end'. Yet there are some non-tertiary careers considered acceptable. These preferably have 'ties with the good life', allow the opportunity for glamour and excitement, demonstrate a particular flair or talent and reveal great 'individuality' or 'originality'. Acting, modelling or work in the media or the arts will thus be approved by peers, if not so much by parents. Most other work is deemed far beneath the girls' capacities and rightful expectations.

The concept of ability is also deployed as a means of justifying class differences. As one Year 10 girl pointed out, 'Our particular class are all intelligent. The large majority of intelligent people will take on a *career*, professional or otherwise.' So, too, is the mental-manual distinction. Commenting on the possibility of an apprenticeship, a girl in Year 10 made the following remark: 'The school would demand to know what has possessed me to become involved in a manual trade. This is because they push you to choose the highest that YOU can achieve. I would be asked many times to reconsider my choice.' Interestingly, such responses are not without exception. Some girls find the prospect of manual work attractive. However, the school is neither prepared to cater for nor to promote such interests. As another Year 10 girl observed: 'Our school teaches you practically nothing in trades like other schools do. Our education is focused on the mental part of labour and not the physical side of it' [Year 10]. The vast majority of girls believe that, were they to choose a job outside the school norm, their peers and parents would be variously 'shocked', 'scathing', 'embarrassed', 'resentful' and 'a little disappointed'.

Vocation must give way before the forces of 'ability' and prospects.

> If I chose to be a phys. ed. teacher, the school, my friends and my parents would all feel that it is a bit of a waste. I have the intelligence to become something more and I would receive pressure about doing something more fulfilling. They would say, 'it's such a waste; it's a dead-end job, etc.' I would know, however that they would only be doing this for my benefit. If that was what I really wanted they would respect my choice. My own feelings about this future are extremely mixed. I would really enjoy being a phys. ed. teacher but do feel that it is a dead-end job. I want to aim for a greater degree of success.

After this little autobiography the following remark from another Year 10 rings rather poignantly true: 'They don't really push you to be something high, but if you can just sort of make it to be a doctor they'll try and get you into that kind of thing — and it doesn't really matter a lot whether you want to do it, or not.'

The school contains a wider range of abilities and prospects than the image so far enunciated suggests. Those who have learned that they don't have 'ability' either leave to go to a despised state or technical school, or stay on and reap the other benefits of the school, while enjoying what the principal calls 'the right to fail'. The school's narrow definitions of ability and success and its accompanying hot-house academic atmosphere contain considerable hurt for some.

> G: It makes you feel dumb. You are not good if you don't get good marks.
> G: I'm not brainy, I'm nobody.
> G: My mum and dad used to say to me, 'Nothing matters if you've done your best', but even your best isn't always good enough here.
> G: 'You're capable of better than that you know' [teacherly tones].
> G: There's too much stress on brains and not education and that's everywhere it's not just here.
> G: You have to be brainy or you don't count. [Year 10]

These girls are the school's sacrifices to the interests and values of the educational marketplace.

So far, through the eyes of the students we see a school intent on reproducing its class but also engaged in some intra-class restructuring along gender lines. We observe also some of the mechanisms at work in producing class distinctions and some of the means by which a school, and by extension its students, generate a positive self-image. In summary, these produce such a totalitarian taxonomy of values that choice, as a process, loses its meaning. In the 'push society' of this private school whole social horizons are not just cut off, but derided. Only through certain choices can the school's and a person's esteem be gained. This can barely be seen as feminist. The girls may make inroads upon the prestigious professions, but notions of 'independent womanhood' cannot encompass low status jobs or any 'manual labour', nor do they encompass in any adequate way the domestic sphere.

The school's discourses on the domestic sphere are the least privileged, their consumers considered 'the least able', this no doubt contributing to many girls' derogatory and sexist perception of women's domestic labour. Rather than taking a productively critical view of the family and at least recognizing the worth of its associated nurturing values, the girls have in effect rejected them, associating 'relationships' with romantic ideology and domestic labour with drudgery. Given that most plan for themselves dual career families and children, one wonders about the consequences of their adoption of the individualistic, competitive value system of the world of careers. It is a very conservative feminism which suggests that simply putting women in the professions and rearranging domestic responsibilities is a big step forward for women, let alone humanity.

Ladies

The second primary discourse which the girls identify is concerned with style, manners and morals. In constructing subjectivities it is markedly less successful than that on careers and, as I will show later, is translated to have its most significant effects within the terms of the school-girl culture.

'Ladies' is the girls' chorused response when asked what the school wants them to be. Being a lady is very much tied up with appearances. 'We have been taught that what we appear to be, is what people think we are.' The appropriate appearance is:

Feminine....
Genteel....
Pretty....
Nothing like short hair and....
Nice looking — all pretty and jossed up.
Yeah, ribbons, hair tied away, some of it up.
This is a *ladies* school, it's not a mixed school, so there's nothing rough about it, it's really feminine.

This message is transmitted at its most intense through meticulous requirements concerning the school uniform. These include an exact change-over day from the winter to the summer uniform, an insistence that hair must be up, that only ribbons of certain colours may be worn, only one ear-ring in each ear, no other jewellery, no make-up, blazers worn to and from school, the top button on the shirt always done up.... The LSP girl has to look 'perfect', and here is how some Year 10 girls responded to such calls for perfection.

> G: It's posh wealth — it's all the hair cut, the clothes. I mean at another school you don't get blazers and ties and *school* shoes and polish them every day.
> G: So you look expensive, like a piece of material.

Pride in the uniform, worn correctly, is supposed to be associated with 'pride in ourselves and in the school'. To breach the uniform code in public is 'a let-down for your school' and causes severe pangs of conscience.

> This morning on the way to school I had my hair down and I thought if someone sees me what are they going to think. I'll have to put it up as soon as I get to school. Also, wearing your jumper to and from school. I do that but I really shouldn't and when I actually do it I know I'm doing it and I think I shouldn't be. You feel guilty about it.

Notions of being a lady, of wrong and right, reason and maturity, loyalty and pride have become symbolized in the uniform.
Being a lady also involves certain prohibitions.

> G: Not eating in the street.
> G: Not writing on walls and things the public wouldn't appreciate.

G: Not picking up male — um — male — um [laughter] no — not picking up male characters.

G: Not being very boisterous.

G: Learning how to conduct a conversation without swearing.

G: No running in the corridors and no holes in your stockings and dress neatly with your....

G: Your top button done up. [Year 10]

For some, it is associated with being well-mannered, and the boarding school offers particular assistance with manners. 'We were given a couple of years ago a little pink pamphlet on manners, what you can and can't do and you had to know it — we were supposed to go home and learn it by heart.' The possibility that there may be some ethnocentricity about manners seems unconsidered, as a Chinese-Malay boarder's comment indicates: 'When I came here in first term I was told off by a senior because I didn't have any table manners. In my country we don't really care about table manners. I was told by a senior girl not to put the elbows on the table. I didn't know that was bad manners.'

To be a proper person — a lady — also demands the 'right attitudes, socially and morally': 'They want us to *do* the right thing but if we're not doing it they like to think that we *know* the right thing ... act the right way in front of people, fit the rules for the set even if we don't agree to them' [Year 12]. There is some uncertainty among the girls about whether the LSP's concept of a lady is old-fashioned, stereotyped, realistic or, indeed, feminist. Some feel it arises from the history of the LSP as a finishing school for richer girls. A Year 12 said: 'You get the feeling that it's all been happening for hundreds of years. It sort of registers in cycles, sort of churning out young ladies.' Others implied that the school was pushing them towards a new notion of female adulthood. Only some saw the contradictions: 'They want us to be really feminine but I still think they want us to be really liberated at the same time — they want us to be really clean cut, well groomed, frilly and beautiful, but at the same time they want us to go out and get what we want' [Year 10].

The other-worldly quality of the look-alike ladies the girls are expected to be is often mentally rejected. The school claims to value individuality but 'the principal just thinks we're a whole lot of sheep underneath her.' Ladies must conform but girls becoming 'independent' women need not. The girls also learn about the importance of appearances. Appearing to conform, while believing that they do not, allows them to continue to believe in their free will and independence. This disjunction between appearing and thinking is very much what the school

140

is about. Contradiction is at its centre. In one discourse it wants the students to be 'independent', yet in that on ladies and style it treats them like children, taking from them even the choice of colour for their hair ribbons. Behaving responsibly means doing what one knows the school wants. Like choice, even though the rhetoric remains, it is only meaning-ful for the students as a delusion, offering a sense of responsibility where little exists. Again, a very restricted notion of womanhood is offered, one which sets itself up as superior, refusing other versions as worthy of merit.

Internal Differences and the School-girl Culture

The girls recognize that the school's social catchment is restricted, but that within the restrictions there is a range of levels of wealth and occupation. In public discussion they claim that these internal differences have little social impact, yet in their *private* writing a number of girls wish to add certain riders. These point to differences which are experienced by the students, suggest the lines along which social distinctions are made at the level of the school-girl culture and show another basis upon which self-esteem is constructed. This translates the school's discourse on appearances and uses it within the logic of consumption which dominates the suburbs which the school serves and the youth markets which, alongside schooling, provide the girls with mechanisms of self-definition and social closure. What divides the girls among themselves and what divides them from outsiders are fashion and leisure consumption patterns and social life.

To talk of friendships among the LSP girls is to identify divisions and tensions among a supposedly cohesive population, to pick up the effects of the school's structuring mechanisms and the effects of those from outside and to identify differing value systems in operation. Very quickly, apparently, the girls who live in the boarding house take on and are given an identity. Being a boarder does not simply signify where one lives, it marks out a set of social relationships and is accompanied by a social definition. The boarding house consists mainly of girls from the establishment class of rural districts, but includes a small minority from South-East Asia. Boarders see themselves and know that they are seen as different. In the pecking order of the school-girl culture they feel looked down upon socially, culturally and educationally by girls who 'don't have a very good idea' about them. From the day-girls' point of view, 'boarders are set apart from the other pupils, simply because they are not familiar with city life and perhaps their speech and manners are a little different.' Certainly grammar and accent are distinguishing features. Further, as a group of boarders pointed out:

> B: They think we are abnormal. [laughter]
> B: Country people live in these old sheds out the back and have different ideas.
> B: I think the day girls view us as being a bit dumb.
> B: We are sort of from outbush and we are locked up here and we don't know anything. [Year 11]

The boarders proudly assert their country values in discussion and present themselves as less class conscious than the day-girls and less concerned with appearances.

> B: On the camp it was really noticeable — all the trendies brought these brand new jodhpurs for the rides. There's nothing against that but ... half hour rides?
> B: New jodhpurs just for a camp — new Wellington boots and everything and they'd never use them in the city.
> B: ... and there's all the Boarders in the oldest clothes out. [shared laughter]
> B: They even went out and got *new-old* clothes so they'd look used. [Year 11]

Low on the pecking order in the school and claiming to resent snobbery, the boarders feel rather aggrieved that back in their country home towns it is they who are perceived as snobs. Self-protective segregation and insularity in the city are transposed to the country where feelings of inferiority are replaced by feelings of superiority or at least difference.

> B: It's a horrible thing to say but people who live in small country towns all their life do tend to be a bit narrow minded. They don't like the idea of changing. I mean I've changed a lot since I've been here and when I go back I think — 'Oh, was I like that?'
> B: If a lot have been away, then you all sort of group together but if you are the only one from that place — I came from a place where there is only a very small school and I was the only one who came to a private school and everyone treats me like a snob now.

Where the city clusters can continue, they do, thus reinforcing social division in the country. Where they cannot, it is socially pragmatic to mix.

In addition to the vertical divisions between boarders and day-girls there also exists among the girls what they regard as a hierarchical structure of groups. At the top are the 'trendies' or 'trendites' and at the bottom the 'rejects', 'loners', 'squares' or 'dags'. In between, some say, are groups descending in status, depending upon whether their characteristics are more like the top or the bottom end of the hierarchy. Some girls like to describe those 'in the middle' as 'normals'. A girl new to the school said:

> There's so many groups of day girls it's really amazing. As a new girl at school last year I couldn't believe it that 'Oh, so and so just got kicked out of so and so's group'. Coming from a public school, so and so just had a group and I just got accepted into a group. I really couldn't get used to this new type of 'Oh, there's a dags group' or 'There's a so and so group.' [Year 10]

Let us consider each end of the spectrum of school-girl social esteem. The trendies demonstrate a capacity to excel in school activities, particularly sport and those areas associated with the arts. They also project the highest status image, part of which is associated with good looks and fashionable dress and is often, but not exclusively, associated with their parents' wealth. The trendies are regarded as the 'main dominating clique' in each year level. They are 'full of themselves', 'very confident', 'extrovert', have the most power and status among the girls and are the school's 'snobs'. 'They treat you like you're dirt, they sort of sneer at you, patronise you. They come up and go "Hi!" and you don't know whether or not they are stirring you.' Also associated with being a trendite are family freedom and certain boys.

> What about the girls' dress and the boys' dress? I mean the top boys' group always goes out with the top girls' group. It's natural.

> Out of school they smoke, go out with guys, go to pubs, to shows on Saturday night, and smoke pot, and in school they sit beside the canteen and rub coconut oil on their legs and they talk about boys and clothes and boys and drugs and boys and smoking and boys and....

The 'normal' girls are fascinated by the trendites, attracted, repelled, indignant and envious, their talk is filled with theorizations of the source of the 'top' group's power and prestige. In contrast, they are considerably less interested in and more tactful about the 'reject' group. A reject is defined as follows:

G: Someone nobody really likes, they don't just fit in with anybody or if they fit in with somebody that other person might be a reject. All rejects get shoved together.
G: You can think oh they're really brainy and some people are jealous of them but it's not just one thing it's their whole personality.
G: Or lack of it. [laughter]
G: It's not because they are absolutely ugly or poor.
G: Squares turn up to school wearing this and that and everybody turns around and starts talking about what they're wearing.
G: Squares have no social life — or not much of a social life. [giggles]
G: Really intellectuals....
G: They're not really in a group. They're just loners.
J: What proportion would you say in each year?
G: There's very few, four — three — four. [Year 11]

One group not mentioned within the girls' social taxonomies is that consisting of girls from South-East Asia. They are the only other racial group within the school, and very visibly separate. These girls find the topic of their separateness very embarrassing to discuss, particularly in a 'mixed' group. Here, however, is how one discussion evolved.

SEA: Well [reluctant], I think the girls are keeping away from us and don't want to talk to us. We've got a group of our own — Asians.... On the other hand we found out that the girls think that we don't want to mix with them — so we've got different points of view.
G: Misunderstanding. Vicious circle.
G: But I don't think people can be bothered making the effort. Most of the time it's not as if they don't like each other — it's just that you've got your own set of friends and you just keep going.
G: I think it takes two to tango. I think that both groups would have to try.

> SEA: Like with all the Christmas Islanders, Malaysians and
> things, everyone has got their own little group and they
> don't want to branch out, and you don't.

The cliquishness which is typical of the girls lends itself well to a form of
racial apartheid which is redefined simply as cultural difference between
groups of equal stature, a separation freely chosen or else brought about
by joint apathy and misunderstanding. By such means, and by processes
of individualization, any structural racism is denied.

While there is a good deal of unity about the two ends of the
spectrum, there is little about what constitutes the 60–70 per cent of girls
who constitute the middle ground. Some argue that a hierarchy exists in
which 'subtrendies' may be distinguished from trendies according to
degrees of snobbishness. Others, while recognizing that 'definite sets'
exist, prefer to think of the groups as 'just friendship groups', not
arranged in any sort of hierarchy and generally harmonious, more 'individual' and less cliquish. The more general opinion is that the groups are
slightly fluid, highly competitive and formed according to their members'
social life, style, morality, 'maturity' and relationship to schoolwork.
Each group is seen to have its own distinguishing features and each to
elevate itself and to monitor and criticize the other groups. 'I reckon
every group thinks they've got the right thing, the best thing to wear,
and they have their own sort of morals.'

These divisions most clearly exist in the girls' middle secondary
years. Among the 'seniors' divisions are seen to be 'wearing out', there is
more 'mixing'. The processes of attrition by non-conformers and failures
and bonding practices have been effective. Even so, it takes very little
surface-scratching to identify tensions, and these are based more on
out-of-school activities than those inside. Even though the senior girls
deny vehemently that income differences have any effect upon whom
they mix with, social life's arrangements are circumscribed by 'what you
can afford'. Films, video evenings, group dinners in restaurants, gather-
ing in friends' homes, weekend sport, private parties, going to pubs and
discos are among the activities which most girls value and appear to have
in common.

> G: If you have friends that have got that sort of stuff you just
> expect it [girls protest] — not expect it but you become used
> to it.
> G: I'm average in money's ways — and we've got a wind-surfer
> and a video — and when I worked in my Dad's office a girl
> my age says, 'What did you do on the weekend?' 'Oh, I

went wind-surfing' — 'Oh, how lucky! You've got a wind-surfer.' She didn't have what we have — it was obvious.

G: Often people with the same amount of money have got similar ideas and tastes and interests anyway, so *naturally* they gravitate together.

Consumption patterns are important in structuring hierarchies of esteem and social relations in and out of school, and educational consumption is no less important than other forms. Living in the private school suburban belt, the girls talk of 'growing up mixing with people from private schools', of a social environment where a private education is the norm and insular mixing is natural. Although holding a sense of common identity with other similar, private schools and interacting socially, the rivalry generated by academic, sporting and cultural competition between the schools spills over into the process of definition within youth cultural terms. While recognizing educational, religious and cost (fee) differences between the schools, the girls express most interest in and gain most delight in discussing the schools' 'reputations' which, as one Year 10 writes, 'whether it being one as athletic, scholastic, snobby, bitchy'. Here are some typical comments on the reputations of their 'sister' schools.

G: People at St Jerome's are Micks and thought of as less elite by those at the LSP as not only is it co-ed but the fees aren't as high.

G: Most of the differences are social, St Anne's girls are supposed to be 'snobby', while St Jerome's girls perhaps 'tarty', Mentone girls are what we call 'dogs'. All of these names are obviously RASH generalisations. However, schools, like girls, get reputations.

G: Mentone girls are thought of as 'Bush Pigs' [desperate for boys] and Piedmont are rarely mentioned, so far away.

G: Piedmont are not very nice — you just don't think of it as if you were saying private schools.

These remarks show how clearly the girls' thinking is caught up in matters connecting social status, religion and suburban location to schooling. The lower status private schools are not thought of at all. The other distinctive feature is related to sexuality. In employing such terms as 'tarts' and 'bush pigs' the girls define each other within male categories concerning female sexuality. Co-education is seen to confer a lower status on a school and its students because of this. Ultimately, though, despite these gradations, a sense of commonality with other private schools remains. The girls have similar sets of typologies for the private boys' schools, and matters of esteem and status are very evidently caught up with 'having a boyfriend' from the esteemed boys' schools.

The Negative Other

What I am about to show is another side to the production of a positive image of self and school, the definition of 'the other' designed for insiders. Included in the process of class/gender identity construction and formation is a vision of outsiders, those who are them and not us. The private school/state school division, although blurred along class lines at times, provides a convenient means of making such distinctions. Each of the discourses so far outlined has its negative referent in the state system.

Education and Careers

Essentially, what is seen by most girls to distinguish their type of private school from state schools are the 'strictness about the students' appearance, behaviour and their academic standards'. The value of the private school, in its girls' eyes, is its capacity to produce academic and career successes. The failure of the state school is not simply its perceived incapacity to do so but its lack of interest in such a project. Sadly for its students, the state system is usually seen to have less adequate teachers and, in addition, it fails to 'push' them. 'You are left to do your own thing, and nobody cares.' A failure to push indicates a failure to care and results in a lack of student motivation and ambition.

> G: At a state school, if you don't want to work, you don't and you can get away with it.
> G: You can, it's incredible. If these kids are seeing teachers who are totally disinterested in life and everything, what motivation will they have?

State school students' lack of ability and/or ambition is seen to be reflected in their 'choices' for their futures. As one tactful student, educational observer noted, 'Half the kids in dumber schools leave after Year 10.'

> G: Of the whole class at Nanwarren High last year, only two of them wanted to do something professional, all the rest of

  them wanted to do apprenticeships and work in Nanwarren. Girls in co-ed. get the feeling, 'Oh, I'll get married.'

G: If this was co-ed, you would be wearing make up and shaving your legs everyday and because here, you're free for your studies, you're not sort of impressing boys.

 In contrast with the standards of private schools, those at state schools are usually seen to be much lower — usually, not always.

G: When I came here from a government school at the end of grade six I was really shot ... I found that I was really backward in things like English and just basic things like that.

G: I found that coming to this school I was totally equal, I knew more. We did science last year that you guys haven't done yet, we did our. ... In maths we were equal, in every other subject we were equal.

G: I was talking to a girl yesterday and she was, in every way one of the top classes at Seacomb High and she came to the LSP and she was dumb. [Year 11]

Like parents and some private school teachers, most students have a hair-raising story to tell about state schools. Stories revolve around such matters as the low standards, the uncaring teachers, the types of students and particularly the lack of discipline.

 I used to go to Cherwell Primary and we used to walk in school and turn on the television and the teacher would come in and say, 'O.K. we've got maths', and we would all boo and boo, so he'd say, 'Well come out and play cricket', and so we used to go and not do maths at all. We'd do maths about once a week. But it's not good enough. [Year 10]

 Although rather vague concerning the details, there is a belief that because 'we have more money behind us' the school has better facilities, more options and 'extra subjects like careers'. When, in discussion, there is a suggestion that state schools may actually offer more choice, the choice itself is derided.

G: Kids in state schools just get tech drawing, but we get stuff like computer and cooking.

G: They get computer now, they do.

G: We get computer, we get cooking, we get um, sewing, we get media. . . .

G: Manual arts?

G: . . . what happens if you come into a private school and you want to do manual arts, you want to do metal work or tech drawing?

G: You don't have a chance.

G: . . . that's one thing that really got me when I came here was I couldn't do my tech drawing anymore, and I loved it.

G: You don't love tech drawing! [scorn] [Year 10]

While some girls disagree, most others point to the 'better choice', 'better chance' of private school girls. 'Otherwise why would our parents put us here?' asks a Year 10 girl, employing impeccable logic. In the job market private schooling is, by and large, seen to give girls the edge. Private schools are seen to equip their students with the right style, manners, dress and accent. 'People who go to private schools they have more manners and they know how to act and everything. You see people from Seaholm High [laughter] and they'll go to a job, you know, they won't know how to . . . you know, they'll dress really revolting and everything.'

Classed Youth Cultures

'It's just two completely separate groups, private school kids and state school kids', says a Year 11, capturing the strong sense among the girls of the difference between state and private school students.

G: Different values. . . .

G: They are different people, the state school community.

G: It also depends on the school.

G: Their values may not be alright for us but alright for them. And the values that we're taught, they're alright for us. So there's basically different kinds of people go to private schools. [Year 10]

While the matters already mentioned concerning formal schooling are important in the process of employing the mode of educational use as a means of social differentiation and distinction, again the greatest distinctions in the students' minds occur as a consequence of values, style, modes of consumption and sexuality. The girls associate all sorts of unsavoury behaviour with state schools, particularly with city schools.

G: Country high schools, oh from what I know are fun. But the image of city high schools it's more tough, bogan.

G: I think of kids going to school, make-up all over their faces and smoking.

G: You get more radical groups in government schools — you know you'll get groups of punks and you'll get groups of skinheads, and you'll get groups of hippies and....

G: You can't be that radical in a school like this or you get expelled.

G: A lot of them are on drugs and everything.

J: Aren't there any girls at the LSP on drugs?

G: Yes.

G: It's just that you don't hear about it.

G: They just do it nicely.

G: They wouldn't do things like breaking in and vandalizing houses while they're wagging school and things like that. [Year 11]

Some girls do seek to inject a more democratic spirit into such discussions, often noting that there are some nice people in state schools, but the general mood is not changed by such arguments. 'Bogans' is the usual term for classifying state school students, but state school girls are also suspected of being 'tarts', their freedom from discipline and the presence of boys in co-education apparently being too much of a heady mix for them. In Western Australia prestigious private schooling has historically been single sex, all state schools are co-educational.

G: There's a lot of girls who go to the public schools who — are probably tarts because — um — I think because the boys are around....

G: and they have the opportunity....

G: Yeah and their freedom is completely different to what ours is. Going out after school and at public schools you can get away with a lot more, so —

J: Like what?

G: Like wagging school, oh — just general behaviour in the classrooms.

G: I went to a state high school to Year 10. I don't feel like a tart or a bogan [laughter]. I don't think my friends are tarts or boguns either. It's —

J: Do you think there might be a few tarts, as you say, in this school?

G: But it's hidden.

J: How?

G: It's hidden because private schools have got to look — I mean people look at private schools as being snobbish schools — and — people just overlook those types of things — but there really are girls. . . .

G: They think it wouldn't happen here.

G: No [giggles].

G: I think it's hidden in the school because, for a start, there's no boys around — so that sort of behaviour can't be seen at school, and at school they're kept quite on a low level. You know, the teachers make sure they act right in class. But outside school, gosh, sure. [Year 11]

In one sense state school girls are seen to be at a social advantage.

G: They do get to do a lot more intermixing with boys.

G: I know there's a lot of girls at the LSP who don't have boyfriends now and I mean they worry about it, they shouldn't.

G: Lots of girls that have been at private schools all their lives just don't know how to mix with boys.

G: They only know — the only way they associate with them is in a party — and they can't actually talk to them in a — normal, natural way — a normal life. [Year 10]

Many girls find it difficult to imagine how girls might interact comfortably with boys and envy state school girls' opportunities in this regard. For them, boys are an absent presence, romanticized and glamorized, and they seem to project their own sexual preoccupations onto girls in co-educational schools. Owing to their single sex schooling they have not learned to interact with boys in a relaxed unaffected manner. From a number of their earlier comments it is clear how conscious they are of the male gaze and many have devised a restricted code of behaviour to be brought forward in the presence of the opposite sex. Yet given their own limitations in this regard, they can still define their single sex schooling as an advantage. As the following exchange indicates, while some girls believe that they win out in the end, others are not so certain.

G: People who've been to an all girls school all their life and they leave school and go to university and all of a sudden it's boys all the time and they sort of like. . . .

G: But what happens here is you get the chance to create your own personality and you don't have to worry about boys watching you and all that....

G: When you're with a boy you're always aware that they are watching you and you're always inside yourself and you don't sort of speak, clam up.

There is a mixture of envy and resentment in the girls' discussions of the freedom with which state school girls mix with boys. They feel that their school is failing them in this regard, that they are not learning the necessary social skills and are too confined. From what the girls say, mixing would appear not to be their forte. Many find it particularly difficult to mix with public school students, those who are 'not on the same sort of social level', although 'it depends how much lower they are.' There are certain high schools which do receive approval, which 'could almost be a private school' on the basis of their catchment suburbs, their academic results and their students' styles of consumption.

G: But Hall is a better high school.

G: It's in a better area.

G: Most of them dress the way we do, speak the way we do ... like Hall is a really good school even though it's a state school.

G: Like if you get kicked out of the LSP, I mean you could go to Hall.

G: It's where all the kids who've been expelled go.

G: Lots of state school girls have bogun images but you look at the state schools and you look at places like Chatfield, Seatown and they're just average schools and they've got just as many trendies as we have. [Year 10]

Predictably, when it comes to mixing with the opposite sex, the girls show a strong preference for private school 'guys'. In any comparisons between boys from the two sectors, state school boys inevitably fare badly.

G: Seaholm boys treat you like shit.

G: There are a few nice ones, but PBG boys are so much more refined.

G: They treat you like a lady.

G: They talk to you and your parents nicely.

G: They are the kind of guys that you're brought up to expect to love.

G: They respect girls. They seem more mature and their family. . . .

G: It's partly their background, but a lot of it's school 'cos like, I know guys from my primary school and some went to Hall and some went to St Steven's and PBG and the ones from St Steven's and PBG most of them are real gentlemen but I don't know any of the ones from Hall that are gentlemen, they are just a load of bogans. [Year 10]

The image of state school boys is:

G: Really crude and tough sort of bogun.

G: They are more tough, they are crude, they are disgusting and they are older than their age.

G: Yeh, and smoking and stuff like that, drugs.

G: In private schools there are more individuals. In government schools, high schools, they are more like little sheep.

G: When we went to that sports thing and we were sitting next to those kids and they all had their Joseph Banks High bags and everyone immediately thought, 'Oh, yuk'. We knew what they were like.

G: They don't shop around, they like to shop somewhere like Target.

G: They don't all come up here and get the real expensive boutique clothes. [Year 10]

To prefer private school boys is 'natural', often because similarities of wealth are seen to produce similar patterns of leisure consumption.

G: We do all the same things as private school boys do. We go wind-surfing, we've got the money to do it.

G: That's it money, money. If I went out with someone from Glengala, or Yutha, I probably get as much pocket money in one week as he got in a year, I'd probably sort of be paying for him. I've been brought up to expect things like — you know — he can pay for the movies, he can pay for the. . . .

G: You think about the things that you do with them like on

the weekend, 'Oh yeh, oh yeh, I got my licence too, I've got a car' or 'Come wind-surfing, I've got a surf-cat, come out with me.'

Gs: [everyone talking at once] Exactly.

G: Video, they've all got videos. Instead of skateboarding and riding bikes they do other things. Spas, saunas and other things.

G: For Rowallen guys [interjections : 'Boguns'] an ideal Friday night is to go to the bowling alley — don't bowl — sit there and watch everyone — pick up a few chicks — you know — go over to the oval and get drunk or stoned, then go over to Cape Arthur in the car and have a big drink-up.

J: What's an ideal night to the boys you mix with? [screams of laughter]

G: That's got more a trendy — an ultra-trendy party or show — great big mansion, pool and everything [more screams], and the parents might be there but they're out of the way — and everything's just happy.

Boarders feel equally remote from country boys, and again it is a matter of style. The selection of appropriate male company also falls along manual/mental labour lines and only the latter are acceptable. 'Maree said that Joc was an apprentice fitter and turner. Everyone went "Oohh!" . . . if she had gone out with some smart boy in his second year at university it would be different' [Year 10]. To go out with a boy from a state school is almost to invite the raised eyebrow, the condescending 'Oohh!', the sarcastic 'that's nice!' Yet not all high school boys are dismissed out of hand. They may redeem themselves by being 'cute' or 'gorgeous' looking or by 'dressing trendy and wearing whatever the rest of us do'. The following comment is a rarity: 'No, I said I like boys from public schools better than I like ones from private schools. More natural and not snobby.' And some girls feel this way:

G: I like, I like. . . .

G: All boys? Yeah!

G: Older boys.

G: Any boys [laughter]. [Year 10]

Implications for the Self-esteem Discourse

What are the mechanisms by which the school keeps up its reputation for superiority, one which its girls sustain and are sustained by, from which they gain their sense of being different and superior? Those strong components of the LSP's alter ideology which have been alluded to here include such matters as obsessive public impression management, constructing a hierarchy of concern in which appearances and the private school market have top priority and in which individual preferences and feelings must be reconstructed in the interests of 'the image'. The girls must live their education always with an eye to the gaze of the outsider, who must be taught the superiority of the LSP and that LSP girls have a right to claim educational success, social honour *and* high self-esteem.

The ego ideology involves a severe set of circumscriptions through which the girls learn the codes of the social class, its canons of acceptable choice and taste and *only* within these can social and thus self-esteem be gained. None can be gained outside the boundaries, and within them desires are produced through the glorification and emulation of the most prestigious. While a failure to reach the heights may have poor self-esteem consequences, these are offset by an insular narcissistic ethic which asserts that it is better to fail in a culture of conspicuous success than to succeed in matters despised. Further, such insularity permits the private school system's circuit of positive self-regard to remain largely unbroken. Most difference is defined as deviant. The codes of the class include its negative referents, people whose disreputable identity and baser instincts are exhibited in their 'choice' of school, labour and leisure and in their use of ignoble consumer goods.

There is a tendency to equate high self-esteem with the confidence which many private school girls exude, but such confidence may be illusory, as the girls have learned that 'what we appear to be is what people think we are.' What matters is appearing confident, just as what matters is appearing in the right clothing. Self-esteem may be bought via the right 'casual-chic' designer label. In the culture of consumption within which private schools are immersed, success also can be bought alongside approval, acceptance and social honour. They also learn that it must be displayed. The fact that the process of social definition is so caught up in appearances and in the logic of consumption is a matter warranting concern.

Self-esteem, as it is conceived of by liberal feminists, is not a particular issue for these girls, as their discussion on achievement and success illustrates. However, feminists who are concerned about the intersection of class and gender and about the problems for girls associated with sexuality, romantic ideology and consumption cannot but regard the culture of this expensive private school as in need of feminist intervention seeking to build these girls' self-esteem upon a more personally and socially liberating set of values. What this study suggests further is that feelings of self-worth are not necessarily a universal good. It shows how certain educational orthodoxies may be used not simply to enhance self-esteem but to claim a monopoly on it while defining others as less worthy. The LSP girls' positive identity is clearly linked with the distinction between private and state schooling, and by extension with class distinction. To me, the social and educational costs of these girls' supposedly high self-esteem are too expensive.

References

KENWAY, J. (1987a) *Private Schooling in Australia and the Production of an Educational Hegemony*, Unpublished PhD Thesis, Murdoch University, Perth.

KENWAY, J. (1987b) 'Left right out: The politics of signifying Australian education', *Journal of Education Policy*, 2, 3, pp. 189–203.

KENWAY, J. and WILLIS, S. (1986) 'Feminist single-sex educational strategies: Some theoretical flaws and practical fallacies', *Discourse*, 7, 1, pp. 1–30.

THERBORN, (1980) *The Ideology of Power and the Power of Ideology*, London, Verso.

Part III

Curriculum

Chapter 8

Cultural Differences and Self-esteem: Alternative Curriculum Approaches

Bill Cope and Mary Kalantzis

The Problem

Some of the literature on self-esteem gives the impression that the problem boils down to a minority of students being treated prejudicially by a school system and curriculum dominated by a single cultural viewpoint. So, students of non-English-speaking background are discriminated against by a curriculum which is 'Anglo' in its cultural emphasis. Students of working-class background find the middle-class, academic culture of mainstream curriculum alien. Girls face a persistent culture of sexism which forces them into particular 'aptitudes' and subject choices. It follows from this that curriculum, as a compensatory and empowering counter-move to this cultural dominance, needs to re-value those cultures of ethnicity, class and gender which are excluded by their difference, their non-'normality' as defined in terms of the dominant Anglo, middle-class male culture.

This counter-move is based on a very proper reading of power relations in the curriculum. Not only this, it is based on simple pedagogical common sense: that students learn what they want to learn and that what they want to learn is very much defined by what is relevant to their own particular cultural context. The traditional academic curriculum was simply a mechanism for defining certain students as failures. It appeared to be equitable because it was comprehensive. But, in a subtle and pernicious way, it condemned particular social groups to exclusion by virtue of its discriminatory cultural presupposition that the Anglo, male culture of competitive academic success is universally superior.

This analysis, however, is not the end of our problems, but the beginning. For a start, any implication that cultural differences are a problem for minorities or marginal groups is far from true. Those culturally excluded — students of non-English-speaking background (NESB), working–class students and girls — together constitute by far the greatest proportion of the school population. But quite significant groups of these groups seem to be performing 'well' in terms of the dominant culture.

A newly emerging Australian literature on ethnicity and education is beginning to argue that some of the conventional wisdoms of compensatory education, that being of non-English-speaking background contributes to educational disadvantage, are in fact based on myth. The proponents of this view cite statistics which show that certain NESB groups demonstrate considerable intergenerational mobility and that education is a critical factor in this mobility. Indeed, many NESB groups seem to be doing better than the ESB Australian-born. There are serious methodological and social distortions in the revisionist literature on ethnicity and education, which we document and analyze fully elsewhere (Kalantzis and Cope, 1987c). Nevertheless, the prima facie truth is inescapable: that some significant strata of some NESB groups, both boys and girls, are succeeding in dominant cultural terms. In other words, dominant and ostensibly minority ethnic cultures are by no means mutually exclusive. Educational programs which emphasize raising self-esteem by granting respect to differences through curriculum might be based on an oversimplified reading of the situation. The educational revisionists conclude much more crudely: compensatory education catering to differences through raising self-esteem is simply a waste of money.

Similar observations about the complex overlay of cultures of difference and cultures of success could be made about all-girls' schools, which in certain, very specific privileged contexts construct a female culture which is just as compatible with academic success and social power as is that of equivalent (and culturally very different) privileged boys' schools (see Kenway, Chapter 7). And then there are the 'working-class-kid-made-good' academic success stories. It is not simply and unproblematically the case that working-class culture eschews academic success and social power.

From this point of cultural complexity and cultural overlay our problems become even worse. Progressivist educators, concerned with the cultural insensitivity and discriminatory power of the traditional academic curriculum, have increasingly come to advocate diversified curriculum, based on culturally specific needs and relevance. This is the practical program that comes with their critical counter-move against traditional curriculum. But immediate problems arise. Cultural differences are not innocent, colourful and simply worthy of celebration. They also embody relations of inequality. Reproducing the difference can also mean reproducing a power relation, but with a smile. The macrame/

international cooking/communications skills curriculum not only trivial-
izes what it classifies as cultural difference but is ironically all too relevant
to a society divided by class, gender and ethnicity. It is relevant in a
populist conception of democracy: people should have what, at first
glance, it seems they want and therefore need. Recognizing and reproducing a culture in school supposedly raises self-esteem and satisfaction
with one's lot. This, of course, is highly relevant to a society which is
going to stay, quietly and happily, unequally divided (Kalantzis, Cope
and Hughes, 1983). It is not surprising that progressivism at this point
frequently comes to blows with the 'conservative', 'unrealistic' parental
expectations of some working-class or NESB parents who work hard to
send their children to expensive, single sex private schools, for example.

Is self-esteem raised by celebrating cultural difference or by success
measured in the dominant terms of the academic curriculum and the
careers market? The answer one gives to this question, one way or the
other, has implications for curriculum practice. A cultural pluralist model
founded on the paradigm of difference means school-based, diversified,
democratic, culturally relevant curriculum. A model based on explicit and
direct channels of access and participation measured by outcomes in terms
of social empowerment mostly means some permutation of the conventional academic curriculum. The former model, despite best intentions,
can be a liberal pluralist reproduction of inequality and existing power
relations. It streams curriculum and tries to tell 'non-academic' students
that they have succeeded on their own cultural terms. The latter can be a
form of cultural assimilation which alienates, excludes and raises the
hurdles for those who do not fit 'naturally' into its norms and modes of
operation. But this sort of curriculum need not be conservative in its
intent and effect, as English as a second language (ESL) programs and
feminist moves to get more girls into traditional boys' subjects attest, for
example. It is a problem of this dichotomy, between self-esteem through
celebration of difference and self-esteem as access to dominant structures
of education and social power, that this chapter addresses.

Having thus problematized the field, the chapter will first discuss the
basic alternative conceptual presuppositions of the self-esteem debate. As
the argument here can be no more than schematic, we refer to other
places where we have undertaken empirical work or literature reviews.
Then we describe the experimental practice of the Social Literacy Project,
which has attempted to link a concern for cultural pluralism with
strategies for social equity. The main tangible result of this project has
been a series of social studies/social science curriculum materials now
used in approximately 100 Australian primary and secondary schools.

Ethnicity/Class/Gender: Alternative Curriculum Approaches

The esteem/achievement equation is not simply a chicken and egg problem. Putting either esteem or achievement as a primarily causal factor usually indicates one's approach to the question of cultural differences. Putting self-esteem first is generally a progressivist, pluralist move which stresses that curriculum fosters self-esteem by giving credence to cultural difference. Raising self-esteem in this way raises satisfaction with school and thus participation and achievement rates. On the other hand, putting the objective of achievement in the mainstream first is generally a move based on the paradigm of disadvantage and the challenge of securing access to core culture. Self-esteem follows, as a late 'post'-industrial society grants economic and social status to a particular set of abstract, technical and linguistic competencies. The intended curriculum consequences of these two equations we will call respectively, in a terminology we have already foreshadowed in our introduction, cultural pluralism and social equity. We should note, incidentally, that both approaches can have very regressive manifestations: rigidly streamed and segregated curriculum in the case of the former and crude cultural assimilation in the case of the latter. We have deliberately used a positive terminology as we want to analyze critically, not crude or discredited curriculum approaches, but sophisticated attempts at social reform through curriculum. In drawing up the paradigmatic lines, moreover, we do not want to imply that the two approaches are always or even frequently mutually exclusive in practice. Indeed, at the end of this section we argue that curriculum should transcend simplistic versions of each approach to foster social equity through cultural pluralism.

'Multicultural' education programs approaching the issue of ethnicity and schooling are to be found mainly in the form of socio-cultural programs, English as a second language (ESL) and 'community languages' (Cope *et al.*, 1986; Cope and Alcorso, 1987). A cultural pluralist approach to the socio-cultural element of the multicultural curriculum frequently emphasizes and celebrates cultural differences. For example, traditional social studies curricula in Australian schools had a purely Anglo and assimilationist view of Australian 'discovery', 'settlement' and progress. The school environment showed no signs of recognizing the diversity of students' cultural backgrounds. Activities with parents (fêtes and canteen committees) simply alienated NESB parents. It was thus considered to be time to redress the balance. Social studies came to involve a study of the different cultures in the school. The school environment came to reflect the diversity of its population with multilingual signs and multicultural artwork going up, and NESB parents became involved in 'national days' in which the colourful variety of food and dance was put on show. This, it was supposed, would help raise the cultural pride and self-esteem of NESB students in the school context.

But what has this socio-cultural renewal produced in terms of outcomes? Putting the bleakest construction on this sort of cultural pluralism, too horribly true in too many cases, the effects have been as bad as the old cultural-assimilationist curriculum, even if in quite different ways. Cultures are constructed as stereotypes, as the colourul and the visible: traditional food, 'national' dress and folk dancing; not MacDonalds, jeans and discos. Division is exacerbated as differences are emphasized. Cultural difference is frequently aligned with nationality (countries, flag symbolism), a particularly inept move given that migration is frequently the result of the non-coincidence of ethnic affiliation with nation-state affiliation. Ethnic groups, frequently bitterly divided by politics, class, dialect, length of residence in Australia and generational differences, are naively aggregated around the stereotypical 'national' symbolism. The not-so-hidden agenda, moreover, is that culture is traditionalism and that cultural conservation is a good thing. Neither of these assumptions is necessarily true. Culture is dynamic as much as it is founded in tradition. Indeed, moving away from some aspects of traditionalism (such as sexism and racism) is in all probability a good thing. As a corollary to this type of cultural pluralism, the 'ethnics' are de facto separated from the rest, as they are the only ones with significant elements of traditional folk culture that can be made visible. All this happens in 'multicultural' schools, not 'academic' schools where traditional history and geography continue for their supposed intellectual 'seriousness'. The net effect is to divide schooling between soft-option curriculum which attempts to raise the self-esteem of NESB students by celebrating their differences, and 'serious' schooling which aims at 'academic' results and produces self-esteem as a by-product (Kalantzis and Cope, 1986a, 1984; Kalantzis, Cope and Hughes, 1985).

Alternatively, an equitable socio-cultural approach to the question of ethnic differences can include programs which explain 'Australian ways'. In terms of institutional access, this might include learning about the political and welfare systems. In terms of social values, it might include the officially promulgated policies of non-sexism and non-racism, neither of which is unproblematically compatible with the cultural traditions of either NESB or ESB students. Indeed, the project of social equity itself is often not a matter of cultural preservation, but of active cultural change. Many parents correctly perceive the ethics of cultural freedom and individual choice to mean children assimilating to 'Australian ways'. Both progressive education and peer context actively contribute to this. Self-esteem, it is assumed, is produced by participation and access to the mainstream culture. The most serious difficulty with this approach, however, is that it is relatively insensitive to students' starting points and implicitly devalues these. Students will not necessarily respond to messages outside their own cultural framework. There is also a serious ethical question about directly intervening in a situation of institutional power (the school, credentialing, etc.) to effect cultural change.

Other elements of multicultural education include ESL and 'community' languages. ESL has an almost exclusively equitable and participatory objective, except where it is pragmatically limited to 'communications skills' and where no systematic attempt is made to take NESB students to levels of language competence necessary to give them the genuine choice to participate in the full range of post-compulsory education. Furthermore, 'community' languages with a pluralist rationale might aim to raise self-esteem simply by their tokenistic appearance in the school curriculum. When self-esteem through the school's ostentatious but inevitably underresourced recognition of difference is seen to be enough, we frequently find very limited and ineffective programs. Not unusual in the primary school, for example, are short-term esteem-oriented community language programs which seem to have served their purpose simply by their minimal presence for a lesson or two per week. Meanwhile, traditional 'foreign' language teaching operates in the secondary school with quite different cognitive objectives, in which academic success produces self-esteem, incidentally and in the long run. On the other hand, advocates of equitable approaches to the language question often stress that meagre resources would be more efficiently channelled into ESL teaching; that transitional bilingualism is a useful, if expensive, means to educational access and social participation; and that 'community' languages, if they are to be taught at all, have to aim at the same intellectual seriousness as so-called 'foreign' languages (Kalantzis, Cope and Slade, 1986; Kalantzis, 1986a).

Pluralistic and equitable approaches to the issue of differences of social class are best encapsulated in the positions of proponents of diversified and common curriculum respectively. In a diversified curriculum, students not destined for academic success and not culturally attuned to the competitive, credential-oriented formality of the traditional education system undertake 'relevant' subjects such as 'living skills', motor mechanics, international cooking, 'maths in society' or 'communication skills'. Diversifying the curriculum, it is hoped, will thus raise the self-esteem of students whom the comprehensive curriculum only served to define as failures. They will succeed because these subjects are designed, qua re-

levant, as something in which they can succeed. This process of diversification has had a considerable degree of success. 'Non-academically
inclined' students are participating more and more in the alternative
curriculum, if only because the employment situation leaves them with
few options. On the other hand, there is an institutional and social reality
— social power — that means that the alternative subjects in the diversified curriculum are not relative and equal. Diversification leaves the
traditional academic curriculum untouched. It does nothing to right inequities of access to social power. Students doing the alternative curriculum know very well from their peer culture that 'communication skills'
really means 'veggie English' and 'maths in society' is 'veggie maths'
(Cope, 1986; Cope and Kalantzis, 1985).

Common, comprehensive curriculum, equally inadequately, was the
idealistic facade, the supposed guarantee of equality of opportunity, that
in fact failed most working-class students. It is true that cognitive and
affective 'aptitudes' to educational success and social power are profoundly class-based. Equitable approaches to this problem are often the weaker
for ignoring the specificity of class-cultural background. It is not enough
to view the problem as one of cultural deficit and remediation. As the
cultural pluralists are, in their own way, so aware, teaching has to begin
from where students are at.

The majority of interventions to meet the challenge of cultured
differences around the gender divide have aimed at social equity. The
strongest connotation of the concept 'inclusive' curriculum is that girls
can participate in subjects and jobs that were the traditional preserve of
male culture. The politics of equality of genders means the active support
of the trend towards the erasure of their cultural differences. Self-esteem
for women is created by joining the world of men on an equal footing
(Kalantzis, 1986b; Kalantzis and Cope, 1986b, 1987a). Already, however,
there has been a reaction to this. Should not schools aim to preserve
female culture as much as they give girls the chance to join the male
world of power manipulation and competitive individualism? Are not
skills and values of caring and domestic competence, for example, equally
important? Why should schools devalue this difference in the structure of
their curriculum, thereby reproducing the broader social devaluation of
what was traditionally female culture and female work? Women's history, for example, is as important as getting more girls into technical and
scientific subjects. Self-esteem is created by celebrating rather than erasing
female cultural difference. Again, this difference is not one that should be
reproduced unproblematically, as it embodies relations of inequality.

Thus far we have caricatured approaches to the question of cultural
differences of ethnicity, class and gender which alternatively emphasize

cultural difference or social equity. The basic problem of the former approach is that, despite best intentions, it is frequently tokenistic and patronizing in its effect because it sits in a broader context of unequal power relations. Positing differences as formally equal for the purpose of valuing all different cultures and then introducing curriculum diversification leaves larger power structures untouched in which these differences are not separate, equal and relative but simultaneously embody powerful and pervasive relations of inequality. Self-esteem programs can easily become a patronizing and socially quiescent educational exercise. The basic problem of the latter approach, on the other hand, is that of all reformist, compensatory education based on the paradigm of disadvantage. Despite best intentions, this paradigm implicitly condemns cultural differences; it is assimilative and uncritical of dominant cultures and structures of power in its attempt to incorporate the culturally marginalized; and it is pedagogically inept in failing to build positively on students' own cultures. Self-esteem is the reward of success on the dominant culture's own terms.

How do we reconstruct self-esteem programs so that they are more socially effective? A curriculum approach which attempts to develop both cultural pluralism and social equity will be quite different from either approach simplistically opposed to the other. Curriculum which genuinely aims to increase self-esteem has to work critically with both dominant and marginalized cultures. The dominant culture has to be reconstructed so that its empowering essence, not its Anglo, middle-class male embodiment, is accessible to all. At root, there are certain cultural and cognitive factors which are necessary for social power in this particular historical context. Certain forms of abstraction and reasoning form the linguistic basis for the technical and social literacy of those who wield power (Cope, 1986). It happens at the moment that particular groups get more of this through education, and this is at least in part because much 'elite' education is currently cloaked in the exclusivist garb of the competitive academic curriculum, quite understandably alienating to students from many cultural contexts. The task is neither to create self-esteem to make some groups feel better in their cultural context nor to establish compensatory programs to let a select few succeed who will later feel better for having acquired a new culture of power and success. Rather, a curriculum which aimed at social equity without prejudice to cultural pluralism would remove its class/gender/ethnic bias. This might allow, not sycophantic cultural mobility, but genuinely chosen (rather than structurally and educationally predestined and thus marginalized and excluded) counter-cultures.

On the other hand, the same curriculum that has this universalistic intent has to be open to differences, but without simply and uncritically aiming to 'respect' and preserve these. Differential curriculum means are necessary to equitable ends. Cultural pluralism is one of the great virtues of the menagerie of social experimentation that is late industrialism. Of course, certain elements of the project of social equity are incompatible with traditional cultures. Pluralist approaches to the problem of self-esteem not only mostly came with a set of singular assumptions about non-sexism and non-racism, for example. In recognizing our own singular culturedness in valuing pluralism, we remove some of the self-delusion frequently to be found in simplistic pluralist approaches to the question of curriculum and self-esteem.

The Social Literacy Experiment

The pluralist emphasis on establishing difference can ignore the common denominators that students from all cultural backgrounds face in Australia. That is, it can ignore the mainstream processes and requirements of schooling and social enablement. A focus on the process of negotiating with the core Australian culture, however, must also be able to cater to differing paths of access. The Social Literacy Project set out to meet this challenge.

The objectives of the Social Literacy Project are summed up as an ability to understand a complex and interdependent social world, and skills of active, confident social participation. This simultaneously involves acquiring a universalistic language with which to read large social structures and developing a framework for understanding cultural differences (Kalantzis and Cope, 1987b). Rather more prosaically, the main product of the project is a series of social studies/social science curriculum units for upper primary and lower secondary school. The project has been very much an experiment, involving extensive conferencing with teachers, trialling in a variety of school situations and re-drafting in the light of the consolidated school experience.

On the side of equity and participation, 'social literacy' is an ability to abstract. We cannot know all the details, all the names to all the faces in the modern world: the 'peer group', 'women', 'social class', the 'news media', the 'Third World'; these are significant generalizing concepts which help us to describe and explain large social structures. Social processes are not intelligible simply as the actions of different individuals. The everyday structures of our lives are shaped within the larger structures of industrialism. To see this connectedness and to have some degree of control over our lives, we need to read the world and discern or impose patterns by generalization or abstraction.

On the side of plurality, 'social literacy' also means making sense of differences within individual experience. Immigrants with traits developed in different parts of the globe; mundane commodities from exotic-sounding places and exotic commodities produced in mundane factories; genders and subcultures and styles; industrialisms meeting pre-industrialisms; languages, and discourses within languages, and genres within discourses; wealth beside poverty; varieties of family and domestic relationship: all these cultural phenomena affect us each as individuals. Racism and sexism, parochialism and bigotry are ill-thought reactions to these differences. 'Social literacy' is a process of understanding and explaining people's differences.

More than this, the skills of understanding are of little value if they are not practical skills. 'Social literacy' involves more than just passive understanding. It involves acquiring the skills of social action. Without an ability to manipulate and negotiate the structures of industrialism and to handle the differences encountered in everyday life, people can be marginalized. Such skills are acquired through activities in which students make their own knowledge and gain experience in social action. The emphasis on the development of a language of abstract social concepts in the Social Literacy Project is not simply academic. This language and these concepts are practical tools for active, confident social participation, and the materials themselves actively engage the learner in social investigation and intervention.

With these fundamental rationales in mind, we will discuss the Social Literacy materials, illustrating how they work by way of example. The project's general aim is to present a model that mainstreams the issues of non-sexism, multiculturalism and Aboriginal studies into a core social studies/science program. The last two units of the series of materials for Year 7 (12-year-old students) have as their content the issues of gender and culture. These units place students in learning experiences in which they have to assess the factors that contribute to the construction of gender, the consequences of social relations of gender, the history of inequality and discrimination that can occur when culturally constructed features like gender and race are presented as natural and casual, as determined roles and behaviour. The units culminate in an investigation of what students themselves have been exposed to through a study of childhood, the family, school, media and so on. They examine the factors that have shaped their practices, roles and beliefs.

These units incorporate the prime social and conceptual goals of the Year 7 materials. Their aim is the understanding of self as cultured and one's own role in making culture in the broadest sense. But in order that the students are equipped to explore these issues without feeling immediately threatened, and so that the teacher is not placed in a position of preaching a particular emotive line to the students, a foundation is built up in the previous four units that enables this task to be more an exercise in critical and objective self-analysis than something which evokes an emotive reaction.

The preceding unit (unit G4) investigates the concept of socialization. The content involves an investigation of stories and articles about feral children, observation of kindergarten practices, anthropological-type research and social surveys. The content in this, as in all units, is only suggestive. The critical dimension is the bringing together of a series of experiences that enable the student to explore the possible variety of human activity and behaviour and the way in which cultural practices and norms are acquired. For example, all people, if not biologically impaired, have the ability to learn language. But the environment they are placed in determines which language they learn, how well they learn it and to what ends. The concepts of environment, social, natural, biological potential, human potential, formal learning, informal learning, culture and family are thus prerequisites for the later units on gender and culture. They lay a foundation for viewing gender and ethnicity as learnt and socially constituted rather than genetic and fixed. The purpose of this unit is to help students develop, through a variety of active experiences, concepts and skills of inquiry, as well as to introduce them to the idea that what is called human nature has a very wide range of possibilities. Human beings are creative in their responses to the same basic human needs, and a lot that we often assume to be natural is in fact learnt.

This learning, however, goes on within certain social structures, and the previous unit (unit G3) takes as its starting point the exploration of the social structure that people are born into and its effects. Its key concepts include social groups, social class, roles, rules, relationships, law and equality. Ancient Greece is taken as a case study, but again this is only in order to build up the concepts and skills necessary for the subsequent units on socialization, gender and culture. Ancient Greece was chosen not only because it is a popular area of study in Year 7, but because it was distant enough to allow for a relatively non-threatening experience of the concepts. This unit, nevertheless, as do all the units, regularly comes back to an application of the concepts to life in Australia.

To prepare for this examination of large social structures, the previous unit (unit G2) places students in experiences that explore relationships in small-scale structures such as schools and sports teams. The main concepts used are structure, function, roles, rules, relationships, written rules and change. This unit explores not only the mechanics of the relation between structure and function but the dynamic dimension of social relations. Social structures are investigated as a series of social activities reproduced in specific ways to specific ends. The way in which they satisfy individual and group needs is also explored.

Preceding this, the very first unit of the Year 7 materials (unit G1) explores social values. The students examine values, not as tied to things and practices in an abstract way, but as matters of action and choice. The object is not just to clarify values, but to conceptualize values as a framework for analyzing one of the bases of social activity.

The central goal of these six units is to explore the ways in which gender and ethnicity are socially constructed and dynamic. The developing framework of concepts is of general use as a means to explaining both broader social structures and the phenomenon of cultural difference. At the same time, being conceptually oriented, the content of the materials is only presented by way of example, open to substitution of locally relevant and school-based concerns by teachers and students.

It should also be evident from this discussion that the Social Literacy Project has aimed principally at cognitive, rather than affective, modes of raising self-esteem: assisting students to develop a language with which to explain culture and differences, rather than submersing them in the colourful details of difference and hoping they will absorb respect for themselves and tolerance of others by osmosis.

Furthermore, given the plurality that exists in their classrooms and the barriers produced by inadequate language skills, all teachers need to regard themselves as teachers of the English language, irrespective of their discipline area. For example, many students are likely to come from homes where English is not used as the major medium of discourse, or, if it is, it is used unevenly and perhaps in a restricted manner. Peer group dialogue and limited teacher-student linguistic interaction are insufficient sources to compensate for this. It is imperative that curriculum in general address the issue of language competence in a sustained and systematic way. Accordingly, the Social Literacy materials integrate experiences which develop language skills both in the reception and production of a variety of linguistic genres.

Conclusions

This chapter began by discussing, in general terms, the question of self-esteem and the contrasting consequences of alternative curriculum approaches. On the one hand, cultural pluralist approaches support and promote cultural differences by attempting to raise students' self-esteem through recognition of their particular cultural backgrounds and thereby improving achievement and participation. On the other hand, approaches whose objective is social equity, such as those that work within the compensatory paradigm of disadvantage, aim first to improve levels of achievement and participation, thereby secondarily improving students' self-esteem. As we have argued, simplistic versions of each approach have potentially serious limitations. An approach is needed which concerns itself with both cultural pluralism and social equity.

The Social Literacy Project is a curriculum experiment which aims to address the question of social equity, not through the culturally biased medium of the traditional academic curriculum, but by placing students in a context of social inquiry in which they develop a conceptual framework with which to understand and actively manipulate the culturally and institutionally complex world of late industrial society. Given an orientation to practical and abstracting concepts, rather than curriculum as facts and content, the Social Literacy materials, despite providing content by way of suggestion and example, leave themselves open to the injection of local community content and school-based concerns. This is one element of Social Literacy's concern with cultural pluralism. More importantly, moving beyond the stereotyping and trivializing of 'multi-cultural' curriculum which celebrates colourful differences, Social Literacy attempts to provide students with a framework within which to explain and negotiate cultural differences.

References

COPE, BILL (1986) 'Traditional versus progressivist pedagogy', *Social Literacy Monograph*, 11.

COPE, B. and ALCORSO, C. (1987) 'A review of Australian multicultural education policies, 1979–1986', Position paper for the National Advisory and Consultative Committee on Multicultural Education, Commonwealth Department of Education, Canberra.

COPE, B. and KALANTZIS, M. (1985) 'Pedagogy after progressivism', *Education Links*, 27, p. 15.

COPE, B., KALANTZIS, M., BOOTH, T. and ROWSE, G. (1986) *Seeing the Need: A National Review of Inservice Programs for Teachers of Adolescents of Non-English Speaking Bankground*, Canberra, Commonwealth Department of Education.

KALANTZIS, M. (1986a) 'A community language: Politics or pedagogy'?, *Australian Review of Applied Linguistics*, Series S, 2, pp. 168–79.

KALANTZIS, M. (1986b) 'Opening doors: Keys or sledgehammers? Non-sexist education for a multicultural sociey', *Social Literacy Mongraph*, 25, Australian Women's Education Coalition Conference, Sydney, 1986, Keynote Address.

KALANTZIS, M. and COPE, B. (1984) 'Multiculturalism and education policy', in BOTTOMLEY, G. and DE LEPERVANCHE, M. (Eds), *Class, Gender and Ethnicity*, Sydney, George Allen and Unwin, reprinted in Rizvi, Fazal (Ed.) (1986), *Ethnicity, Class and Multicultural Education*, Geelong, Deakin University Press.

KALANTZIS, M. and COPE, B. (1986a) 'Pluralism and equitability: Multicultural curriculum strategies for schools', *Social Literacy Monograph*, 16, Position paper for the National Advisory and Consultative Committee on Multicultural Education; also, NACCME, Canberra, 1987.

KALANTZIS, M. and COPE, B. (1986b) 'Some issues in the education of girls of non-English speaking background', *Social Literacy Monograph, 20,* Position paper for the New South Wales Department of Education's Work Opportunities for Women Project, Sydney.

KALANTZIS, M. and COPE, B. (1987a) 'Gender differences, cultural differences: Towards inclusive curriculum', *Curriculum Perspectives*, 7, 1, pp. 64–8.

KALANTZIS, M. and COPE, B. (1987b) *An Overview: Teaching/Learning Social Literacy*, Sydney, Common Ground.

KALANTZIS, M. and COPE, B. (1987c) 'Why we need multicultural education: A review of the ethnic disadvantage debate', *Occasional Paper No. 3*, Centre for Multicultural Studies, University of Wollongong.

KALANTZIS, M., COPE, B. and Hughes, C. (1983) 'Shaping the curriculum: Some unanswered questions', *Curriculum Perspectives*, 3, 3, pp. 66–9.

KALANTZIS, M., COPE, B. and HUGHES, C. (1985) 'Pluralism and social reform: A review of multiculturalism in Australian education', *Thesis Eleven*, 10/11, pp. 195–215.

KALANTZIS M., COPE, B. and SLADE, D. (1986) *The Language Question: The Maintenance of Languages Other Than English, 1: Research Findings, 2: Methodology and Empirical Results*, Canberra, Department of Immigration and Ethnic Affairs.

SOCIAL LITERACY (1982–87) A Series G: Unit G1, *Social Values*; Unit G2, *Social Structures*; Unit G3, *Groups in Society*; Unit G4, *Socialisation*; Unit G5, *Gender*; Unit G6, *Culture*, Sydney, Common Ground.

Chapter 9

Personal Growth or Critical Resistance? Self-esteem in the English Curriculum

Pam Gilbert

As a subject in Australian secondary schools, English has undergone significant changes in the past twenty years. It has played a major role in general moves to humanize the curriculum by emphasizing the value and significance, for the classroom, of students' experiences. Attention to the role of language in learning and of language across the curriculum has been compatible with the redefinition of English, and the resultant emphasis on language and language matters has contributed noticeably to the individualization of school learning. The result has been that the total language environment of schools has become much more an object of critical attention.

However, this 'personalism' and 'individualism' within English curriculum matters have not been without some cost; in this chapter some of the implicit dangers associated with a language study which focuses on the person rather than on socio-cultural contexts will be addressed. In addressing English in this way, some parallels will be drawn with self-esteem projects within secondary schools. As with English, self-esteem programs have played an important role in the secondary school curriculum and have focused attention on areas that had previously been neglected. As detailed by Pam Jonas in Chapter 11, important political work with girls has resulted, and many schools and classrooms have altered policies as a result of the impact of the self-esteem literature.

Projects which are couched in personal and individual terms need, however, to be scrutinized carefully. While for many educationists, English and its adjacent discourse of self-esteem offer classroom opportunities to make critical assessments of the way in which gender or race or class are constructed culturally, there is nothing explicit in the discourses which promotes these opportunities. While the personal and the individual are such key concepts within the two discourses, both are vulnerable to substantial depoliticization.

English, therefore, is an interesting subject to address in a collection such as this. This chapter, which focuses on the English curriculum, makes the claim that the personal and individualist nature of currently acceptable concepts of English works against, rather than in support of, a critical social questioning of phallocentric social organization. The chapter suggests that any pedagogy which does not question the ideological construction of language and language products cannot begin to redress gender inequalities. Prevailing assumptions about the nature of English are critically reconsidered, as are the implications for girls in English classrooms. The chapter looks for alternatives to self-esteem or personal growth in the empowerment of girls, as a group, in schools.

The English Curriculum: Self-esteem through Personal Growth

Adjacent Discourses

One of the noticeable features of several of the Australian self-esteem projects for girls is the emphasis placed upon developing positive self-concepts through expressionist writing and creative language use. For instance, *Wings* (1983), one of the better known self-esteem schemes, describes the development of 'self-knowledge skills' (through writing, poetry, video, films, etc.) as well as the development of 'communication skills' (talking and expressing ideas, opinions and feelings to others). By suggesting, as *Wings* does, that language activities can be instrumental in understanding the nature of the 'self', in building and expanding 'self-esteem', in enabling girls to assume responsibility for their own lives by developing new images of themselves, in expanding the skills of creativity, intuition, feeling and holism, the discourse on self-esteem takes on many of the concepts dominant in the discourse of English pedagogy. In fact, the two discourses are adjacent. Both are aligned to child-centred learning, to romantic conceptions of creativity and personal expression and to a common-sense approach to language as communication. Both fail to give due emphasis to the socio-cultural nature of language: to the central role language plays in the workings of ideology.

If ideology is taken to mean, as Althusser (1971) would put it, those systems of beliefs and assumptions (unconscious, unexamined, invisible) which represent the imaginary relationships of individuals to their real conditions of existence, then language plays a key role in ideological formations. The social construction of gender, for instance, must take account of a language system which has been labelled 'man-made' (Spender, 1980): a language system which perpetuates gender inequalities and divisions. Language cannot be considered a neutral, innocent field. Claims that individuals are free to express themselves personally through language, to come to 'self-knowledge' through language, assume a language system which is ideologically neutral.

Language is far from this. Indeed, many feminists would argue that language is a patriarchal practice. Language practices market and sell images of women compatible with a patriarchal society; language practices silence, deride and frequently by-pass women; language practices help to maintain women as the second sex. However, it is also language practices which provide the opportunity to resist the social construction of gender, although resistance can only follow when the seemingly natural and ideologically innocent discourses that constitute the social fabric of the world are questioned and critically re-read. A subject like English, which has language as its content and its process, is a particularly important curriculum area to examine, and a reappraisal of the assumptions dominating a language-based subject in the secondary school is likely to have important consequences for programs like the self-esteem projects which operate so heavily through language and language practices.

English: A Personalist and Individualist Discourse

The liberation of the 'self' through expressionist and creative language use has long been seen as a goal of English in the secondary school curriculum. The dominant assumptions underlying prevailing concepts about English are firmly rooted in personalist and expressionist discourses, and have been so since the late 1960s as an aftermath of a transatlantic English conference held at Dartmouth in England. The proceedings of the watershed Dartmouth conference of 1966 were enshrined in a monograph prepared by John Dixon, *Growth through English* (1967), in which Dixon suggested that there were three dominant models of English: a 'skills' model, a 'cultural heritage' model, and a 'personal growth' model. He strongly preferred the third, making the claim that:

> In English, pupils meet to share their encounters with life, and to do this effectively they move freely between dialogue and mono-logue — between talk, drama and writing; and literature, by bringing new voices into the classroom, adds to the store of shared experience. Each pupil takes from the store what he [sic]

can and what he needs. In so doing he learns to use language to build his own representational world and works to make this fit reality as he experiences it. . . .

In ordering and composing situations that in some way symbolize life as we know it, we bring order and composure to our inner selves.

When a pupil is steeped in language in operation we expect, as he matures, a conceptualizing of his earlier awareness of language, and with this perhaps new insight into himself (as creator of his own world). (Dixon, 1967, p. 13)

There is little doubt that the development of English curriculum concerns in Britain, North America and Australia, in the wake of Dartmouth and of Dixon's book, has followed this model (Allen, 1980). As Protherough notes:

The apparent shift in the 1960's seems to be away from emphasis on qualities of language displayed for their own sake towards stress on the sincerity, the vividness, the truth to life with which experience is displayed. The aim moved from adult models of impersonality towards the revelation of personal ideas and feelings appropriate to the age of the writer, from generally accepted truths and attitudes to unique perceptions. (1983, pp. 193–4)

This emphasis on the 'personalist' nature of language sat well with the images popularized in the 'creative writing' movement of the 1960s, and received additional support from two other significant directions in the 1970s. James Britton published *Language and Learning* in 1970, and in that book argued that language played a key role in the transformation of personal experience into personal knowledge. His work was complemented by the growing popularity in the 1970s of a reader response aesthetics which was positing new approaches to reading.

The 'reader liberationists', notably Iser (1974) and Rosenblatt (1978), challenged traditional forms of literary criticism as not making adequate allowance for the role of the individual reader in the literary endeavour, and argued for a reconsideration of the relationship between reader and text. Such an approach to reading could sit easily with the language, learning and personal growth cluster which was emerging in the 1970s as a preferred model for English (see Gilbert, 1987 for a fuller discussion of this). In fact, literature could be seen to complement the cluster, because traditional assumptions about literature assume that it, too, is a personal vision of the world created by a single creative being, the author. By reading the book, the reader could come to terms with the author's intentions and to share the author's feelings and vision: to enter into the universality of experience that the text offered. In this way the preferred contemporary approach to literary study became the personal one: the linking of the individual student's mind to that of the creative artist's.

The personalist emphasis in English now encompassed both writing and speaking, as well as reading and listening. Language and literature classrooms were to be places where children could 'grow' through language, and where the language that children brought with them to school became an important early learning medium. The ideals were high, but practice has been a little more difficult.

English in the Classroom

Not surprisingly, the prevailing personalist and individualist assumptions made in the pedagogy about English have run aground when confronted with the power structures of schooling. Like the prevailing discourse on self-esteem, English assumes the ability of the individual to operate freely: outside the subcultures of the school, the family, the dominant peer group, and outside considerations of gender, race or class. In English, like any other subject, teachers and students have to juggle with the demands of set curriculum matter, set texts, assessment tasks, bureaucratic and parental demands — the 'work' of school.

Far from being an avenue of personal expression and individual development, language within secondary schools is frequently used to discipline and to sort, to mystify and to alienate. The contradictions and paradoxes within English confuse both students and teachers. The attractive and beguiling notion of language as a personal and creative act struggles with the more pragmatic and realistic concept of school literacy as an agent of social control and selection. As one baffled Year 12 English student remarked:

> I don't think often teachers want to know the truth. They want to know what they want to hear. You can't just write something and say that's your true feelings. You have to say why you feel that and why you feel this....

> We can hardly do anything right really.... I think by grade twelve you should be able to write how you feel. To write what

you really want. There shouldn't be rights and wrongs in English. (Gilbert, 1989)

Currently acceptable pedagogy has constructed an elaborate edifice of 'creativity' over the work of the school, masking the construction and production of school language tasks, and ignoring the ideological construction of language practices. Such models are constructed on assumptions that language is personal, individual and idiosyncratic; that literature is personal, individual and idiosyncratic; and that the act of reading literary texts is also personal, individual and idiosyncratic.

Yet despite its claims to such subjectivity and personalism, English does not operate unequivocally as a 'growth' and 'self-esteem' subject in secondary schools and may well undermine the very goals it holds so firmly. One direction that contemporary Australian classroom-based language work has taken is to unveil the hidden agenda of subject writing (Martin, 1985; Gilbert, 1989), and to suggest ways in which 'self-expression' might be taught. Rather than have students claim that they cannot do well at English because they are not creative or original, research can attempt to isolate the writing and reading practices which produce the effects of creativity and originality.

Dominant models of English take as their starting point that language is personal and individual, and that reading is personal and individual. The salient omission from the dominant ideology about English is a critical appraisal of the cultural construction of language practices and, in particular, the cultural construction of a group of texts labelled as literary texts and of specific reading practices which will produce such texts as literary texts. English discourses are so laced with assumptions about 'uniqueness', 'creativity', 'individuality', 'personalism' and 'originality' that writing and reading processes within English classrooms and the printed texts that are used in English classrooms are often regarded as natural because they are seen to stem from individual consciousness. Consequently, such texts are regarded as ideologically free: 'innocent' texts. This has important ramifications for the education of girls.

Literature and Ideology

Feminist literary criticism has challenged the ideological valorization of innocence or 'truth' in literature by demonstrating how particular groups and certain values are privileged within traditional literary discourse. Texts like Millett's *Sexual Politics* (1977) offered readings of the supposedly ideologically innocent literary tradition. Widdowson *et al.*'s *Re-Reading*

English (1982) and more recently Batsleer *et al.'s Rewriting English* (1985) have unveiled many of the historical and specifically cultural conditions operating to privilege certain literary texts over others.

The nature of literature — of what constitutes a literary text — has itself been under fire. As it stands, 'literature' clearly does not mark out a domain of language which is in some way different from other language domains. There are no criteria which will serve objectively to label certain types of language as discretely belonging to 'literature'. If literature is defined as 'fine' or 'good' writing, then immediately the criteria for deciding such categories are suspect when one considers why, as Eagleton illustrates, 'Lamb, Macaulay and Mill are literature but not, generally speaking, Bentham, Marx and Darwin' (1983, p. 10).

What literature does mark out, and this has often been obscured by the dazzle of 'the author', and 'the truth of the work', is: '... not a neutral totality of imaginative or fictional writing, but an ideologically constructed canon or corpus of texts operating in specific and determinate ways in and around the apparatus of education' (Davies, n.d., p. 13). Althusser (1971) includes literature among the ideological apparatuses which contribute to the process of reproducing the relations of production, claiming that the role of ideology is to construct people as subjects, and Balibar and Macherey (1981) regard literature as inseparable from:

> ... an academic or schooling practice which defines both the conditions for the consumption of literature and the very conditions of its production also ... literature is historically constituted in the bourgeois epoch as an ensemble of language — or rather of specific linguistic practices — inserted in a general schooling process so as to provide appropriate fictional effects, thereby reproducing bourgeois ideology as the dominant ideology. (Balibar and Macherey, 1981, p. 84)

Literature has acted as one of the mainstays of a phallocentric society. The selection, production and distribution of literary texts has managed to silence many women writers, to devalue women's writing and to portray masculinist texts as universally significant texts. To consider literature as personal, creative and expressive, is to lose sight of its ideological nature. This is, of course, a direct parallel to the self-esteem question. To consider the personal and individual nature of subjects is to lose a firm grip on the social power structures within which individuals are sited, and to lose a focus on the ways in which individuals are inscribed by, constructed by, those power structures.

Girls and the English Curriculum

Girls and School Literacy

A consideration of the role girls play in English classrooms needs to be grafted onto this critical reappraisal of the assumption that language can unlock the 'self' or that language can be ideologically 'free'. Research studies of girls and school literacy provide some interesting, although rather predictable, findings. Girls do well at English: they like it, choose it and are successful with it. Females' greater verbal fluency is claimed to be apparent at about age 10 or 11 (Stockard *et al.*, 1980) and to continue through high school and tertiary studies, generally making itself manifest in measures of specific skills like spelling, punctuation or some comprehension tests (Maccoby and Jacklin, 1974). Girls have traditionally displayed greater ease in adapting to school literacy demands than have boys, and Maccoby and Jacklin (1974) maintain that in few other areas can female superiority be established as strongly as it can in reading ability. Significantly higher numbers of boys than girls, for instance, require some form of reading remediation.

The fact that massive injections of funds are provided for such reading remediation programs (and for reading research generally), and yet so little media attention is given to male failure with reading, points to an interesting comparison with the situation in mathematics. Maths remediation programs until recently have secured little or no funding, and yet the 'problem' of girls and mathematics, as Sue Willis has demonstrated in this volume (see Chapter 10), is a well publicized media event. Whose interests are best served by constructing media copy about girls' maths failures? And why is so little made of girls' verbal successes? Are boys' failures regarded as failures on the part of the school? Female teachers? Inappropriate curriculum materials? The unattractive nature and style of classroom reading instruction? Are girls' failures regarded as evidence of girls' intellectual inferiority?

The reasons for female reading superiority are perhaps more complex than would seem apparent at first. Kagen (1964) and Stein and Smithells (1969) suggest that boys tend to view reading as an activity more appropriate for girls than for boys, and Neale, Gill and Tismer (1970) have demonstrated that boys tend to have more negative attitudes to reading than girls do. Stockard *et al.* (1980) indicate how difficult it is to make any consistent statements about the reading achievement of boys as opposed to girls, indicating how studies in countries other than the United States do not present clearcut differences between the sexes. Studies which indicate how boys are able to read as well as girls, if the material they have to read has been rated by them as 'highly interesting' (Asher and Markell, 1974), suggest that boys may tend to view school, and in particular reading and language work, as feminine areas and therefore not worthy of particular attention. Again, the comparison with mathematics education is telling. While girls are expected to enter the masculinist world of mathematics curriculum style — or to fail — the language curriculum is often deliberately adjusted to make it more attractive to boys. Reading materials are notoriously sexist and are strongly aligned to masculine interest, and class texts are frequently chosen for their interest for the boys, rather than their interest for the girls.

As well, boys demand, and are given, more linguistic space in classrooms — a situation which, as Gill and Dyer (1987) have claimed, 'refracts and reflects' divisions in society in general. In Gill and Dyer's research boys regularly broke the classroom discourse rules of putting hands up to answer questions or of not calling out answers, and teachers were found to be much less critical of such behaviour when it came from boys rather than girls. The rules for classroom talk are that girls will sit silently, and if they do 'muck around', they will do it quietly. How do concepts of 'personal growth' or 'self-esteem' sit beside such masculine power games?

The situation with writing is not dissimilar. In an earlier paper I have argued that the generic constraints upon girls' texts serve to make alternative messages about female identity difficult to write (Gilbert, 1988a). Far from allowing for self-expression or personal growth, most school writing tasks serve to anchor girls even more securely to patriarchal discourse patterns. Girls have to learn to write outside the tyranny of gendered generic forms, to construct alternative texts with alternative gender roles. Ironically, the English curriculum — the subject area in which girls have demonstrated superior achievement — locks them tightly into specific gender roles. Resistance to these can clearly be read in girls' writing (see Gilbert, 1988a), but readings that will produce such resistance are not practices that are familiar to teacher readers.

The case needs also to be put that developing a competence as a writer of stories may have little academic value for girls in secondary schools. Studies of school writing have demonstrated time and again the preponderance of 'transactional' — to use Britton's (1970) term — writing: writing which is not the 'creative' or 'personal' writing traditionally associated with English classrooms. So, at the level of power that matters — academic success across a range of secondary school subjects — competent 'mastery' of conventional narrative form is relatively insignificant.

Not surprisingly, while reading ability and general verbal fluency may be areas in which girls — for whatever reason — demonstrate some gender-specific superiority, such success has not brought changes in the power structure which controls the canon of literary acceptability in this country, and has not brought with it any corresponding access to academic jobs. The situation in the United Kingdom, as presented by Batsleer *et al.* (1985), is depressingly similar.

> Girls are commonly held to be 'good' at English, of all the subjects that women go on to study, English is the most popular, women in teaching are well represented in English and there are women writers firmly established at the heart of the national literature. Yet there are few women professors of English, and the few critics of recognized authority who are women do not derive their authority from what they say either about women or as women. The power of utterance rests with men. Women, as students of literature, are apprenticed to a system which is, despite its reverence or perplexity in the face of a Jane Austen or an Emily Bronte, fundamentally and normatively masculine. (p. 107)

There is still only one female English professor in Australia, and still a disproportionately high number of male literary critics pronouncing on the literary merit of Australian books. Females are still outnumbered by males in university appointments, particularly in tenured permanent lecturing positions, and in the two professions other than teaching which might expect to tap 'verbal fluency' — law professionals and university academics — women constitute less than 20 per cent of the group (FAUSA, 1983). Interestingly enough, the only profession substantially occupied by women — although only in its lower echelons — is teaching, and teaching is one of the least respected and least well paid of all the professions.

On one level, all that girls' English competence may perhaps have led to is the development of a large reading market for a steady stream of romance literature and glossy magazines (Christian-Smith, 1988), and the establishment of a substantial group of social letter writers who provide not only an important family interconnectedness but also a body of stationery consumers (a further example of capitalism and the patriarchy working hand in hand?)! But both of these need to be seen in an historical perspective, for both have traditionally been the pursuits of women. The novel's origins, for instance, lie in the autobiographical writing by women in the seventeenth century, and it has been through such writing that women constructed identities as women and sought to make sense of the masculinist world they lived in (Mitchell, 1984). But novel writing, like letter writing, has often been trivialized, and women's novels have often been considered much less significant than men's. It would seem as if women are only able to have control over a literacy that does not count: a domestic, romantic, 'feminized' literacy. Women of ideas, as Dale Spender has argued (1982), have frequently been overlooked and ridiculed. Philosophy, for instance, is predominantly a masculinist domain.

Gender Concerns in English: Beyond Self-esteem and Personal Growth

In a small research study in 1985 student teachers in a children's literature course studied sexism in children's literature by identifying stereotypes. At the end of the course, when they constructed their own children's stories, the students relied on many of those same stereotypes to build their narratives. In discussion about the sexism in their stories, students made these remarks:

> It somehow seemed wrong to have the animals being mean to a little girl wombat.
> It was easier to think of boys' names. Boys' names seemed to fit better.
> I just didn't think about it. I got the idea for a story, and then the characters seemed to be right in that way.
> I can't believe it. I even changed the sex of the bees in my story from female to male deliberately.
> I could have just as easily had a girl at the centre of my story. I don't know why I didn't. (Gilbert, 1985, p. 19)

Attempts to focus on building students' self-confidence with language, as argued by English curriculum writers such as Arnold (1983) and Ashcroft (1987), need to face this dilemma: to be concerned to expose the limitations on attaining self-knowledge through an ideological language system whose commonplace 'innocence' masks its political power, and to explore the relationship between 'self-knowledge' and particular cultural conditions. What 'self-knowledge' about being a woman is possible for girls given the prevailing gender constructs in literature and in the media masquerading as natural and universal concepts of womanhood or girlhood? Is it 'self-knowledge' that will be useful to girls, or a critical understanding of the social construction of gender, and of how that construction operates to oppress women?

Linguistic studies which demonstrate how power is manifested through terms of address, particular conversational moves and strategies, syntactical structures and lexical choices focus attention on the ways in which oral discourse operates ideologically (Poynton, 1985). Understanding how power is asserted and maintained within speech goes some way towards shifting the traditional location of such power, and towards adopting alternative exchange structures which do not rely on such dominance and single control. In the power-infused discourses of the classroom, such knowledge is politically important. Similarly, attempts to consider the images of women in literary texts need to confront the ideological nature of the production of literary discourse and of the way in which 'woman' has been constructed within that discourse — including the nature of 'woman writer' and 'women's writing'.

Mainstream literature is masculinist in that it is masculinist reading practices which produce the illusion of a text's unity and coherence. Feminist reading practices are able to indicate how textual harmony is threatened when texts are read differently, and feminist literary historians have unearthed many texts which seem to have been neglected in the development of the Great Tradition (Showalter, 1978). Recently in this country the editor of *The Oxford History of Australian Literature* (Kramer, 1981) chose not to include most of Australia's well-regarded contemporary women writers in this version of the history of Australian literature. As seeming proof that gender is socially constructed rather than biologically determined, this particular editor was a woman: then the only female professor of English in Australia. Not all women's research will break loose of the patriarchal mantle, nor will all women's writing, as Rosalind Coward (1986) makes eloquently clear in her paper, 'Are Women's Novels Feminist Novels?'

Within the literary domain specific to education, it is common to find research studies of sexist stereotyping in children's literature (Czaplinski, 1976) and in early reading schemes (Anderson and Yip, 1987), but less common to find studies of gender constructions in adolescent literature or in the set literary texts studied in senior English classrooms. Literature that seems to have been written for a specific purpose — for instance, children's literature — appears to be regarded as a more acceptable field for critical analysis than does 'proper' literature. 'Proper' literature is seen, on the whole, to be beyond criticism because its goals are pure. 'Proper' literature presents various facets of the human experience in such a way that individual readers can share the experience vicariously. Its purposes are not regarded as didactic or propagandist. Indeed, such qualities are likely to be responsible for the omission of certain texts from the canon.

However, secondary English classrooms, like college and university

English departments (Ryan, 1982), present a strongly male-oriented set of mainstream texts to students. Few contemporary women writers are included on set lists (Gilbert, 1983), and while the dominant literary tradition in teaching is the personal response mode, a critical re-reading of the Great Tradition does not occur. The construction of gender through literary texts has not been part of mainstream English traditions. Sexist stereotypes may be identified (Rasmussen, 1982), but the overarching concerns of discursive power frameworks in the construction of such stereotypes are too frequently by-passed.

Yet feminist research has meticulously unpicked the male domination of literary production (see, for example, Greene and Kahn, 1985), highlighting the omission of women writers from serious critical acceptance, the assumption that male experience is the universal experience, and the way in which the most common literary genres rely on female oppression and passivity to function (DuPlessis, 1985). Feminist re-readings of literary texts have also demonstrated how it is possible to be a 'resisting reader' to this canonization of male experience and male domination (Fetterly, 1978), and feminist re-writings have posed alternative texts which challenge the supposed 'universality' of the male literary genre. In earlier papers, I have argued that school writing needs to be unpicked in similar ways (Gilbert, 1988a, 1988b). Girls' texts, in particular, need to be read in terms of the seduction of generic forms, and of girls' texts' resistance to gendered generic formulas. The necessity for girls to be able to read non-sexist texts, and texts that try to write beyond the tyranny of masculinist genres, is obviously crucial. Neither text type is in abundance in secondary classrooms.

But while it is necessary to keep identifying sexist stereotypes in literature and to keep providing alternative women's texts for secondary school English classes, it is primarily important that the basic premise of language as an innocent resource for the development of self-esteem or personal growth be challenged. It is imperative that students learn to become 'resisting readers' and 'resisting writers'. Rather than entering into the text, as reader-response theorists would ask students to do, so that the world of the book and the world of the student become one, it is far more productive for students to engage with the textuality of the book; to unravel the many strands in the work and resist that apparent seamless coherence of purpose that the work expects. It is far more important for teachers to become critical readers of student texts: readers who look for ways in which students have resisted narrow gender and generic stereotyping. In this way it is the production of the text that is under scrutiny: the natural and commonplace becomes the object of critical attention.

Conclusion

English is presumably a girls' subject. Yet girls' greater competence with English, and with the school notions of literacy that underpin this subject, has not led to greater access to academic success for girls beyond the secondary school — even in academic areas that rely upon literacy-based competency. The competence that girls display with English seems to be channelled into low status domestic literacy pursuits: romance reading and letter writing. Any verbal competence that girls might display with oral language is usually frustrated within the power games of the classroom, where boys break the classroom discourse rules for order and so guarantee significantly more attention and linguistic space for themselves. Girls who play the game by the rules lose.

The discourses of English are predominantly personalist, and their basic assumptions rest with the power of language and language practices to develop an individual consciousness. Such assumptions deny the role that language practices play in the construction of any concept of 'individual consciousness' and ignore the ideological nature of language. Girls in secondary classrooms have difficulty resisting the prevailing and oppressive gender constructions offered them through traditional literature, contemporary media, classroom discourse patterns and the apparently innocent language of everyday use. 'Man' is everywhere and everywhere superior. 'Woman' is the second sex, the hidden, often ridiculed subordinate.

But it is the resistance to this subordination that should be looked for, not the acquiescence. It is cultural consciousness rather than personal self-esteem that is most powerful for girls. Not until the apparently innocent discourses are unpicked and opened out for and with students can the ideology upon which they are based be examined, and psychological concepts of self-esteem are part of that ideology. It is naive to assume that increased self-esteem or increased self-confidence can lead to any real change in social and cultural practices. In many ways it is 'gender' esteem that is more important, and while that may be developed through self-esteem work, it should be the purpose, not the spin-off, of such work, However, the discourses that produce 'subjects', and in particular gendered subjects, work against the recognition of such social consciousness.

While English has the potential to be a radical force in the school curriculum, able to offer critical readings of dominant ideological power formations, and the opportunity to write new versions of female experience, it frequently fails to take up this challenge, and instead loses itself in the hedonism of self-expression and personal creativity. A re-reading of

English has much to offer to adjacent discourses such as that of self-esteem. Both discourses appear to have drawn substantially upon narrow psychological definitions of personal growth, and neglected the sociological and cultural dimensions of education and of gender. As a result their potential, as radicalizing discourses within the school, is not maximized. The opportunity to turn in upon the language and language practices that are basic to both discourses, 'and to focus upon the gender constructions each relies upon, is often lost. More importantly, by cloaking both discourses in the false and misleading concepts of personal and individual linguistic freedoms, the two discourses frequently help to oppress girls by locking them into, rather than freeing them from, a set of patriarchal language practices.

Acknowledgment

Acknowledgment is given and thanks offered to Rob Gilbert, Allan Luke, Lyn Martinez, and Sandra Taylor for their advice with aspects of this chapter.

References

ALLEN, D. (1980) *English Teaching Since 1965: How Much Growth?* London, Heinemann Educational.

ALTHUSSER, L. (1971) 'Ideology and ideological state apparatuses', in *Lenin and Philosophy and Other Essays*, trans. B. Brewster, London, New Left Books, pp. 127–86.

ANDERSON, J. and YIP, L. (1987) 'Are sex roles represented fairly in children's books? A content analysis of old and new readers', *Unicorn*, 13, 3, pp. 155–61.

ARNOLD, R. (1983) 'How to make the audience clap: Children's writing and self esteem', in ARNOLD, R. (Ed.), *Timely Voices: English Teaching in the 80's*, Melbourne, Oxford University Press, pp. 123–37.

ASHCROFT, L. (1987) 'Defusing "empowering": The what and the why', *Language Arts*, 64, 2, pp. 142–56.

ASHER, S. and GOFFMAN, J. (1973) 'Sex of teacher and student reading achievement', *Journal of Educational Psychology*, 65, pp. 168–71.

ASHER, S. and MARKELL, R. (1974) 'Sex differences in comprehension of high- and low-interest reading material', *Journal of Educational Psychology*, 66, pp. 680–87.

BALIBAR, E. and MACHEREY, P. (1981) 'On literature as an ideological form', in YOUNG, R. (Ed.), *Untying the Text: A Post-Structuralist Reader*, London, Routledge and Kegan Paul, pp. 79–100.

BATSLEER, J., DAVIES, T., O'ROURKE, R. and WEEDON, C. (1985) *Rewriting English: Cultural Politics of Gender and Class*, London, Methuen.

BRITTON, J. (1970) *Language and Learning*, Harmondsworth, Penguin.

CHRISTIAN-SMITH, L. (1988) 'Power, knowledge and curriculum: Constructing femininity in adolescent romance novels', in DE CASTELL, S., LUKE, A. and LUKE, C. (Eds), *Language, Authority and Criticism: Readings on the School Textbook*, Lewes, Falmer Press.

COWARD, R. (1986) 'Are women's novels feminist novels'?, in SHOWALTER, E. (Ed.), *The New Feminist Criticism: Essays on Women, Literature and Theory*, London, Virago, pp. 225–40.

CZAPLINSKI, S. (1976) 'Sexism in award winning picture books', in *Sexism in Children's Books*, London, Writers and Readers Publishing Cooperative, pp. 31–7.

DAVIES, T. (n.d.) 'Education, ideology and criticism', *Red Letters*, 7, pp. 4–14.

DIXON, J. (1967) *Growth through English*, London, Oxford University Press.

DUPLESSIS, R. (1985) *Writing beyond the Ending*, Bloomington, Ind., Indiana University Press.

EAGLETON, T. (1983) *Literary Theory: An Introduction*, Oxford, Basil Blackwell.

FAUSA (1983) *Trends in Contract Appointments in Universities*, Melbourne, Federation of Australian University Staff Associations.

FETTERLY, J. (1978) *The Resisting Reader*, Bloomington, Ind., Indiana University Press.

GILBERT, P. (1983) 'Down among the women: Girls as readers and writers', *English in Australia*, 64, pp. 26–9.

GILBERT, P. (1985) 'Stereotypes for the classroom: Student teachers write sexist children's stories', *Australian Journal of Reading*, 8, 1, pp. 14–20.

GILBERT, P. (1987) 'Post reader-response: The deconstructive critique', in CORCORAN, B. and EVANS, E. (Eds), *Readers, Texts and Teachers*, Montclair, N.J., Boynton/Cook Publishers.

GILBERT, P. (1988a) 'Stoning the romance: Girls as resistant readers and writers', *Curriculum Perspectives*, 8, 2, pp. 13–18.

GILBERT, P. (1988b) 'Student text as pedagogical text', in DE CASTELL, S., LUKE, A. and LUKE, C. (Eds), *Language, Authority and Criticism: Readings on the School Textbook*, Lewes, Falmer Press.

GILBERT, P. (1989) *Writing, Schooling and Deconstruction*, London, Routledge and Kegan Paul.

GILL, J. and DYER, M. (1987) 'Out of order: Rethinking the rules of classroom talk', *Curriculum Perspectives*, 7, 1, pp. 61–4.

GREENE, G. and KAHN, C. (1985) *Making a Difference: Feminist Literary Criticism*, London, Methuen.

ISER, W. (1974) *The Implied Reader*, Baltimore, Md, Johns Hopkins University Press.

KAGEN, J. (1964) 'The child's sex role classification of school objects', *Child Development*, 35, pp. 1051–6.

KRAMER, L. (Ed.) (1981) *The Oxford History of Australian Literature*, Melbourne, Oxford University Press.

MACCOBY, E. and JACKLIN, L. (1974) *The Psychology of Sex Differences*, Stanford, Calif., Stanford University Press.

MARTIN, J. (1985) *Factual Writing: Exploring and Changing the World*, Geelong, Deakin University Press.

MILLETT, K. (1977) *Sexual Politics*, London, Virago.

MITCHELL, J. (1984) *Women: The Longest Revolution*, London, Virago.

NEALE, D., GILL, N. and TISMER, W. (1970) 'Relationship between attitudes towards school subjects and school achievement', *Journal of Educational Research*, 63, pp. 232–7.

POYNTON, C. (1985) *Language and Gender: Making the Difference*, Geelong, Deakin University Press.

PROTHEROUGH, R. (1983) *Encouraging Writing*, London, Methuen Educational.

RASMUSSEN, B. (1982) 'Dealing with sexism and ethnocentrism in literature', *English in Australia*, 60, June, pp. 54–7.

ROSENBLATT, L. (1978) *The Reader, the Text, the Poem*, Carbondale, Ill., Southern Illinois University Press.

RYAN, J. (1982) 'Feminism and curriculum: A case study of ACT colleges and senior schools', *Ideals in Education*, 1, pp. 11–15.

SHOWALTER, E. (1978) *A Literature of Their Own: British Women Novelists from Bronte to Lessing*, London, Virago Press.

SPENDER, D. (1980) *Man-Made Language*, London, Routledge and Kegan Paul.

SPENDER, D. (1982) *Women of Ideas: What Men Have Done to Them*, London, Routledge and Kegan Paul.

STEIN, A. and SMITHELLS, J. (1969) 'Age and sex differences in children's sex-role standards about achievement', *Developmental Psychology*, 1, pp. 252–9.

STOCKARD, J., SCHMUCK, P., KEMPNER, K., WILLIAMS, P., EDSON, S. and SMITH, M. (1980) *Sex Equity and Education*, New York, Academic Press.

WIDDOWSON, P. *et al.* (Eds) (1982) *Re-Reading English*, London, Methuen.

Wings: A Pilot Project to Enhance Self Esteem in Girls (1983) Hobart, Education Department of Tasmania.

Chapter 10

The Power of Mathematics:
For Whom?

Sue Willis

Few people working in any field of education have not heard of the problem of girls and mathematics; yet one could argue that the problem is of recent origin. Until about two decades ago the lower participation and achievement in mathematics of girls than boys was regarded as natural and normal, almost certainly genetically determined and neither a problem for girls nor for society. While there are still those who believe it to be 'in the nature of things' that girls should be 'less mathematically inclined' than boys, on the whole the situation today is different from twenty years ago. Schools Commission Projects of National Significance are devoted to overcoming the 'problem' which, depending upon one's perspective, is either that girls do not share equally in the bounty that is to be had by those who are mathematically 'well prepared' or that girls provide relatively low 'mathematical yield' to the nation.

The past two decades have also seen a change in the popular conception of girls and mathematics. Just as it was once regarded as common sense that girls could not, should not and would not want to do advanced mathematics, now it has become almost equally accepted that girls can, should and would do advanced mathematics if only their conceptions of themselves with regard to mathematics and their prospective futures were improved. For many, this common sense has expanded to include their poor self-esteem as the location of girls' problem with mathematics.

The purpose of this volume is to add new dimensions to the work on girls, self-esteem and education, and my brief here is to discuss issues of girls' self-esteem with particular reference to the learning of mathematics. I will begin by describing something of our changing interpretation of the problem of girls and mathematics, considering next the question of girls' self-esteem and their participation and achievement in mathematics. Following this I will argue that girls' attitudes and actions with regard to mathematics may be understood by considering the reality of school mathematics, used as it is for intimidation, socialization and selection and, furthermore, that any attempt to improve educational and occupational opportunities for girls should focus upon the problems of school mathematics and the structural processes through which it is used as a critical filter between school and higher education or employment.

The 'Problem' of Girls and Mathematics

Thirty years ago it was widely and complacently accepted in Australia that girls are less mathematically able than boys. The 1960s, however, saw the development of an extensive research literature devoted to explaining girls' poor achievement in mathematics ('Why can't girls do as well as boys in mathematics?') with a particular emphasis on psychological explanations. For example, in 1964 Smith, a Scottish psychologist, suggested that sex differences in mathematics achievement could be explained by genetically determined differences in spatial ability. In the following years many alternative biological explanations of sex differences in mathematical ability (related to innate abilities and natural urges) were offered and argued (cf. Harris, 1978; McGee, 1979, regarding spatial ability, and Widdup, 1980, regarding mathematical ability). This led (both in Australia and internationally) to a classic nature/nurture debate fueled, in part, by competing psychological theories about intellectual development, but also by the re-emergence of feminism as a social force and by changing social, political and economic realities. It was during the early 1970s that the reputed lower achievement and participation of girls in mathematics became regarded as a problem for the girls themselves and for the community as a whole. While it was now held to be both right and necessary that girls be prepared for a wider range of employment opportunities than previously, it was accepted that girls on the whole did achieve less well in mathematics than boys. For many researchers, however, the question had changed from 'Why *can't* girls do as well as boys in mathematics?' to 'Why *don't* girls do as well as boys in mathematics?'

A considerable research literature on affective influences on girls' achievement in mathematics developed during the early 1970s. For primary and secondary school levels, and contrary to some common beliefs, little evidence was found to show that girls enjoyed mathematics any less than boys, and attempts to relate achievement to attitude toward the subject (liking/disliking) on the whole failed. Similarly, explanations of difference were sought in studies of 'achievement motivation' which were, in turn, related to differential societal expectations of girls and boys with regard to assertiveness, independence, competitiveness, success and so on. Gilah Leder (1980), for example, following Horner (1972), studied the 'fear of success' construct, finding it to be particularly prevalent among 'mathematically able' girls. The effect of task variables such as the context in which problems are set on the relative success of girls and boys and sex stereotyping of textbooks were also explored. That girls do not do well at mathematics remained largely unchallenged.

By the late 1970s, however, researchers were beginning to report the results of extensive studies of mathematics achievement which suggested that male superiority to females in mathematics is by no means certain. Many of the earlier studies which suggested sex differences in mathematics achievement had significant sampling problems and, in particular, in many such studies little account had been taken of the number of mathematics courses taken by the students in the samples. By the beginning of the 1980s it was clear that in many (although certainly not all) countries some differences in mathematics achievement do exist, but typically they are small, do not appear at all ability and age levels and are not consistent for all types of mathematical learning or for all mathematical topics. In particular:

1   Australian and American research tends to suggest that girls as a group outperform boys as a group in school mathematics in the primary years, although the large-scale APU (Assessment of Performance Unit) assessments in the United Kingdom and some Australian studies suggest that sex differences are task-specific, with girls excelling in some areas and boys in others (Keeves and Bourke, 1976; Clements and Wattanawaha, 1977; Rosier, 1980; Joffe and Foxman, 1986).

2   Typically, girls and boys perform equally well in lower secondary mathematics (Parker and Offer, 1987) although, where differences appear, it is likely to be in the areas of logic and numeration that girls excel and space that boys excel (Keeves and Bourke, 1976; Clements and Wattanawaha, 1977; Rosier, 1980). Whether or not gender differences occur at all and, if they do, the direction, extent and nature depend on the country (Hanna and Kuendiger, 1986) and, in Australia, on the state (Rosier, 1980; Moss, 1982).

3   During the secondary school years girls, it appears, are generally underrepresented (or are boys overrepresented?) at both extremes of the mathematics achievement spectrum, that is, from as early as 12 years of age fewer girls than boys demonstrate either special giftedness or handicap in mathematics (Eddowes, 1983). In par-

ticular, of those girls and boys in Australia completing Year 12 mathematics courses about the same proportion 'pass', but consistently more boys than girls achieve in the highest bands; that is, receive A grades or the equivalent in the highest level courses (Leder, 1980; Parker, 1984).

4   While it appears that for the higher levels of mathematics achievement there are differences in favour of males even when the extent of participation in mathematics courses is equivalent, it is less clear that these differences remain when the effect of participation in mathematics-related courses (e.g. physics) is controlled. When allowance is made for the factors of age, social class and hours of mathematics learning, sex differences in achievement often disappear (Moss, 1982).

On the evidence now available we should be able to dispose of the myth that all girls or even a large proportion of girls in Australia are performing poorly in mathematics by comparison with boys. It is now generally regarded that fewer girls than boys exhibit extreme giftedness or achieve in the very highest achievement levels in upper secondary mathematics (upper 1 per cent), but that other differences in mathematics achievement typically are exaggerated and, in any case, favour girls as often as boys.

There are those who argue for a genetic basis to girls' lower representation among the mathematically gifted (Benbow and Stanley, 1980), although the weight of the arguments lies with social/cultural explanations such as that girls and boys have different 'opportunities to learn' and that anxiety about the possible social consequences of exceptionally high attainment in mathematics may depress achievement (e.g. Leder, 1977). Regardless of the explanation offered, these differences are so limited in extent that they cannot explain the level of underrepresentation of girls in mathematics and mathematics-related occupations. The focus of attention has, therefore, moved away from girls' achievement in mathematics to their participation in mathematics. Girls, it seems, if given the choice, are more likely than boys to choose themselves out of mathematics, or at least higher levels of mathematics. As a consequence, the mathematical 'yield' (Keeves and Mason, 1980; Moss, 1982; Deckers, De Laeter and Malone, 1986) is lower for girls than for boys, and herein lies the source of the current focus of interest in the problems of girls and mathematics: 'Why *won't* girls do as well as boys in mathematics?' From the plaintive way in which this question is often asked it would appear that some believe the girls to be simply perverse, not prepared to be told what's good for them and take the (admittedly unpleasant, some would say) medicine they need; others regard the girls as compliant victims participating in their own oppression. Studies of why girls choose not to participate in mathematics, however, have so far not proven particularly illuminating.

It is perhaps only a slight oversimplification to suggest that thirty years ago there was no problem of girls and mathematics, twenty years ago the problem was that girls *couldn't* do as well as boys in mathematics, ten years ago they *didn't* do as well and now they *won't* do as well. For many who are concerned with equal opportunity, today's problem is that girls limit their career opportunities by selecting themselves out of certain mathematics courses; for others, it is the wastage of talent implied when girls, as a whole, 'underparticipate' in mathematics. In either case the solution is seen to require that more girls be encouraged to undertake more mathematics. Increasingly, two strategies are offered for producing the change in girls necessary to cause them to make 'the right choices': careers advice and self-esteem programs of one kind or other.

Self-esteem and Participation in Mathematics

How does self-esteem relate to the 'problem' of girls and mathematics? As Jane Kenway and I have argued elsewhere (1986), an inspection of much of the literature on self-esteem reveals problems of overinterpretation.

> Work on self esteem is grafted on to work on achievement, on to work on sex stereotyping, and so on. Thus, the much quoted relationship between self esteem and achievement, taken together with the stereotype that girls and women have lower self-esteem than boys and men, is used to 'explain' girls' lower academic participation and achievement and to justify self-esteem programs for girls. (p. 4)

Nowhere is this more clear than in the area of mathematics. The following 'facts':

> that girls underachieve and underparticipate in mathematics,
> that girls have lower self-esteem than boys,
> that self-esteem and achievement are correlated,
> that mathematics is stereotyped as a male domain, and
> that self-esteem, sex stereotyping and occupational aspirations are related,

are taken together as establishing low self-esteem as one cause of girls' lower productivity in mathematics and as justifying programs to raise girls' self-esteem.

Evidence relating self-esteem and achievement is, however, quite contradictory and, even where positive correlations are found, the direction of causality is unclear (e.g. Hansford and Hattie, 1982). There is limited Australian evidence to suggest that girls' self-esteem deteriorates relative to boys as they proceed through secondary schooling and that, taken overall, girls and women exhibit somewhat lower levels of self-esteem than boys and men (e.g. Connell *et al.*, 1975), but how one interprets this evidence is far from clear. In particular, as Peter Renshaw indicates (see Chapter 1), it appears an inappropriate interpretation to suggest that the majority of girls have lower self-esteem than the majority of boys; rather, it seems that small groups of girls have low self-esteem relative to most boys and girls and this acts to make the averages for girls lower than the averages for boys. Also, as has already been suggested, while differences between girls and boys in the rates of participation in mathematics are reasonably well established, differences in achievement are not. Finally, although girls' self-esteem, subject choice and career choice are considered to be related and to some considerable extent underpin Commonwealth and state initiatives in the area of self-esteem, in the case of mathematics the nature of the presumed link is unclear. Even at the simplest level one must ask whether the suggestion is that girls 'underparticipate' in mathematics because they have poor general levels of self-esteem, or because they have poor self-esteem in some particular way (perhaps relating to occupational aspirations) which influences their decision to study mathematics, or whether their poor self-esteem is focused particularly on mathematics. If the last, is this a result of particular experiences they have had with mathematics or is it their perception of mathematics as a male domain or . . . what?

Although much research has been devoted to identifying the reasons girls and women select themselves out of mathematics, the social forces influencing decisions about subject and occupational choice appear to be sufficiently complex and subtle that many decisions are made without a conscious awareness of the contributing factors. Consequently, direct evidence on the factors influencing choices is rather limited. The perception of science as a male domain is, it appears, quite strong among adults and adolescents, but this is not quite so clear for mathematics. The view that girls cannot do mathematics has faded somewhat for adolescents (Joffe and Foxman, 1984), although that *real* (that is, feminine) girls would not want to do mathematics is still quite vivid for some. Nonetheless, most recent evidence suggests that students consider mathematics as equally appropriate and necessary for both boys and girls, although as they proceed through secondary schooling girls become less convinced that mathematics is personally useful (Russell, 1984).

There is also a great deal of evidence to suggest that many people lack confidence in their ability to undertake mathematics (Cockcroft, 1982; Buxton, 1981) and, indeed, that 'panic' is not too strong a word to describe their reactions to mathematics. Anecdotal evidence would have it that this is more prevalent among girls and women than boys and men, and there is a certain common sense in the view that this lack of confidence is a major reason why, relative to boys, few girls choose to study mathematics beyond the minimum levels. Whether mathematics does panic more women than men, or whether they simply are more prepared to admit it, is not clear. Evidence is difficult to find. We have considerable evidence (see, for example, Joffe and Foxman, 1986) that girls express greater uncertainty about their mathematical performance than equivalently achieving boys. The following comment by a first year university student is not at all unusual: 'I always sat at the back of the class and prayed that I wouldn't be asked a question. There's a dim recollection of some pain associated with being asked a question in mathematics, but it's too deep to come to mind.'

Furthermore, boys overrate their performance in mathematics in relation to written test results, while girls underrate their performance. The implication seems to be that girls and women are more anxious about their mathematical capabilities than boys and men. These same statements, however, can be and are made about academic performance generally (secondary students' English essays, university students' psychology exams) and about many spheres of activity — boys and men overestimate and girls and women underestimate their abilities. Even leaving aside the question of why underestimating one's abilities should be regarded as more of a problem than overestimating them, the fact remains that girls are not underrepresented in secondary education or undergraduate education in Australia; presumably underestimating one's capabilities does not necessarily imply non-participation. Thus it seems that we must look elsewhere for explanations of girls' participation levels in mathematics.

Gilah Leder (1977) studied the relationship between results on a mathematics test and long-term occupational aspirations of Victorian boys and girls in Years 10 and 11 (15 and 16 years of age). She found that aspirations and mathematics achievement were related for boys and Year 10 girls, but not for Year 11 girls. Among the boys and younger girls, those who scored well on the test were more likely to aim for male dominated, high status jobs than those who scored low. However, this was not so for the older girls. Furthermore, there was strong evidence that 'motive to avoid success' was strongest in those girls who aimed for male dominated, high status occupations, 'unusual' for woman. Leder commented that it is at the end of Year 10 that decisions with respect to future courses need to be made.

> An increasing realization that attainment of an ambitious goal may be a mixed blessing and may have negative personal consequences may well lead to a lowering of personal goals. Alternatively, the growing anxiety about the consequences of attaining an ambitious goal may act as an impediment on performance.... By contrast, those girls who have decided to opt for a more traditional female career, irrespective of their mathematics performance, no longer seem subject to such conflict. (pp. 186–7)

The students in Leder's study were taking or planning to take upper secondary non-'terminal' mathematics courses, which immediately places them in a relatively select group. What of the broad range of girls? Many are looking to sex stereotyping of occupational aspirations for explanations of girls choosing themselves out of the study of mathematics. It appears likely that rather than limited career choice being a consequence of limited participation in mathematics, just the reverse is true. That is, girls perceive for themselves limited career paths and consequently choose themselves out of mathematics. Many girls also believe that there is a conflict for women between family life and careers. Since in many cases girls are making choices in periods of their lives when they are most likely to be influenced by peer group and pop culture, and by romantic thoughts of boyfriends, marriage and babies, their aspirations are less likely to be directed at careers which do not fit into the feminine stereotype. In England, however, West Indian girls achieve more highly in mathematics than both English boys and West Indian boys at 16+ examinations (Driver, 1980). West Indian women in the UK must often be the family provider, and education for women is regarded as the most likely avenue for the better jobs. These girls regard having a good job as an important part of being a good wife and mother. Evidence of this kind is also available about other cultural groups (for example, see Brandon, 1985, regarding achievement in Hawaii) and adds weight to the suggestion that girls may participate and achieve in mathematics in ways that reflect their perception of the future.

Given the evidence regarding girls' occupational choices, there is some appeal in programs which purport to help girls deal with the conflicts which confront them in making decisions of this kind, and certainly we would all wish that girls (and children generally) would have positive feelings about themselves. Nonetheless, many such programs focus almost completely upon the individual and treat the raising of girls' self-esteem as an isolated problem. In at least three ways this denies the realities of schooling and employment for girls. First, girls are seen as both the source of the problem, in that it is their attitudes which lead them to 'fail' and make 'wrong' choices, and the appropriate location for the solution, in that changing girls is regarded as the appropriate mechanism for changing their participation and achievement in certain school subjects and potentially, therefore, in job entry. Often it fails to confront in any serious way the reality that personal success can be a mixed blessing for girls, and that girls are being asked to shoulder all the responsibility for change. Second, it seems to imply that feeling better about ourselves in school can lead us all to move forward to high status careers, that we can all maximize achievement and self-interest without conflict (a 'promise of happiness' for all). Finally, it accepts, almost without challenge, the status quo in terms of the mathematics curriculum and the institutional structures through which mathematics is used as a sieve.

It is to the realities of school mathematics that we must look for a significant explanation of girls' levels of achievement and participation, and it is on the mathematics curriculum and its role as a critical filter that we should focus our efforts for change.

Changing the Realities of School Mathematics

Mathematics is generally held in high esteem in our society, and this is reflected by the central position it holds in the school curriculum. William Sawyer, in 1948, suggested that 'the fact is nobody knows why mathematics is taught in schools. Teaching mathematics is a custom, like shaking hands. We have got used to it. People cannot imagine schools without the arithmetic lesson.' While agreeing with Sawyer in part, probably many people would argue that mathematics is highly regarded because it is useful. And certainly it is useful. But the ways in which mathematics can be truly useful — as a powerful tool for learning, for dealing with and making sense of our experiences — seem hardly to be the focus of much that is school (or for that matter, tertiary) mathematics. Given the time devoted to it, most people's experience of mathematics provides them with scant preparation for dealing with those aspects of their lives upon which mathematics impinges, or for truly understanding an increasingly technological society. Instead, in our society school mathematics is put to three particularly important uses — socialization, intimidation and selection — and these uses are the reason why so many children, a majority of whom are girls, choose not to engage.

Socialization and School Mathematics

School mathematics (which is most people's experience of mathematics as a body of knowledge) was traditionally, and still is, used to provide a particularly narrow form of socialization: following directions, completing exercises rotely and automatically, doing one's own work, neatness, punctuality and so on. The impact of this use of school mathematics on attempts to change the curriculum is considerable.

Let us consider, for a moment, the area of computational skills. A major part of the primary mathematics curriculum is devoted to the development of computational skills of a traditional kind — which means standardized and written. Notwithstanding the claims of the popular press, a traditionally high level of accuracy, speed and even neatness is the objective; and this despite the fact that it is now well established that those who are mathematically effective in daily life seldom make use of the standard written methods which are taught in the classroom but either adapt them in a personal way or make use of methods which are highly idiosyncratic to themselves and to the task (e.g. Cockcroft, 1982). Furthermore, mechanical performance skills are the ones that will be least required in the future. There are, even now, very few circumstances (outside examination settings) in which speed in formal written calculation is a criterion for success, and with respect to accuracy the real skill is in making informed decisions about how accurate you need to be and in choosing reliable, not necessarily standard, methods. Yet the standard written procedures are drilled over an enormous period of time at the expense of developing other, I would say more important, mathematical and non-mathematical concepts and skills. Why is this? Are they 'good for you'? Do they 'exercise the mind'? I think not, but they are good for authority; they are easy to control; they 'teach' conformity.

There is an apparent dilemma in this. A great deal of evidence has accumulated over the years to suggest that girls are very successful at computational mathematics, and a reduction in its emphasis in the primary curriculum could be regarded as shifting the mathematics curriculum in directions which will make it less accessible to girls. The alternative argument, however, is that it is just because girls become so good at computational mathematics that they experience some difficulties with higher level mathematics. Indeed, it has been suggested that those who become successful in mathematics and mathematics-based careers are those who resisted school mathematics — who have, in essence, taught themselves mathematics. The 'successful' student must adopt the framework of the discipline — the ways of seeing and saying — yet even at the upper levels of the secondary school these are quite in opposition to the narrow socialization of most school mathematics. The implication is that many who have been well socialized to mathematics in the primary school may suffer the consequences as they attempt to move on to more sophisticated mathematics.

> Many girls achieve very strong schema for the algorithm domin-ated mathematics of the top primary school. When the demands of mathematical learning change in the secondary school the early schema are inflexible and make the necessary accommodation difficult. Boys tend to be less effective at upper junior school algorithmic mathematics and thus develop less inflexible schema. (Woodrow, 1984, p. 7)

Paradoxically, it seems that girls' very success at learning primary mathematics is turned against them. As Walkerdine (1983) has argued, female success turns out to be no success at all, girls' early learning is not regarded as *real* learning because they've learned 'in the wrong way, ... instead of thinking properly, girls simply work hard' (p. 84). Walden and Walkerdine (1986) suggest that contradictions between the practice of school mathematics and the discipline of mathematics highlight discon-tinuities in the ways that girls' femininity is defined, described and develops. The social stereotyping of girls' success in mathematics as due to hard work and rule following can turn into caring and protective behaviour on the part of teachers which becomes a self-fulfilling prophe-cy, and girls learn to believe that their success is of a particular and less worthy kind. Girls' poorer performance and increasing anxiety as they proceed through school, Walden and Walkerdine argue, is produced by these practices.

Earlier it was suggested that differences in mathematics achievement in favour of boys are often exaggerated. Where they appear at all, it is likely to be at the highest level of mathematics and the differences often are, in practical terms, very small. Nonetheless, it is arguable that such small differences in achievement as do appear and the rather more signi-ficant differences in participation can be explained in terms of the anxiety induced by the subtle gender-differentiated forms of socialization that take place in many mathematics classrooms. Indeed, there is quite exten-sive anecdotal evidence that some intelligent and successful women experience strong feelings of guilt about the regard in which they are held because they *know* that really they are not able to do mathematics.

> You see I always think people think too well of me and it is important to me that they shouldn't like me for things that I believe I do not possess ..., I have to go out of my way to prove that while I'm quite intelligent, I'm not very intelligent ... it is important that they know I can't add up. (quoted in Buxton, 1981, p. 134)

Buxton (1981) has argued that moral judgments are often made about students' successes and failures with mathematics.

> It happens, of course, not only in maths; but the status of the subject, the clarity of the correctness or incorrectness in answers, and the terms 'right' and 'wrong' with their unfortunate moral connotations, all combine to make the situation in maths more stressful than elsewhere. So failure to get the right answers is somehow seen as morally wrong. (p. 118)

Our inherited and unexamined philosophical dogma is that mathematical truth should possess absolute certainty. Mathematics is about truth — mathematics is not democratic (a claim, as Joseph Agassi (1982) points out, which is used to justify inept, elitist mathematics education), and yet, as the work of Lakatos (1976) and others has shown, mathematical truth, like any other, is both fallible and corrigible (see Davies and Hersh, 1983). Mathematics curricula often convey an entirely false sense of the absoluteness of mathematics: one right answer, true in all possible worlds, dissociated from experience and independent of culture. In several ways this presentation of mathematics may alienate more girls than boys.

First, Buxton suggests that differential socialization of boys and girls with respect to obedience and authority may lead more girls than boys to become intimidated by the 'authority' of mathematics. As a consequence they may be more powerfully influenced by the moral overtones of perceived lack of success in mathematics. Second, teaching strategies informed by such views of mathematics often are based on rote memorization which may be even less appropriate for girls than for boys. There is, for instance, some evidence that girls feel considerably more unhappy than boys when forced to do mathematics which they do not understand (Carss, 1980). Such feelings of unhappiness and stress could discourage even mathematically successful girls from studying the subject. Finally, it may be that for more girls than boys, the conception of mathematics as dissociated from experience inhibits their involvement. It appears that girls, more often than boys, prefer more context-bounded tasks and are less likely to accept the version of mathematics as disembedded thought. Brown (1984) has argued that there is not just one mathematics, that 'what has constituted legitimate thinking in the field has changed considerably over time' (pp. 13–14) and it is a 'male' interpretation of mathematics that produces a curriculum which is '"de-peopled" in that contexts and concepts are for the most part presented ahistorically and unproblematically' (p. 12). Male defined mathematics, like male defined morality, is about absolutes, about 'taken for granted' reality upon which students are to operate, about similarities rather than differences, about problem solving rather than problem posing. A mathematics influenced by female perspectives might, he argues, emphasize context-boundedness, differences between situations and problems and people connectedness.

Before returning to the question of an alternative mathematics curriculum, in the following section I will focus on the use of school mathematics as a selection device. The nature of the school mathematics curriculum and selection processes are not unrelated, since it is not mathematics, but a particular kind of mathematics, which constitutes the selection device, and institutions of higher education and employers place quite rigid constraints on curriculum developments and methods of assessment in mathematics (Bannister, 1987).

Selection and School Mathematics

The use of mathematics for selection is no surprise to even quite young school children, as the following extract from a conversation with a group of Year 8 (about 13 years of age) students indicates.

> *Int*: Do you think you'll use maths in your later life?
> *G1*: What? Do you mean just like when you've got a job or something like that?
> *Int*: Anywhere in your later life.
> [All students indicate in the affirmative simultaneously.]
> *Int*: What do you think you'll use it for?
> *B1*: Anything, anything and everything.
> *Int*: OK Joanne.
> *G2*: No, I don't think I'll use it because I'll have a calculator. [The other students laugh.] Or I'll ask someone else. No,

because we don't have to know the square root of things and everything else for getting a job — because someone won't walk in and say, 'What's the square root of this?'

B2: It just goes on your mark. It's your marks really that they go on when you're going for a job. Say if you want to be a policeman or something, right, you don't need to know all about history and Einstein and everything, I don't think.

Int: Do you need maths?

B1: Yeah. Yeah. But . . . .

G1: You need basic maths — but you don't really need to know this. ['This' is algebra.]

Int: What's basic maths?

G1: You know — adding fractions and timesing and everything. Adding and subtracting. Because that's all really you meet up with. The rest you can do on the calculator.

Int: Saul. Do you reckon you'll need this sort of maths?

B3: You only do it because they use it to see if you understand and if your brain knows how to do it.

Int: And do you think it's important that your brain knows how to do it? Will you need to know how to do it for your later life?

B3: Yeah, you need to know how to do it. That's why we do it. To make sure we know how to do it. [The other students laugh.]

Int: That sounds great. But where in your later life, do you need to do pyramids?

B3: Oh they just use it to see how fast you can work out things and that, how you catch on, and you understand them.

Int: Oh, how you catch on?

B3: And you can work them out.

G2: They just want to see if you don't understand it. (Holland, 1987)

These Year 8 students regard mathematics as a sieve: 'they just use it to see how fast you can work out things . . . how you catch on, and you understand them', rather than a necessary prerequisite, and the evidence is that they are not far wrong. Helen Bannister (1987) cites Clarice Ballendon as arguing that 'the preparatory and selective functions of tertiary course preparation are often confused' (p. 19). Mathematical prerequisites are rarely explicitly justified in terms of the concepts to be studied, even though mathematics often acts as the critical filter between school and higher education. Similar mechanisms often apply to job entry. Recently, a psychologist employed by a state prisons department asked me to assist him to check whether the existing mathematics test for applicant prison officers was consistent with the Year 10 mathematics curriculum. Since the test used only imperial units, I could have answered the question fairly quickly. Instead, I suggested that, rather than preparing a new set of textbook exercises based on the school curriculum, the prisons department identify the kinds of problems and situations (mathematical or otherwise) a prison officer would be likely to confront and design their battery of tests around those. Not too surprisingly, my suggestion met considerable resistance. My off-hand comment that, since applicant prison officers must be several years removed from Year 10, there would always be a time lag in using the school curriculum as a basis for selection was received somewhat more warmly than my argument that entrance tests should relate to the nature of the future position. I was told, essentially, that what I suggested was neither necessary (it does take more resources to do it properly) nor desirable. 'We just use the maths test to pick the most intelligent people. You do think [rather accusingly] that prison officers should be intelligent, and more intelligent ones must be better than less intelligent ones.'

We are told that mathematics is powerful, and that learning mathematics will give us power. In this culture, it is true, learning a lot of mathematics can give you power — but for many people it is not personal power — their experience of learning mathematics is that it makes them feel quite powerless. For them, the power resides not in the mathematics but in the myth of mathematics — in the meritocratic prestige of mathematics as an intellectual discipline.

> And on the eighth day God created mathematics. He took stainless steel, and he rolled it out thin, and he made it into a fence forty cubits high, and infinite cubits long. And on this fence, in fair capitals, he did print rules, theorems, axioms and pointed reminders. 'Invert and multiply.' 'The square on the hypotenuse is three decibels louder than one hand clapping.' 'Always do that's in the parentheses first.' And when he was finished, he said 'On one side of this fence will reside those who are good at math. And on the other will remain those who are bad at math, and woe unto them, for they shall weep and gnash their teeth.'

> Math does make me think of a stainless steel wall — hard, cold, smooth, offering no handhold, all it does is glint back at me. Edge up to it, put your nose against it, it doesn't give anything back, you can't put a dent in it, it doesn't take your shape, it

doesn't have any smell, all it does is make your nose cold. I like the shine of it — it does look smart, intelligent in an icy way. But I resent its cold impenetrability, its supercilious glare. (woman student quoted in Buerk, 1982, p. 19)

The situation that many people feel powerless in the presence of mathematical ideas has been systematically reinforced by our culture, which sees mathematics as accessible to a talented few. As Easley and Easley (1982) argue, such elitist attitudes, with the acute inequities of mathematics learning, have become part of what separates and represses many oppressed groups, including women, working-class people and racial minorities. Over recent centuries mathematics has been seen as the domain of European middle-class males who 'naturally' have defined mathematics in their own light and insisted that their particular conception of mathematics as 'disembedded thought' was the only proper conception (Joseph, 1987). Furthermore, mathematics and mathematics-related disciplines and occupations are regarded as more prestigious than those which involve little mathematics. Our society does not choose to accept mathematics as the birthright of all — mathematics is the 'silver spoon' of a fortunate few. Mathematics is not used as a selection device because it is held in high esteem but rather the reverse. It is powerful as a selection device because it plays the role of now widely discredited IQ tests, yet without receiving the same criticism (after all, mathematics is generally regarded as culture free). That it serves the interests of certain groups to keep mathematics as the preserve of the 'few' has been amply demonstrated by studies of tertiary admissions processes in Australia (Bannister, 1987).

As suggested earlier, mathematics is also used as part of selection strategies for many forms of employment. Yet we should question efforts to convince girls into mathematics on the basis of improved job prospects on at least two grounds. First, convincing more girls into mathematics does not create employment; all it can do at best is to redistribute the available jobs. It seems unlikely that increasing girls' mathematical 'yield' will reduce the institutionalized sexism involved in job entry and progress. Second, there is reason to doubt the assumption that future job growth will be in areas requiring higher levels of mathematics. Consider the following extracts from the *Quality of Education Review Committee Report* (QERC, 1985).

For the future the types of employment most likely to grow appear to be those in installation, maintenance and repair, information processing, administration, clerical and other office

activities, and personal services, both public and private. They are
... not clearly associated with particular formal educational qualifications. At the same time they tend to involve high degrees of
client contact and interpersonal skills. (p. 57)

A much greater proportion of young Australians will have to
complete full secondary school and receive a broad general education as a foundation on which to build the occupational skills
necessary to operate in a labour market in a state of flux and in
which the capacity to deal with people will become a growing
requirement. (pp. 59–60)

According to the QERC report, then, future jobs are likely to require
those very interpersonal skills at which girls and women often are regarded as excelling. This, together with their general high level of educational success, should prepare them well for the areas in which future jobs
are likely to lie.

Of course, girls (and others) who select themselves out of school
mathematics *do* restrict their access to many tertiary courses and occupations whose entrance requirements include certain levels of mathematics.
Many feminists wish to use self-esteem programs, careers advice and
various other strategies to assist more girls to survive the filtering process, but they leave unchallenged the structures which are in place explicitly to exclude a rather large proportion of the population. We are
deluding ourselves if we believe that the underparticipation of girls in
mathematics and in a wide range of 'male' occupations can be overcome
by career counselling and self-esteem programs. While these may well
have value in their own right, changing girls is insufficient to change the
system. As Lyn Yates (1985) has asked, what is a 'friendly' act for girls in
this period of unemployment and rapid change?

A truly 'friendly' act for girls would be to place the problem of girls
and mathematics where it belongs — with the selection and exclusion
structures which underpin the education system. It seems both unrealistic
and insensitive to the realities of many girls' lives to expect exhortations
about distant futures to influence them, and in any case, given the nature
of much that is offered in school mathematics, many girls must consider
that we are asking them to sacrifice their present to their future; that they
substitute subjects they value and enjoy for subjects they value and enjoy
less, and replace their own set of values in terms of the relevance of the
curriculum to their lives with ours.

Nonetheless, even given this and having argued that convincing girls
to do mathematics because of hypothetical job prospects seems problema-

tical, I would now like to suggest that, indeed, girls (and educationally disadvantaged groups generally) *should* have increased access to mathematics. For those who do not continue in school beyond the school leaving age, the problems are perhaps more urgent because mathematics does have another powerful role in our community related to its roles of selection and socialization. That is, mathematics is widely used to intimidate those whose access to it is limited. In an excellent paper entitled 'Mathematics as Propaganda' Neal Koblitz (1981) has described many examples, often taken from 'respectable' publications, of the use of mathematics in highly ambiguous ways to produce mystification and an impression of precision and profundity. Arguments that would be ridiculed if explained in everyday language are accepted when presented 'mathematically'; they are then regarded as scientific because they involve 'hard' data. Invoking numbers, statistics and formula can be more persuasive than well-known authorities, and in the presence of mathematics many of us suspend our disbelief. For example, why don't more of us argue about the mathematically defined tertiary admissions strategies that so many of us distrust? Perhaps we are intimidated by the apparent authority and sureness of the mathematics; after all, 'numbers don't lie.'

Many adults are intimidated by mathematics, they do feel inadequate in its presence and there is some evidence that these people are disproportionately women. For this reason, girls and women (and other disadvantaged groups) must gain access to the kind of mathematics that enables them to resist such attempts to intimidate. Encouraging more girls (and working-class children generally) to do more mathematics is necessary but not sufficient. We must ensure that the mathematics they do is truly empowering. As Brown (1984) has suggested, 'What may be called for is an ever more intellectually demanding curriculum, but one in which mathematics is embedded in a web of concerns that are more "real world" oriented than any of us have begun to imagine' (p. 14). All students need the kind of mathematics which will assist them to participate fully but critically in the processes which determine how we all live. The task is to produce such a mathematics, not by providing an alternative curriculum for girls with all the attendant problems of marginalization and possibly even alienation, but by challenging and changing existing mathematics and some of the uses to which it is put.

Conclusion

We would all regard as desirable that girls experience education, and in particular mathematics education, in ways that increase their sense of confidence and competence. Programs aimed at improving self-esteem generally or self-esteem with regard to mathematics specifically, in isolation from considerations of the curriculum or credentialing structures are, however, not only limited but potentially damaging in that they encourage a focus on individual problems rather than social problems. In the case of mathematics, the implicit assumption is that individual girls are the problem. We ask of them that they should become 'free' by giving up the forms of school knowledge which they value and enjoy for forms which they value or enjoy for less. Currently, the majority of boys and girls do not gain intrinsic rewards from continued participation in mathematics; those rewards which are available are extrinsic through credentials and prospective careers. It seems that the influence of these extrinsic rewards is, for whatever reasons, less powerful on girls than boys, and we define this as a 'problem'. Certainly, girls and women should have access to the same rewards and satisfaction as boys and men, but the preferred route should provide, for all students, a different experience of mathematics, that is the intrinsic rewards that an intellectually demanding and culturally rich mathematics curriculum could provide.

References

AGASSI, J. (1982) 'Mathematics education as training for freedom', *For the Learning of Mathematics, 2*, 3, pp. 28–32.

BANNISTER, H. (1987) *Gender and Tertiary Selection: Research Paper No. 2*, Melbourne, Ministry of Education, Participation and Equity Program.

BENBOW, C. and STANLEY, J. (1980) 'Sex differences in mathematical ability: Fact or artifact'? *Science*, 210, pp. 1262–4.

BRANDON, P. *et al.* (1985) 'The superiority of girls over boys in mathematics achievement in Hawaii', Paper presented at the Annual Meeting of the American Educational Research Association, Chicago.

BROWN, S. (1984) 'The logic of problem generation: From morality and solving to deposing and rebellion', *For the Learning of Mathematics*, 4, 1, pp. 9–20.

BUERK, D. (1982) 'Experience with some able women who avoid mathematics', *For the Learning of Mathematics*, 2, 3, pp. 28–32.

BUXTON, L. (1981) *Do You Panic about Maths?* London, Heinemann Educational Books.

CARSS, M. (1980) 'Girls, mathematics and language: Some observations from classrooms', *Improving Maths for Girls*, Report of a conference held at Raywood Inservice Centre, Adelaide, Education Research and Development Committee, May/June.

CLEMENTS, M. and WATTANAWAHA, N. (1977) 'Sex and age — within-grade differences in mathematical achievement of Victorian children', in CLEMENTS, M. and FOYSTER, J. (Eds), *Research in Mathematics Education in Australia: Volume 2*, Mathematics Education Research Group of Australasia (MERGA), Melbourne, Monash University.

COCKCROFT, W. (1982) *Mathematics Counts*, London, HMSO.

CONNELL, W.F., STROOBANT, R.E., SINCLAIR, K.E., CONNELL, R.W. and ROGERS, K.W. (1975) *12 to 20: Studies of City Youth*, Sydney, Hicks Smith and Sons.

DAVIS, P. and HERSH, R. (1983) *The Mathematical Experience*, Harmondsworth, Penguin.

DEKKERS, J., DE LAETER, J. and MALONE, J. (1986) *Upper Secondary School Science and Mathematics Enrolment Patterns in Australia, 1970–1985*, Bentley, WA, Curtin University of Technology.

DRIVER, G. (1980) 'How West Indians do better at school (especially the girls)', *New Society*, 51, 902, pp. 111–14.

EASLEY, J. and EASLEY, E. (1982) *Math Can Be Natural: Kitamaeno Priorities Introduced to American Teachers*, Urbana, Ill., University of Illinois at Urbana Champaign, Committee on Culture and Cognition.

EDDOWES, M. (1983) *Humble Pi: The Mathematics Education of Girls*, York, Longman for Schools Council.

HANNA, G. and KUENDIGER, E. (1986) *Differences in Mathematical Achievement Levels and in Attitudes for Girls and Boys in Twenty Countries*, Toronto, Ontario Institute for Studies in Education.

HANSFORD, B.C. and HATTIE, J.A. (1982) 'The relationship between self and achievement/performance measures', *Review of Educational Research*, 52, 1, pp. 123–42.

HARRIS, L. (1978) 'Sex differences in spatial ability: Possible environmental, genetic and neurological factors', in KINSBOURNE, M. (Ed.), *Asymmetrical Function of the Brain*, New York, Cambridge University Press.

HOLLAND, P. (1987) *Formalization in Children's Initial Learning of Algebra*, MEd Dissertation, Murdoch University, Perth.

HORNER, M. (1972) 'Towards an understanding of achievement-related conflicts in women', *Journal of Social Issues*, 28, pp. 157–75.

JOFFE, L. and FOXMAN, D. (1984) 'Assessing mathematics: Sex attitudes and sex differences', *Mathematics in Schools,* September, pp. 22–6.

JOSEPH, G.C. (1987) 'Foundations of eurocentism in mathematics', *Race and Class*, 27, 3, pp. 1–12.

KEEVES, J. and BOURKE, S. (1976) *Australian Studies in School Performance, Volume 1*, Melbourne, Education Research and Development Committee, Australian Government Publishing Service.

KEEVES, J. and MASON J. (1980) 'Sex differences in attitudes towards achievement in and participation in mathematics in school', *Improving Maths for Girls*, Report of a Conference Held at Raywood Inservice Centre, Adelaide, Education Research and Development Committee, May/June.

KENWAY, J. and WILLIS, S. (1986) 'Girls, self esteem and education: From the personal to the political and from the universal to the specific', Paper presented at the Australian Association for Research in Education Annual Conference, Melbourne.

KOBLITZ, N. (1981) 'Mathematics as propaganda', in STEEN, LYN A. (Ed.), *Mathematics To-morrow*, New York, Springer-Verlag, pp. 111–20.

LAKATOS, I. (1976) *Proofs and Refutations: The Logic of Mathematical Discovery*, Cambridge, Cambridge University Press.

LEDER, G. (1977) 'Mathematics performance and future occupations: Are they related'? *Research in Mathematics Education in Australia*, 1, pp. 179–88.

LEDER, G. (1980) 'Bright girls, mathematics and fear of success', *Educational Studies in Mathematics*, 11, 4, pp. 411–22.

McGEE, M. (1979) 'Human spatial abilities: Psychometric studies and environmental, genetic, hormonal and neurological studies', *Psychological Bulletin*, 86, 5, pp. 889–918.

MOSS, J. (1982) *Towards Equality: Progress by Girls in Mathematics in Australian Secondary Schools*, ACER Occasional Papers No. 16, Hawthorn, Vic.

PARKER, L. (1984) 'Sex differences in mathematics trends in participation and achievement 1976–1983', Paper presented to the Annual Conference of the Australian Association for Research in Education, Perth.

PARKER, L. and OFFER, J. (1987) 'Girls, boys and lower secondary school achievement: The shifting scene 1972–1986', *Unicorn*, 13, 3, pp. 148–54.

QUALITY OF EDUCATION IN AUSTRALIA REVIEW COMMITTEE (1985) *Report*, Canberra, Australian Government Publishing Service.

ROSIER, M. (1980) *Changes in Secondary School Mathematics in Australia: 1964–1978*, Hawthorn, Vic., Australian Council of Educational Research.

RUSSELL, S. (1984) 'A captive audience?' *Mathematics in School*, 134, 1, 31–4.

SMITH, I.M. (1964) *Spatial Ability: Its Educational and Social Significance*, San Diego, Calif., Robert P. Knapp.

WALDEN, R. and WALKERDINE, D. (1986) 'Characteristics, views and relationships in the classroom', in BURTON, L. (Ed.), *Girls into Maths Can Go,* London, Holt, Rinehart and Winston.

WALKERDINE, V. (1983) 'It's only natural: Rethinking child-centred pedagogy', in WOLPE, A. and DONALD, J. (Eds), *Is There Anyone Here from Education?* London, Pluto Press.

WIDDUP, D (1980) 'Review of research on sex differences in mathematics', *Improving Maths for Girls*, Report of a Conference Held at Raywood Inservice Centre, Adelaide, Education Research and Development Committee, May/June.

WOODROW, D. (1984) 'Cultural impacts on children learning mathematics', *Mathematics in Schools*, 13, 5, pp. 5–7.

YATES, L. (1985) 'Is "girl friendly schooling" really what girls need'? in WHYTE, J., DUM, R., KANT, L. and CRUICKSHANK, M. (Eds), *Girl Friendly Schooling*, London, Methuen.

Chapter 11

Improving Self-esteem:
A Whole School Approach

Pam Jonas

Critics of the girls and self-esteem literature argue that it often tends to 'blame the victim', treating girls as if their low self-esteem is their fault and offering them compensatory 'remedial' programs (see Kenway and Willis, 1986). This chapter offers a short case history of an approach to school reform in the Australian state of Victoria which, in part, is informed by the self-esteem literature but which includes no hint of this 'victim' or 'compensatory' mentality. In this case girls' self-esteem is recognized and confronted as a social problem, as a school administrative and structural problem and as a curriculum problem. The value of conceiving of the self-esteem issue in this way will be demonstrated, as will some of the many difficulties and dilemmas which such an approach involves.

The School

Malvern Girls' High School is a small school with an enrolment of 200 students in a suburb of the city of Melbourne. It is unzoned and students come from many other suburbs to attend. The school does not, therefore, have a strong 'local' community core, in fact, many students and parents have little contact with the school outside school hours. The students represent a variety of ethnic groups, the predominant one being Greek, but the Cambodian and Vietnamese population is growing. A significant proportion of the students receive some form of welfare maintenance, and single parent families are not uncommon. Most students are of the working class and a number of the parents are unemployed. Malvern is classed as a 'disadvantaged school' and as such is in receipt of quite significant Commonwealth funding from the programs which, over the years, have been designed to offer extra support to such schools. The school has also been involved in a number of educational initiatives which have occurred at the state level, the most pertinent for our purposes here being its adoption of the Schools Year Twelve and Tertiary Entrance Certificate (STC) — VCAB Approved Study Structure V, which I will explain shortly.

Currently, the learning process at the school includes a broad general education for Years 7 to 11, with an underlying emphasis on improving students' self-image and self-confidence, and seeks to develop the students as informed participants in society. Promotion from Years 7 to 11 is automatic. Students' entry into Year 12 depends upon their degree of subject competency, occurs after interviews and counselling, and is assisted through early orientation programs. Their assessment at all levels is based on demonstration of improvement in subject areas, and is collaborative, non-competitive and descriptive.

The school staff defines curriculum as the sum of all planned and unplanned experiences offered by the school. It includes not only what is taught and approaches to teaching and learning, but also the way the school is organized. Notwithstanding difficulties associated with being an unzoned school, attempts have been made to involve the local community and parents in developing the curriculum. Such participation in the school and in the development of the curriculum has been encouraged through the Commonwealth programs in which the school is involved, the school newspaper, the school council, and public meetings called to discuss curriculum changes in the school. In an attempt to encourage constructive debate on its policies and operations the school is 'open house' to parents and other visitors.

These features of the education which we offer to our students are the result of major curriculum change. This has arisen from the staff's and administration's energetic commitment over the last decade or so to providing the students with high quality education tailored to their particular needs. The concept of 'educational needs' is notoriously difficult to pin down in theory, let alone in practice. Yet, of necessity, the question, 'What are the particular needs of our particular students?' plagued us from the beginning of our attempts to rethink our school's offerings. Indeed, this question continues to plague us as the present state government's policies threaten to jeopardize those very programs which we believe best serve our students' needs.

School Reform: A Democratic Approach

From our early attempts to assess the needs of our students and from the conclusions which we reached in collaboration with students, parents and interested community members it became painfully obvious that the needs which we did identify were not being adequately served by the curriculum at the school. One of the needs which featured often and prominently was that of developing in the girls self-confidence, motivation for learning and greater self-esteem. Parents, students and staff alike saw strong self-esteem as fundamental to the development of each girl's full potential.

The initial task which we set ourselves was to make a positive attempt to address students' needs, particularly that of self-esteem, by investigating and adopting models or strategies which would make these needs an integral part of school policy, decision-making structures and school curriculum. We were concerned not to marginalize the idea of self-esteem by piecemeal attempts to 'teach' it, and recognized that we needed to develop a strategy for enhancing and encouraging self-esteem through both the learning process and the organizational structure of the school.

Prior to 1981 the school lacked any forum in which educational ideas could be properly talked through. Single curriculum days were certainly inadequate. However, in 1981 we introduced the school's Annual Curriculum Conference and this has remained the single most important forum for initiating change and for developing school-based curriculum. From the outset the residential conference included staff, parents and students. It allowed us to achieve a far more coordinated approach to evaluating the experiences which we offered our students. Initially, it also helped to equip the staff with the range of ideas and skills needed to address the needs which we had identified. As teachers, it was also fundamental that we develop the knowledge and skills which would enable us to work effectively and cooperatively on whole issues. In fact, teacher development was considered so central that the first conference was devoted entirely to it.

Since 1981 school-based curriculum development via the conference and follow-up activities has enabled us to explore a range of educational issues and to effect substantial changes in the realms of curriculum/teaching practice, students' non-academic development, professional/personal performance, administration/organization, and external relations. Broadly, the school's curriculum has become student-centred and now attempts to deal with much more than the academic needs of students.

A particular breakthrough in our attempts to tackle the problem of self-esteem, among others, came with our close examination of the senior school. The hard facts were that, although on the whole students in Year 12 tried hard, they were largely unsuccessful with the Group One HSC

(Higher School Certificate) subjects which we taught. Group One subjects are considered the most academic subjects offered at Year 12 and provide the most direct entry to post-school tertiary study. Due to the nature of the curriculum from Years 7 to 11, students were not 'schooled' in their junior/middle years to cope with the pressures of Year 12 (the final school year), especially those associated with external examinations. Students could not understand why they were successful from Years 7 to 11 and then performed badly at HSC level. Teachers felt frustrated with a teaching process which they believed inhibited their students' learning by forcing them to conform to an imposed course outline. In addition, the Group One subjects were designed primarily for university entrance, and the majority of our students did not aspire to this type of tertiary education. Staff were concerned about their capacity to enhance students' self-esteem under the existing Group One system when the assessment process itself presumed failure on the part of a significant proportion of them. While acknowledging the need to retain a twelfth year of study, the staff agreed to look for an alternative which would suit students with differing ability levels and varied post-school intentions, and that was more sympathetic to developing their non-academic needs.

Of all the possible Higher School Certificate options offered under the umbrella of the Victorian Institute of Secondary Education (now known as the Victorian Curriculum and Assessment Board, VCAB), the Schools Years Twelve and Tertiary Entrance Certificate (STC) Approved Study Structure course seemed to be the most compatible with our developing philosophy. The features of the course which appeared likely to enhance students' self-esteem centred on a negotiated or collaborative learning process, where students are actively involved in subject/course design and where they are expected to take responsibility for their own learning. Course development is school-based and assessment is collaborative, non-competitive and descriptive. More specifically, the STC course had, among others, the following stated intentions.

To promote each student's learning and intellectual growth, taking into account the needs of the student, the expressed goals of the student and the previous educational experiences of the student.

To promote students' personal growth in self-confidence, independence, self awareness and initiative through their participation in the organization, design and management of the course.

To promote students' ability to make realistic choices concerning future work and/or future study.

To promote students' ability to work co-operatively with others in the development of appropriate skills and understanding.

To promote students' ability to exercise mature control over their own lives (*STC Approved Study Structure V Handbook*, 1981, pp. 3–4)

Given the significant place which the STC course was eventually to assume in the school, it is appropriate that I outline its intentions, history and achievements (see also Freeman, Batten and Anwyl, 1986).

The STC

The STC Committee was developed in 1977 as the formal expression of the curriculum concerns of its seven original member high schools, Edenhope, Ferntree Gully, Flemington, Lynall Hall, Moreland Annexe, St Kilda Community School and Sydney Road Community School. This group was supported by the Victorian Secondary Teachers' Association and funded by the Commonwealth Schools Commission. Their concerns related to the rise in retention rates at the secondary school level and the failure of the existing Year 12 curriculum (basically the competitive academic style) to meet the educational needs of large numbers of senior students. The original STC group mounted a serious critique of the existing educational processes at the senior school level, showing essentially that the HSC was narrow, exclusive and discriminatory. The group recognized that schools needed to develop a curriculum that could be flexible and responsive to particular students' needs and to changing circumstances. The diversity of students' backgrounds and individual needs, the variety of tertiary courses and entry requirements and the uncertainty of employment were seen to make a single fixed syllabus inappropriate.

The group took as its most essential premise the principle that secondary schooling was for everyone and should be inclusive of all students' experiences, backgrounds and values. The STC group rejected the easy solution of streaming students into 'soft option' types of courses operating alongside unchanged, traditional courses. Such courses, it was recognized, held no credence with the community, were not accepted by tertiary institutions or many employers and were accorded little value by parents, students and teachers. The challenge was to develop a course that would not be seen as a soft option, one which would offer those students who might otherwise have left school a substantial educational opportunity in a well developed comprehensive curriculum which met the needs of its client group without disadvantaging them.

The STC was to become a strong statement about the right of every student to be successful and to have access to a means of success through education. In a very real sense the STC approach to curriculum may thus be defined as democratic. It took a stance against the inequities of a system which sifted, sorted, graded and classified students according to an assessment process designed for the failure of a large number of them. In so doing the STC represented a radical departure from established practice. It combined the elements of recognized good teaching practice to challenge the notion that a Year 12 course of study was only for the relatively small group of students who were heading for tertiary education. The group shaped a course which responded to a wide range of students' needs, interests and aspirations, while encouraging them to consider seriously the possibility that their post-school options might include tertiary education.

In order that undertaking the STC did not close off students' opportunities for tertiary study, the STC group challenged tertiary institutions to work with the group to develop more flexible admissions processes. These were to be based on more diverse criteria which would deal with students who brought with them both descriptive assessments and profiles on their suitability for further study, and who had been actively involved in the admission procedure. Such an approach strongly contrasted STC students with those who anonymously presented themselves through a rank ordering system with a numerical score.

The STC reacted to externally set syllabuses and assessment procedures that placed restrictions on classroom learning, failed to take account of a wide range of learning styles and failed to promote successful and challenging learning for all students. STC was based on the premise that the school should be the focus for course construction and take the responsibility for assessment of its students. In the pursuit of these aims the group also responded to advice and reports to the government of the day which suggested that schools should be responsible for developing curriculum and teaching methods (Committee on Arrangements for Secondary Courses and Assessment, 1974); that tertiary institutions and secondary schools should work together on transition problems (the Buchanan Committee, 1975); and that school-based assessment was preferable to external examinations ('Transition from School to Work or Further Study' after a review of education policy in Australia, 1976).

The range of contexts in which STC has been adopted has been indicative of its success as a whole course, with centrally accredited guidelines which allow schools to develop a Year 12 curriculum to suit the needs of their own students. Recent research has elucidated the value of the course on a variety of academic and social levels as a counterpart to the more traditional approach to Year 12. Of particular relevance to this case study are the research findings in the area of self-esteem.

An Australian Council for Educational Research (ACER) study followed a group of Year 12 students in Victorian schools from 1984, when they were completing Year 11, through Year 12 in 1985 and into their first post-school year in 1986. Malvern was one of the schools involved in this project. The students involved were a cross-section from those who did STC and those who did HSC Group One subjects. The aim of the study was to identify the effects of Year 12 courses on the students from their own perceptions of: measures of self-esteem; the aims of their Year 12 and achievement; and the quality of school life they experienced. The questionnaire in the Appendix to this chapter was the one administered in this survey. The overall findings were quite dramatic. There is an acknowledged importance in STC in the development of self-confidence and self-awareness, therefore through appropriate testing a measure of self-esteem was determined as an indicator for the success of the alternative Year 12 course. In the ACER study authored by Margaret Batten (1989) it was found that

> ... at the beginning of year twelve the measured self esteem of STC students was at a considerably lower level than that of the Group One students, but by the end of year twelve these positions had been reversed. Over that period of time there was a rise in self esteem in both groups of students, *but only with STC students did that rise achieve a level of educational significance.* This outcome would support the conclusion that to the extent it can be measured this way, the important aim of the STC course was achieved for the group of STC students.

Various findings of the study are summarized in Figures 1–4.

By 1989 the STC was being taught in all regions of Victoria, and there were 117 schools servicing some 3000 students in high schools, technical schools, community schools, higher elementary schools, Catholic and other non-government schools, an Aboriginal college and adult learning centre (see Freeman, Batten and Anwyl, 1986a). STC has attracted the interest of many educational reformers and researchers. As a consequence, its achievements are well researched and documented (see

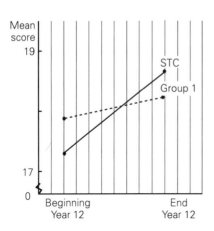

Figure 1: *Change in Self-esteem of Year 12 Students*

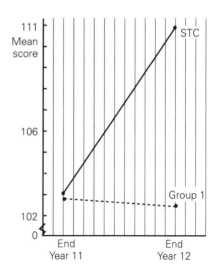

Figure 2: *Perception of Quality of School Life by Year 12 Students*

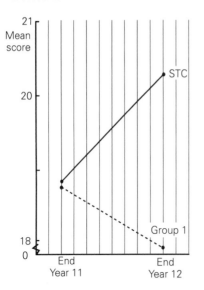

Figure 3: *Perception of Opportunity by Year 12 Students*

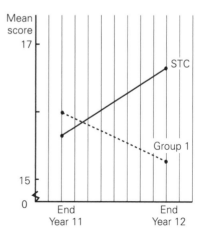

Figure 4: *Perception of Achievement by Year 12 Students*

(*Source*: Batten, M. *Alternative Year 12 Curricula: Working Paper No. 4 — Year 12 Courses and Their Effects on Students*, March 1987. (These working papers have since been published by ACER in a research monograph. The format of the graphic presentation of the result shown in Figures 1–4 has changed, but the findings have not altered significantly.)

Freeman *et al.*, 1986). Another instance is the five working papers which Margaret Batten produced for the Australian Council for Educational Research (1985–87). These not only comprehensively demonstrate the students' and teachers' perceptions of the merits of STC, but also, in a less subjective manner, compare the attitudes and outlooks of STC students and those in other HSC courses both prior to and including tertiary study. The benefits which accrue to Year 12 students through the STC are vividly demonstrated in Figures 1–4. The STC students' levels of satisfaction with the achievement, opportunity and quality of life which they experienced in their course are evident, as is the development of their sense of self-worth.

In the wider educational context STC is obviously a course for all students, not specifically for girls, but it was considered particularly appropriate for the Malvern Girl's High students because it directly addresses self-esteem as one of its aims in a mainstream approach to learning. Let me now return to the matter of school reform at Malvern.

Curriculum Change for Year 12

After further investigation and discussion among all those concerned — staff, students and parents — we decided to adopt STC and its associated principles as our Year 12 course of study. It was decided further that if this move were successful, then STC principles could be used as a guide to curriculum development at the school, and should be filtered down through the school to all year levels.

The implications of this move for the girls' self-esteem have been many. By adopting a new learning process, one in which students were actively engaged in taking responsibility for the organization and running of their own course, we were able to provide the environment and opportunities for them to develop a sense of themselves as valuable and productive members of the school and the wider community in which they would soon take an adult place. This point requires some elaboration.

The learning process which we came to adopt is based on the premise that every student has the right to be successful. In it students are encouraged to exercise their own language on the material being studied; learning is activity-based, focusing on problem solving; students are encouraged to set their own realistic tasks and goals; errors are allowed for in the learning process and students' opinion is valued in the planning of curriculum. The STC is organized to allow for maximum participation by students. As a result of its collaborative and non-competitive nature, assessment is a positive part of the learning process. The differences and experiences of students are treated by the course as a resource and so make learning relevant to girls' knowledge, experience, needs and interests. The rewards from such an approach include increased experience of success and growing confidence, thus changing students' view of themselves and their ability to exercise control and power over their learning and their lives.

By mainstreaming participation as an essential part of each student's course, their schooling experience becomes inclusive, building on the skills students already have and legitimizing their experience. For many girls, it also brings a female dimension to their work, a further empowering experience in which they value what other girls have to say. Girls' knowledge comes to be seen as important. Participation, being asked to have a say, is an important methodology for developing the confidence and self-esteem of all students, and in our case girls. What is critical in this is the real power accorded them when making course development decisions, that their opinions are vital to the course approval/moderation process, and that their continued contribution is integral to its survival. The girls acknowledge these aspects in their comments, they feel confident that people care what they think and that they are listened to :

> I like the independence, being treated like an adult, being asked for my opinion. I've become more confident with teachers and my friends ...

> There is a lot of communicating involved, people ask you what you think, it's important, and you have to learn to be confident in what you say ... What we say is important, it really matters to the course.

The girls, their parents, employers and the staff frequently observe that there is an ease with which they discuss things at home, work and school.

For our Year 12 girls, the STC has had the obvious benefit of improving their self-esteem. For the majority of students, there have been benefits in terms of personal development and more tangible rewards in the form of gaining places in tertiary institutions which would otherwise not have been available to them, simply because they would not have had the confidence to complete their HSC or to apply for further education. Witness this example. A student who initially was too shy to say anything in class became gradually self-confident, more sure of herself, of her ability and of her important contribution to the group. She said of herself, 'I have grown during the year to have higher ambitions (tertiary course) and intend to succeed in it.' This student came from a family where no one else has tertiary qualifications and where it is not traditionally accepted that girls should aim so 'high'. Through the STC she, among many of our girls, has broken through a cultural stereotype.

Devolution through the School

As the principles of this democratic curriculum have been integrated into other year levels, participation in all areas of curriculum development has increased. Students are now active participants on the various committees that exist within the school, and in the wider school community. These include the Discipline and Welfare Committee, Assessment Policy Group, the Curriculum Committee, School Council, Commonwealth Programs Committees, Local Planning Committee (a regional group) and the Regional Board. Their own Students' Representative Council has taken a very high profile in the school, organizing in-service days to discuss student/school-related issues for students from Malvern and other schools. Given the opportunity to communicate their thoughts, feelings and needs to other students and members of the wider community, the students are constantly building their confidence and competence and affirming their position as responsible people who are taken seriously by those with whom they interact.

As a staff we are continually struck by the value of participation for our students. When their ideas and contributions to school policy making groups are accepted by their peers and teachers, they feel a sense of achievement and increasing personal power. As one Year 11 said, 'By talking to different people outside of the school about issues related to the school, I have built up my self-confidence.' Such self-confidence is vividly demonstrated in the following instance. At a parent evening organized by the Students' Representative Council to explain the Victorian Certificate of Education (that is, the new system to be introduced on a statewide basis for Years 11 and 12) the predominantly adult audience sat up and took notice when, after a particularly 'sticky' question on educational standards was asked of the adult 'expert' panel (one teacher and two regional consultants), the 'master of ceremonies' (a Year 12 student) confidently took the floor, asked leave of the experts, 'I'd like to answer that question', and went on to deliver, by word and action, a most convincing reply.

Difficulties and Benefits

There are difficulties in introducing such an approach. We freely admit to the problems which we experienced in adopting this model for change. It is appropriate to list some of these along with the feedback which we have received which indicates the merits of adopting this approach despite the difficulties. Certainly, the reforms which we introduced involved risks for the students and the school.

First, students, staff and parents were presented with an approach to learning which was generally outside their frame of reference. Students and teachers had to be prepared, through intensive in-servicing and orientation, to accept the challenge of negotiating their way through a course. They had to make radical changes in their styles of learning, teaching and assessment. Universal to all groups was both the fear of change and a sense of being inadequately equipped with the skills to cope with such change. Students were being asked to do what they saw as 'the teacher's job', to make decisions about their learning, to decide on content, approach and assessment. Teachers were confronted with learning new methods to cope with course management skills as well as subject skills and knowledge. In negotiating a course with students, in giving students access to real control over course development, their 'power' within the classroom situation was challenged. The time taken to explore these issues meant that frustration levels were high for both parties, even though such time needed to be viewed as a valuable part of the learning program.

The consensus among all staff is that the course and its impact on the rest of the school are worth their enormous effort. They see the development of self-confidence as one of the most important parts of the course, and have no trouble identifying students who have developed both personally and academically, surprising people with their ability and willingness to take control over their own lives and learning. Teachers comment,

> I have seen students working co-operatively, helping each other to check goals and assessments. They develop confidence in expressing their own opinion as there is a chance to develop and explore issues.

> The negotiation process allows a special relationship to develop between teacher and student. The students feel good about their opinions being an important component of the course and it translates into the confidence with which they approach their

work. They enjoy working when they are made to feel what they say and do are important.

Group work helped to clarify her ideas and give her the confidence to tackle things beyond her experience, things she assumed to be beyond her ability.

It's a lot of hard work for everyone but it's worth it.

Although these comments relate specifically to Year 12 students, similar remarks were made of students further down the school in relation to their participation in classroom and other curricular activities.

Second, a major risk for senior students was the certain knowledge that the type of course they were doing was not as publicly acceptable as the Group One HSC course and, therefore, prejudiced their chances of entering tertiary institutions. They had to demonstrate to the wider community (including tertiary institutions) that our course of study was challenging and rigorous, not a soft option of low status achievement. This factor was both damning and liberating. Students' perceptions of themselves and their courses played a vital part in determining their post-school destinations. In the face of stated opposition students who believed their course had improved their knowledge and skills, had prepared them for their future lives and developed their self-confidence were well equipped both to fight the battle of tertiary placement and to convince employers that they should be given jobs.

Students' self-assessments expressed real growth in confidence and satisfaction with their achievements. They commented on their ability to plan work, to reflect on and evaluate their activities, to identify the learning that is important to the planned activity and their intellectual, vocational, personal and social development. Time and time again they spoke of the value of the course for them.

It's helped me with my personal development, I get on well with others now.

I don't feel stupid any more when I speak up.

I believe it [STC] has built my confidence, my friends have noticed a change in me.

I feel more confident in myself and when dealing with other people.

In their post-school lives these sorts of beliefs have indeed helped them compete for the scarce and valued positions in tertiary education and employment.

Work experience employers, in most cases, remark on the self-confidence of the girls, their maturity, enthusiasm and ability to relate well to other staff. Comments quoted here are the norm rather than the exception, and apply to girls from Years 10 to 12.

> N__ is very confident of herself and communicates well with other staff.

> A__ had a very good understanding of what is involved in working in a group situation.

> We were generally impressed with M__. She has developed a maturity and air of self-confidence not generally found (in my experience anyway) in people of her age.

> She not only does what is asked but she sees what needs doing and does it. I was impressed with H__'s independence and confidence.

It is true that students seeking tertiary entry have a harder job than do those in the more traditional Year 12 courses, but imagine the feelings of self-worth of a student who, when told she was ineligible to apply for a computer course at Chisholm Institute of Technology, challenged their course entry requirements with the dean of the faculty by letter, by telephone, and by personal interview and secured for herself a written assurance that her entry would be accepted and considered — all this largely independent of teacher assistance! In her own words, 'I felt powerful when I challenged a big institution and won — even if I don't get a place, they couldn't stop me from trying!' Further, a recent study (Stephens, 1986) undertaken by the PEP access group, focused on the STC students who entered tertiary courses in 1985; it produced evidence of a high measure of first year success among these students, due in large part to the nature of their previous Year 12 course.

Third, parents' fears were mainly concerned with understanding the changes and in particular the assessment procedures. The introduction of descriptive assessment on a non-competitive basis was a radical departure from grades, marks and talking in terms of pass and failure. They could understand the benefits as outlined to them by the staff and the students, but the bias towards grades as the traditionally acceptable and recognizable credential from the educational system was a difficult barrier to penetrate. Even so parent feedback indicates that they are generally happy with their girls' development.

> We've noticed some changes in her, she seems to be more confident, she's more responsible.

> She seems happy with what she is doing.

> She talks a lot more about school and what she's doing.

> The school has done wonders for her, she's really come out of herself.

They acknowledge that 'the assessment system seems fairer', but the concern still surfaces: 'Will the colleges accept it?' Being able to give them details of our exit students and their successes in gaining tertiary places or worthwhile employment has been our most convincing tactic for reassuring parents.

Another area of concern was that, although parents could see the need for girls to build their self-esteem and believed that raising self-esteem in the school setting was worthwhile, it was not necessarily acceptable within the family setting, especially where there were cultural differences over the role of females. This is not to say we have not had positive responses in this area, but it is an issue to which we have been made sensitive. In the words of two teachers, 'Many students from migrant backgrounds whose culture emphasizes passivity do learn to speak out in class when it becomes part of the course requirement'; 'Some show personal moral courage to challenge a cultural stereotype and assume the confidence necessary to join in group discussions or volunteer opinions.'

Fourth, from an organizational point of view there has been the need to maintain the focus of school policy, constantly clarifying the aims with all parties and attempting to evaluate and replan. I say 'attempting' to evaluate, as a primary disadvantage of undertaking this sort of drastic and dynamic curriculum change 'at the chalk face' is that there has been little time to reflect on and evaluate programs in other than an anecdotal and ad hoc manner. Our main concern has been to make this type of change work for the students, undoubtedly the most important people in this exercise. Signs of their improvement on an individual basis have been monitored through assessment procedures (including student self-assessment), their involvement in extra-curricular activities, participation in the classroom, anecdotal information, parent surveys. In addition, we observed their acceptance of a wide variety of learning techniques and the new ways which students themselves have developed of exploring knowledge.

In conclusion, I wish to emphasize the point with which I began. Ours has been a program for action, not a compensatory program seeking to rectify girls' personal and educational deprivations/disadvantages. Rather, it has been an attempt to enhance and encourage girls to think about themselves in a positive way, to raise their self-esteem through a whole school commitment to success and to access. The ramifications of the introduction of STC for the rest of the school have been enormous. The transition has not been without its problems, but the soundness of the decision has rarely been questioned. Significant improvements have taken place and are taking place in the quality of schooling for our students. The confidence with which many of the girls can examine their own experiences and identify benefits and inadequacies in the school is a sign that they are learning skills which are valuable in their own right. An improved retention rate in the senior school (eleven students enrolled in 1984 to thirty-two students enrolled in 1989) and undoubted success in obtaining tertiary placements for students with these aspirations are further testimony to what has been achieved. We should be optimistic about the future, but can we be?

Current changes in education brought about largely by changes in the economic and political environment place at risk the reform programs which have so benefited our girls. The Victorian state government is in the process of altering the Year 11 and 12 curriculum in major ways. Although currently it is possible for students to choose from a variety of courses, the new revised curriculum, the Victorian Certificate of Education (VCE), is to incorporate or replace all such choices. Promises have been made that the best features of the STC will be included in this new curriculum. Nonetheless, as time proceeds it is evident that much of what was possible within the STC course will not be possible in the new comprehensive curriculum which is ambitiously and perhaps unrealistically designed to cater equally for all.

What will our students stand to gain with the introduction of a course that purports to do what we do already? Our students currently enjoy the benefits of an approach to learning based on *sound* pedagogical principles. They experience real personal development; their studies are relevant to their needs, and inclusive of their backgrounds and future aims; they develop commitment to, and ownership of, the learning process; they are a part of assessment practices which promote successful and challenging learning. One wonders how successfully such things will be incorporated in the 'new' common curriculum.

The degree of the sense of ownership and empowerment felt through participation and the resulting effects this has on self-esteem is something we stand to lose as we move towards a system that seeks to replace a proven, successful approach to learning.

> For most of the students in this study, the STC course seems to have achieved its aims. Educators undertaking the restructuring of post-compulsory education should take this success into account and consider the principles underlying the success of the STC course principles of curriculum and teaching and learning processes. (Batten, 1987, p. 18)

We at Malvern Girls' High fear an approach which may 'straight-jacket' our students' learning. The VCE threatens to place restrictions upon teachers' and students' participation in decisions about their study, first, by imposing specific content-based guidelines or specific content-based work requirements and, second, by restrictive assessment practices which control the curriculum and have damaging effects on classroom practice. We believe that the recommended modes of assessment, which grade students by comparing them, will eventually mean that the students' grade will become more important than their learning and, in addition, that the cooperative nature of learning and assessment which we have adopted, and which our students respond to, will be destroyed. Enjoying the benefits of participation in a flexible curriculum design, inclusive of their needs and experiences, our girls show a high level of satisfaction with the quality of their school life and the relevance of the curriculum, and display significant growth in self-esteem. Will we be able to say the same at the end of 1992?

Postscript

The student cited on p. 226 who challenged Chisholm Institute of Technology was offered a place in the computer degree course and accepted. She began her course in 1988, and at the half-year her results included two credits and three distinctions.

References

BATTEN, M. (1985, 1986, 1987) *Alternative Year 12 Curricula — Working Papers 1–5,* Hawthorn, Vic., Australian Council for Educational Research.

BATTEN, M. (1987) 'Year 12 courses and their effects on students', *Alternative Year 12 Curricula: Working Paper No. 14*, Hawthorn, Vic., Australian Council for Educational Research.

BATTEN, M. (1989) 'Year 12 students' expectations and experiences', *Research Monograph No. 33*, Hawthorn, Vic., Australian Council for Educational Research.

FREEMAN, M. (Ed.) (1985) *STC: A Series of Ten Booklets about Year 12 Curriculum*, Melbourne, Ministry of Education, Participation and Equity School Resource Program, Victoria.

FREEMAN, M., BATTEN, M. and ANWYL, J. (1986a) *Towards Universal Secondary Education: The STC Experience*, Melbourne, Ministry of Education, The Brunswick East Symposium, Participation and Equity Program.

FREEMAN, M., BATTEN, M. and ANWYL, J. (1986b) 'Post-compulsory curriculum: The STC Course', Paper presented at Conference of the Australasian Association for Research in Education, Melbourne, November.

KENWAY, J. and WILLIS, S. (1986) 'Girls, schooling and self esteem: From the universal to the specific and from the personal to the political', Paper presented at Conference of the Australasian Association for Research in Education, Melbourne, November.

REID, P. (Ed.) *The STC Book*, Richmond, Vic., Victorian Secondary Teachers Association.

Staff, Student and Parent Evaluation of School Policy and Practice, Caulfield, Vic., Malvern Girls' High.

STC Approved Study Structure V Handbook (1981) Melbourne, Ministry of Education, The Victorian Curriculum and Assessment Board.

STEPHENS, J. (1986) *The PEP Access Study*, Melbourne, Ministry of Education, Participation and Equity Program.

SUGGETT, D. (1987) 'Equity and curriculum', *PEP Discussion Paper No. 2*, Melbourne, Ministry of Education.

Appendix: Item Summary Statistics on Quality of School Life; Data from Term 3 1984, Malvern Girls High School

Item		Number of cases	Percentage agree
Positive Affect Items			
IT8	I like learning	22	100.0
IT9	I get enjoyment from being there	22	90.0
IT31	I really like to go each day	22	68.2
IT2	I feel proud to be a student	22	95.5
IT39	... that learning is a lot of fun	21	100.0
Negative Affect Items			
IT5	I feel depressed	22	9.1
IT11	I feel restless	22	27.3
IT33	I feel worried	22	22.7
IT19	I feel lonely	22	9.1
IT24	I get upset	22	13.6
Teachers' Items			
IT23	Teachers help me to do my best	22	81.8
IT12	Teachers ... the marks I deserve	22	86.4
IT40	Teachers listen to what I say	22	90.9
IT29	Teachers are fair and just	22	86.4
IT16	Teachers ... interest in helping me	22	72.7
IT1	Teachers treat me fairly in class	22	100.0
Status Items			
IT4	People look up to me	22	68.2
IT28	I feel important	22	68.2
IT21	I know people think a lot of me	22	77.3
IT35	I feel proud of myself	20	80.0
IT15	Other people care what I think	22	81.8
IT17	I am treated with respect ...	22	86.4
Identity Items			
IT6	It is easy to get to know people	22	95.5
IT10	Other students are very friendly	22	86.4
IT36	Other students care/accept me as I am	22	95.5
IT38	Get on ... with students ... in class	22	90.9
IT32	I learn to get along with ... people	21	90.5
IT18	... help me to understand myself	22	86.4
Opportunity Items			
IT27	Things ... taught are worth learning	22	95.5
IT3	The things I learn are important	21	100.0
IT34	... good preparation for my future	22	95.5
IT20	... learn will help me in adult life	21	100.0
IT25	I can do interesting work	22	81.8
IT13	I have acquired useful skills	22	81.8
Achievement Items			
IT36	... do well enough to be successful	22	95.5
IT7	I ... get involved in my school work	22	95.5
IT22	I know how to cope with the work	22	100.0
IT37	I have learnt to work hard	22	95.5
IT14	I achieve a satisfactory standard in my work	22	95.5
IT30	I am a success as a student	22	90.9

(cont.)

Item		Number of cases	Percentage agree
Personal/Social Development Items			
IT41	Provide advice on careers and education	22	95.5
IT42	Give experience of responsibility	22	100.0
IT45	... skills and knowledge to get a ... job	22	100.0
IT46	Acquire oral communication skills	22	100.0
IT47	Be able to follow own interests	22	86.4
IT48	Develop ability to think ... for self	22	100.0
IT49	Help to understand oneself	22	95.5
IT50	Help think out ... want to achieve	22	100.0
IT51	Be able to experience success	22	95.5
IT52	Opportunity to work cooperatively	22	100.0
IT56	Acquire skills and ... for leisure	22	68.2
IT57	Equip ... with daily living skills	22	81.8
IT60	Prepare for future career	22	100.0
IT62	Encourage independence	22	100.0
IT66	Develop self-confidence	22	100.0
IT67	... apply learning to real life situations	22	100.0
IT69	... contacts with people outside school	22	100.0
IT71	Help to understand other people	22	100.0
Academic/Intellectual Development Items			
IT43	Encourage wide reading	21	81.0
IT44	Encourage ... involvement in learning	22	100.0
IT53	... study a subject in great depth	22	72.7
IT54	gain understanding of Australian society	22	77.3
IT55	... competitive standards to extend ability	22	86.4
IT58	Help to develop study skills	22	95.5
IT59	Encourage interest in current affairs	22	90.9
IT61	... range of subjects and learning experiences	22	
IT63	Maintain competence ... basic skills		100.0
	... get the place wanted in tertiary education	22	100.0
IT64	See links between different areas ...	22	95.5
IT65	... achieve a high standard of work	22	100.0
IT68	Develop problem solving skills	22	95.5
IT70	Develop questioning attitude ... learning	22	100.0
IT72		22	95.5

Part IV
Conclusion

Conclusion

Jane Kenway and Sue Willis

After consideration of the girls, schooling and self-esteem discourse from a range of different perspectives, what is an apt way to conclude such a discussion? Indeed, are conclusions appropriate after such a journey through so many related but different fields? A common tendency in the conclusions which often follow collections of this kind is for the editors or authors to offer 'ways forward'. These sometimes take the form of rather patronizing 'tips for teachers'. Such attempts often rush towards closure and/or solutions, then falter in the process, dispensing ill-conceived suggestions for practice which not only fail to do justice to both the preceding material and the complexity of education, but also close off the broad array of possible responses which the collection might otherwise have generated. We feel no such compulsion towards closure. Indeed, as the collection's introduction and the chapter by Peter Renshaw (Chapter 1) suggest, the unseemly haste with which educational research has been translated into policy and then into practice for schools, is a particular problem of this field. Renshaw makes very clear the confusion and ambiguity which constitute the area of self-esteem research and, along with the chapters in Part II, points to the dangers of making assumptions about the connection between high self-esteem and high achievement and between low self-esteem and low social status (matters we will return to). Basing policy and practice upon a research literature which suffers such confusion is problematic to say the least.

As we indicated at the outset, our purpose in taking a closer look at this literature was threefold: first, to identify some of its problems, omissions and underlying messages; second, to address some of the more neglected issues; and third, to generate some possible alternative readings. Generally, our intention has been to enhance the field, not to discredit it. As is the case in the development of most knowledge, however, it is often difficult to achieve the former without at least something of the latter. So if, on occasions, our discussion has been a little disrespectful, we offer no apology. Feminism is (or should be) a politics of disrespect, treating all received wisdom, including its own, with a healthy and positive suspicion. Nonetheless, feminism seeks reconstruction as well as deconstruction and so, too, do we in this collection.

In taking a close and critical look at the literature, we have pointed to some of its origins and have suggested something of the manner of its development as a program of feminist educational reform. In so doing, various reasons for its appeal to policy-makers, curriculum developers and teachers have emerged. The chapters by Renshaw, by Kenway, Willis and Nevard and by Gilbert (Chapters 1, 2 and 9) show one clear reason for its resonance with much popular educational thought. The 'self' literature, as it arose out of social psychology, emerged in various guises in many fields in, and associated with, education, and informed a wide range of 'progressive' attempts both to humanize the curriculum and to engineer some sort of educational change which might militate against educational and social 'disadvantage'. In a sense the 'progressive' educational movements of the 1970s, in their various manifestations, provided a complementary body of thought which was to help facilitate the acceptance of the girls, schooling and self-esteem literature. Both pinned their hopes for educational and social progress on micro-politics and individual change. In so doing they painted an educational and social reform scenario in which the teacher was central. Enlightened and humane teachers were to be the vanguard for a movement in which all individuals developed their full potential together, in an atmosphere of unconditional positive regard. Social change was made possible by change at the 'chalk face', an appealing prospect to the socially compassionate teacher, as Jackie Wenner (in Chapter 5) in particular implies.

As this collection has also made clear, this humanist approach to education was but one discourse which intersected with the self-esteem literature. The latter was also a comfortable companion to other more conservative aspects of the education system, particularly to the individualism which is one of its central features. Individualizing educational problems and their solutions is a strong tradition in Australian education, and the many blind spots which may be associated with it have, as Georgina Tsolidis shows (in Chapter 3), also found their way into the material on self-esteem and girls' schooling. In foregrounding the individual, both the self-esteem discourse and the education system generally repress matters of culture, ideology and power. The complex, contradictory and dynamic nature of society and education is lost in any analysis which focuses on the individual and, as Kenway, Willis and Nevard argue in Chapter 2, inevitably such analysis cannot generate a program for educational change with any likelihood of contributing to wider-ranging social change. By its very nature it must stop short of offering a significant challenge to the status quo.

An overarching theme of the collection is that self-esteem research, policy and curriculum must be viewed as theoretically, culturally and historically specific; they cannot be adequately understood unless placed in the context of a particular theory, a particular culture and a particular time. Acknowledging this is important for a number of reasons. One reason emerges in Part II. As the chapters therein demonstrate, a recognition of the field's cultural specificity forces one to look not only at its cultural preferences, biases and omissions but also at what it cannot say. The point is repeatedly made that the self-esteem discourse had difficulty in confronting multicultural issues precisely because it is firmly located within the value system of white, middle-class Anglo-Australia. In attempting to address the educational difficulties which girls from ethnic and racial minorities may experience, it generates a portrayal of such groups which, as Dudgeon, Lazaroo and Pickett (Chapter 4), Wenner (Chapter 5) and Tsolidis (Chapter 3) show, borders on caricature, neglecting any real sense of the diversity of their culture as it is lived, intersects with the dominant culture and changes. Certainly, the caricature is often sketched with good intentions and it may occasionally be affectionate. More often it is negative and always it is simplistic. As these chapters in Part II make clear, such caricatures may have very unfortunate consequences for the manner in which many educators contemplate the education that they offer ethnic minority girls. Not only do the writers in this part perform the valuable service of breaking down stereotypes, they also suggest much more open, positive and potentially helpful ways in which educators might think about, and work with, cultural minorities.

These chapters undermine the comfortable sense of superiority which accompanies ethnocentrism by pointing to the fact that the dominant values of Anglo-Australian society may be questioned, rejected or even held in amused or amazed contempt by minority cultural groupings. For instance, Tsolidis points to the popular but partial equation between 'ethnicity' and disadvantage or deprivation. She makes the point (which should not be necessary) that ethnic minorities often have considerable pride in their culture and, rather than feeling deprived by it, go to considerable lengths to sustain and promote it. These chapters also point to the possibility that the conceptual apparatus of the self-esteem discourse (and by implication much else) may strike no responsive chord at all among people of minority groups. This point is made particularly powerfully by Wenner, who points to the incompatibility between the values associated with self-esteem research and those, such as modesty and reserve, held by Indo-Chinese communities, and by Dudgeon, Lazaroo and Pickett, who show how incompatible the individuality associated with self-esteem is with the strong sense of community among Aboriginal students. On the other hand, as Tsolidis so movingly argues, feminism has a long way to go before it develops any sense of what a 'culture-specific' feminism might look like.

If the field is short-sighted with regard to ethnicity and race, it is positively blind in matters connecting girls' self-esteem and educational achievement to social class and, as Cope and Kalantzis show (in Chapter 8), the overlay of one upon the other remains totally unrecognized, and thus the range of circumstances through which girls' self-esteem may develop and fluctuate is unacknowledged. Social class and its important cultural dimensions are central to the chapters by Wyn and by Kenway (Chapters 6 and 7). Wyn raises provocative questions for those educators who are concerned about working-class girls and their schooling. In adopting a cultural perspective, Wyn points to aspects of the working-class neighbourhood which encourage girls to make matters of community and security central to their lives and which often militate against such girls' success at school. The implication of her argument is that if schools were more cognisant of, and sympathetic towards, the gendered aspects of working-class culture, they might better direct curriculum reform in these girls' interests. A further implication is that much current feminist reform in education is class-centric and thus misdirected. In contrast, Kenway's chapter on privileged girls highlights a negative side to high self-esteem which is captured in the girls' dichotomies between snobs and bogans; us and them. Further, it shows that such girls' apparently high self-esteem is more readily assured because of their connections with dominant values and that the liberal feminism which informs this 'culture of success' has similar and equally strong connections. Kenway's chapter, along with those of Kenway, Willis and Nevard and of Tsolidis, help to clarify some of the limitations of liberal feminism. Indeed, pointing to such limitations is another dominant thread running through a number of the chapters. Of particular significance in this regard is the failure of liberal feminism to promote either gender esteem (to use Pam Gilbert's evocative phrase) or gender solidarity. Its focus on the individual and on individual mobility ensures that neither can be accommodated, let alone encouraged. This critique of liberal feminism is not just an academic exercise but has important implications for the direction of feminist educational policy and practice.

In our view any program for educational or social change embodies three essential complementary aspects: access, critique and alternatives. First, it should be concerned about mechanisms of access (for those whose interests the program serves) to the modalities of power associated with dominant power structures. Second, it should develop a critique of these power structures. Third, and no less importantly, it should offer a new discourse which elaborates alternative forms of practice which people may identify with and operate by. Informed as it is by liberal feminism, the self-esteem literature is more concerned about access than about offering either critique or educational and social alternatives. As the chapters in the final part demonstrate, this is simply not good enough.

Let us begin to address this point by highlighting another theme which emerges in this collection and which revolves around two issues. The first concerns the problematic relationship between self-esteem and academic achievement which Renshaw forcefully identifies and carefully unpicks. This is contextualized within a broader second issue, which Renshaw also unravels, to do with the supposed connection between low self-esteem, low educational achievement and low social status. In one way or another all the chapters gathered here warn educators and policy-makers not to draw any simple causal connection between self-esteem and educational achievement. Further, they warn against the assumption that all students use the academic curriculum as a central mechanism in the construction of their self-esteem. This point is particularly pertinent in regard to the students which the schooling system attempts to stigmatize as failures, many of whom are not from socially dominant backgrounds. So, for instance, as Wyn points out, working-class girls refuse to construct their sense of self in accordance with the values of the competitive academic curriculum but look to their friendship and suburban communities instead. A similar point is made by Dudgeon, Lazaroo and Pickett with regard to Aborigines, who make the further point that the sources of both negative and positive identity must be regarded as multifaceted and constantly shifting. On the other hand, Kenway shows how privileged girls often use the competitive academic curriculum as a means for constructing both their own positive identity and negative definitions of others.

Similarly, but differently, Gilbert (Chapter 9) suggests that any curriculum which places personal growth at its centre must negotiate some very tricky ideological ground. As she shows, the development of such a perspective in the field of subject English was accompanied not only by a certain innocence about the power of language to construct people in gendered ways, but also by a failure to recognize the limits which current approaches to reading and writing place upon girls. While supposedly extending them in an open and free manner, the genres of the curriculum silently but firmly constrain them. Gilbert's remarks in this regard are striking because, more than any other subject in the core curriculum,

English would be most conventionally identified as sympathetic to girls' and women's culture and experience.

Certainly, English is a field in which girls generally achieve more highly than boys and through which, one supposes, they construct a positive identity. However, as Gilbert implies, if personal growth and achievement esteem are attained through success in an ideologically offensive medium, then 'growth' and 'success' cannot be accepted as sufficient. In contrast, as Willis suggests (Chapter 10), mathematics is strongly identified with males, so much so that many commentators are blinded to girls' success in the subject. As Willis indicates, unsubstantiated assumptions about girls' failure have spawned a considerable literature claiming that such 'failure' broadly emanates from low mathematics esteem. Similarly, and more recently, the problem has been reconstructed as girls' lower than preferable participation in mathematics; again, this is explained in low esteem, fear-of-failure terms. Again and again, causal connections between high self-esteem and academic achievement, subject attraction and attachment are drawn. Meanwhile, the critical gaze remains deflected from the curriculum itself.

Like Gilbert and Willis, all the writers in this collection are concerned that many current attempts to enhance students', particularly girls', self-esteem through the school curriculum may not only be limited in their effects but downright misguided. Cope and Kalantzis make this point cogently in their critique of certain reformist curriculum agendas: the liberal pluralist approach which celebrates minority ethnicity while at the same time marginalizing it, and the social access approach which, although providing the fortunate few with an avenue of social mobility, depends for its force upon social, cultural and educational selection and repression. Strongly suggested in the Cope and Kalantzis chapter is the need for continual and careful monitoring of the subtle effects of educational reform programs.

The implication arising particularly from the curriculum chapters in Part III is this. The competitive academic curriculum may well improve the esteem of its most successful appropriators, but this is hardly the point; the curriculum itself must be recognized as complicit in, and the outcome of, gender, class, ethnic and racial power relations and thus as deeply discriminatory. This recognition leads in a number of different, but not incompatible, directions, which nonetheless coincide in the agreement that the mainstream curriculum rather than the students should be the target for close and critical scrutiny. The social mobility strategy, which largely promotes only access to this flawed curriculum for the so-called minority, is roundly condemned.

While acknowledging that the mainstream curriculum, and particularly the more prestigious subjects within it, may well smooth the pathway to social power for its most successful consumers, none of the writers in this collection is content with a simple access and success approach to gender equity and all are concerned to identify the good and bad sense which such curricula embody. The associated bad sense emerges very clearly in Part II, where the selective and excluding aspects of the curriculum are stressed. In addition, in Part III Willis points to the power of mathematics to intimidate and beguile (Chapter 10), while Gilbert alerts us to the tendency of English to naturalize the commonplace disparities of power between males and females (Chapter 9), and Jonas clarifies the ways in which the conventional manner in which schools administer, transmit, process and assess knowledge disempower many students — not only encouraging their passivity but indeed inviting their failure (Chapter 11).

As we suggested earlier, the oppositional thinking embodied in these sorts of critique can, of course, only take us so far, and all the writers, but particularly those in Part III, are concerned not to restrict their discussions to critique alone. The chapters by Cope and Kalantzis and by Willis urge us to resist the temptation to be totally condemnatory about the curriculum. They suggest that, in their subject specialities at least, it does embody empowering components which must be identified and which must provide the basis for a reconstructed curriculum. Cope and Kalantzis offer the example of the Social Literacy Project as such an attempt. In contrast, Gilbert has difficulty in identifying much 'good sense' in subject English as it currently exists. She urges its critical reappraisal in such a way as to enable girls to become 'critically resistant' readers and writers — at least controllers of various genres rather than their subjects and at best genre breakers.

Jonas comes to the problem somewhat differently. In talking about the introduction at Malvern Girls' High of an alternative upper secondary school curriculum, she points to the importance of changing the 'hidden' as well as the 'visible' curriculum. When students are the passive recipients of administrative decisions, knowledge selected by others, and teachers' assessments they cannot, she claims, help but have a limited sense of their capacity to effect change. Jonas argues that by involving students, both individually and collectively, in the negotiation of such matters, they come to recognize their individual and collective capacity to act upon the world and thus their sense of self-worth is tied directly to their sense of empowerment. This argument resonates strongly with the final theme of the collection which we have chosen to highlight here.

In developing this theme, let us return to the 'Introduction' and to the chapter by Kenway, Willis and Nevard, both of which, in discussing the self-esteem discourse, highlighted its central tenets and some of their ideological problems. Of particular concern here is the field's tendency to paint girls as the passive victims of negative stereotyping and its search for a range of mechanisms through which girls may be encouraged to feel positive about themselves in circumstances which would normally lead them to feel otherwise. Self-esteem programs supposedly equip girls with the confidence to act for personal advancement, in ways unconstrained by gender, across a wide range of circumstances. However, as we noted in the 'Introduction', many self-esteem enhancement programs are little more than a marginalized form of educational therapy. The appropriate transfer of the feelings and interpersonal skills learned through such programs is too frequently left largely to chance.

This is neither an image of girls nor a view of feminist education with which any of the writers in this collection concur. As the chapters in Part III imply, self-esteem curricula tend not to teach girls the 'really useful' skills, competencies and knowledge which might help them critically to read and consciously to rewrite their culture. Indeed, consciousness and intentionality tend to be denied. No longer helplessly positioned by negative images, girls are now to be similarly helplessly positioned by positivity. They are still not to be agents in their own destiny.

Kenway, Willis and Nevard point out that the self-esteem literature and, indeed, liberal feminism paint a rather insipid picture of girls and women, capturing mainly the oppressive aspects of their lives and consciousness and doing so in an extremely simplistic fashion. Yet, as demonstrated by the stories of Aboriginal women offered in Chapter 4 and in Chapters 6 and 11, working-class girls, members of the female sex are much more than the intricate and diffuse forces which would oppress us, and such forces are only part of our culture and experience. Indeed, underlying this collection is the belief that no feminist discourse which addresses girls should offer them a weak image of themselves. The girls mentioned here do 'make history, but not in conditions of their own choosing' (as Marx said of the other sex). It is implied throughout this study that girls' esteem is best secured through an educational approach which emphasizes their agency — girl power. In saying this, we are also saying that while access to, and successful control of, male genres of power are important, they are only the beginning of the process of empowering girls. However, if high self-esteem helps them in this regard, well and good. Further, in advocating 'girl power' we are not advocating any simple exercise of free will but rather an educational agenda informed by the belief that girls should learn about those aspects of their worlds and themselves which limit them. Equally, it is regarded as important that they learn to be 'critically resistant' readers of themselves, their experiences and their socio-cultural environment. This means helping them, individually and collectively, to develop both the skills to identify what is working against them and the competencies to negotiate a new, more equitable and just reality.

Earlier we noted the importance to any movement for social and educational change of access, critique and alternatives. It has been demonstrated throughout that the self-esteem discourse is essentially directed towards access but that even in its own terms it suffers quite serious limitations. This collection has offered a critique of the self-esteem field and demonstrated the merits for feminist educational projects of subjecting to critical scrutiny not only 'male stream' but also feminist thought. However, it has also sought to move beyond critique towards a new discourse by suggesting ways of shifting and adjusting the meaning of the self-esteem project within feminist educational politics.

Notes on Contributors

Bill Cope is a senior research fellow at the Centre for Multicultural Studies at the University of Wollongong. His main areas of interest are multicultural education and historical research into the questions of Australian identity. On this latter theme his PhD traced changes in Australian identity as reflected in history and social studies textbooks since 1945. He is a co-author of *Mistaken Identity: Multiculturalism and the Demise of Nationalism in Australia* (Pluto Press, 1988). He has published widely on multicultural education and curriculum theory, as well as being actively involved in the Social Literacy Curriculum Project since 1979.

Pat Dudgeon is currently Head of the Centre for Aboriginal Studies, Curtin University of Technology. She was born and grew up in Darwin of Broome parents — Aboriginal (Asian); she holds a BAppSc (Psychology) and a GradDip in Psychology (Counselling). Her special interests are in tertiary Aboriginal education.

Pam Gilbert taught in secondary schools for many years, but is now a lecturer in education at James Cook University. Her research and teaching interests are in the connections between language, literature, education and gender, and recent publications include *Coming Out from Under: Contemporary Australian Women's Writing, Writing, Schooling and Deconstruction* and *Gender, Literacy and the Classroom*.

Pam Jonas taught at Malvern Girls' High in Victoria for ten years. She has had extensive involvement in the development of alternative curriculum for senior school students and is currently the executive officer of the STC group.

Mary Kalantzis is a senior research fellow at the Centre for Multicultural Studies at the University of Wollongong, where she has worked since

1984. Her main publications include *Minority Languages and Dominant Culture: Issues of Education, Assessment and Social Equity* (1989) and *Cultures of Schooling: Pedagogies for Cultural Difference and Social Access* (1990), both published by Falmer Press. She is also the author of numerous commissioned research reports and academic articles in the areas of multiculturalism and education, and co-authorship of the extensive Social Literacy series of books for primary and secondary schools.

Jane Kenway currently works as a senior lecturer in social and administrative studies in the School of Education at Deakin University. Her research interests and publications are concerned with the relationship between social class, gender and education with particular reference to private schooling, the state/private school interface and to gender reform policies. Prior to her working in the tertiary sector she taught in state primary and secondary schools.

Simone Lazaroo, originally from Singapore, taught secondary Aboriginal students in a remote Kimberley community and has taught secondary Aboriginal girls in all core areas of curriculum and art. She has tutored secondary Aboriginal students from both urban and remote areas, and currently works with Aboriginal staff, schools and communities to produce the magazine *Djwal-Idi* in the Ministry of Education, Western Australia. Involving Aboriginal members of the community in the education of younger students has been the most interesting aspect of her work in Aboriginal education.

Mary O'Connor, after a Catholic school education, attended Macquarie University to complete a BA DipEd. For the following ten years she taught science and maths. Since retiring from teaching she has become more interested in the research side of education, including part-time work as a graduate research assistant at the University of New England and at Murdoch University. She recently began a masters degree in special education at the University of Western Australia.

Jenny Nevard runs a learning centre at Canning Senior College, Perth. She is currently completing further study at Murdoch University in the area of literacy education. She has taught (and learnt) in a variety of institutions in Australia over the last two decades.

Harry Pickett is a travelled second-generation Australian with experience, studies and research over the past ten years in cross-cultural counselling in tertiary education. In addition to working with students and staff of mainstream Australian culture, his specialization has been with overseas students, refugees and migrants and with Australian Aborigines. This follows an earlier career in tertiary lecturing and research, and in applied psychology.

Peter Renshaw is senior lecturer in education at Murdoch University. He teaches undergraduate and graduate courses in educational psychology with a particular emphasis on the social context of learning. His current research focuses on the processes of peer interaction in school settings, and the developmental theories of Vygotsky and Leontev.

Anne Stevens is presently working as a clerk typist in the School of Education at Murdoch University and worked previously in a similar job at the University of Western Australia.

Leonie Taylor currently works as a secretary in the School of Education at Deakin University.

Georgina Tsolidis is of Greek background and arrived in Australia at the age of 10. She taught in Victorian secondary schools before becoming an ESL consultant. In 1984 she began working on the MACMME NESB Girls and Education Project which culminated in the report *Educating Voula*. Subsequently, she has worked with the Victorian Ministry for Education in the multicultural area and on recommendations arising from the report, including a national curriculum development project aimed at breaking down stereotypes of ethnic minority women and girls.

Marilyn Walker has worked at Murdoch University as a secretary for fifteen years and is currently secretary to the Institute for Social Program Evaluation at Murdoch.

Jackie Wenner is an ESL teacher working with pre-English literate new arrivals in a secondary language and literacy unit. She has also worked as a primary school teacher, coordinator of a Women's Studies Resource Centre and as a teacher/researcher for the PEP First Phase Language Learners' Project.

Sue Willis began her career in education as a secondary school mathematics teacher. Since then she has worked in the curriculum branch of the Education Department of Western Australia and is a senior lecturer in mathematics education at Murdoch University. She is currently seconded to the Curriculum Policy Unit of the Commonwealth Department of Employment, Education and Training.

Johanna Wyn has been working with and carrying out research on young people in Melbourne since 1982, with a focus on their experiences of education, gender relations and the labour process, and has completed her PhD in this field. Johanna is a senior lecturer in sociology at the Institute of Education, University of Melbourne. She is also a researcher in the Youth Research Centre at the Institute of Education in which she is involved in research projects on young people, education and the labour market. Johanna is the author of many reports, monographs and papers, and with Bruce Wilson is co-author of *Shaping Futures: Youth Action for Livelihood*.

Index

Aboriginal children
  see also Aboriginal girls
  and cultural deprivation, 73
  and cultural focus of education, 81
  and mainstream education, 71–2, 79–83
Aboriginal education, 73, 79–80, 82–3, 89, 94
  national workshop on [1971], 79–80
Aboriginal girls
  see also Aboriginal children;
    Aboriginal people
  and body language, 91–2
  employment prospects of, 88–9
  and ethnocentric self-esteem programs, 90–2; *see also* Aboriginal girls, and self-esteem programs in schools
  and mainstream education, 88–9
  and naming, 90–1
  and race, class and gender, 87–93
  and racism and sexism, 86–7, 88–9
  removal from families of, 72
  and self-esteem programs in schools, 11, 87–93
  and self-esteem, 11, 71, 83–94, 238
Aboriginal people
  see also Aboriginal children;
    Aboriginal girls; Aboriginal students; Aboriginal women
  assimilation policies regarding, 72, 73
  and communality of self-concept, 78–9, 89–90, 94
  and cultural deprivation, 79–80

denigration of, 75–6
diversity among, 76–7
and educational self-determination, *see* Aboriginal education
emergent cultural reality of, 76–7
and external referents, 75–6
and gender relations, 83–7
and group consciousness, 78–9, 81, 89–90, 94
and identity, 71–96, 239
and individualism, 78–9, 94
integration policies regarding, 72
and land, 76, 77, 84
and locus of self-esteem, 77–8
and pan-Aboriginal identity, 77
and poverty dependency, 76, 79
protection acts regarding, 72
and self-determination, 94
and self-esteem as community-based, 79, 89–90, 94, 238
and self-esteem concept, 74–83, 89–90
separatist policies regarding, 71–2
and transitional society, 76–7, 85
unemployment among, 87–8
and Western influences, 76–8
Aboriginal students
  see also Aboriginal children;
    Aboriginal girls
  achievement levels among, 73, 79–80
  and counselling, 79
  and participation in schooling, 72, 73
  and peer group pressure, 81
  retention rates among, 73